The Which? Guide to Money in Retirement

This guide reflects the law and tax position in spring 2005. Budget 2005 was announced as we went to press and you can find a summary of the main changes on page 283.

About the author

Jonquil Lowe trained as an economist and spent several years in the City as an investment analyst. She is a former head of the Money Group at *Which?* magazine and now works as a freelance researcher and journalist. Jonquil is author of several other books, including *The Which? Guide to Planning Your Pension, The Which? Guide to Giving and Inheriting, The Which? Guide to Shares, Be Your Own Financial Adviser, Money M8* (aimed at 16- to 24-year-olds) and, with Sara Williams, *The Lloyds-TSB Tax Guide.*

The Which? Guide to Money in Retirement

Jonquil Lowe

Which? Books are commissioned by
Consumers' Association and published by
Which? Ltd, 2 Marylebone Road, London NW1 4DF
Email address: books@which.co.uk

First edition April 2003
Second edition 2005

Editorial and production: Robert Gray, Ian Robinson
Original cover concept by Sarah Harmer
Cover photograph by Rob Melnychuk/Digital vision/getty images

Typeset by Saxon Graphics Ltd, Derby
Printed in Great Britain by Creative Print and Design, Wales

Contents

★ An asterisk next to the name of an organisation in the text indicates that their address and/or contact details can be found in this section

Introduction

Life is getting longer. The average person now spends a third of their adult life in retirement[1]. That means a third of your adult life to live at your own pace, to pursue your own ambitions, activities and interests, to do what you want. A crucial ingredient in this rosy picture is having enough money to finance your chosen lifestyle.

Average retirement income is around £10,500 a year for a single person and £20,000 for a couple but this masks a very wide variation between the richest and poorest pensioners. The poorest fifth must manage on around £5,000 a year (single person) or £9,000 a year (couple) while the richest fifth have over £20,000 a year (single person) or £44,500 a year (couple).[2].

What makes the difference is largely an occupational pension, investments and/or earnings. But whatever your income and other resources, there are steps you can take to make the most of your money in retirement.

A Pensions Commission set up by the government recently set out three choices for avoiding financial hardship in retirement: save more, rely on taxpayers to fund state support for pensioners or work longer. The Commission was thinking mainly about people who have time to plan ahead and the big decisions facing the economy as a whole if UK citizens are to have financial security in retirement.

If you are reading this book, you have probably reached retirement, or soon will, and maybe you feel the Commission's message is not relevant to you. But you can use the same basic building blocks to ensure your own financial security when retirement has arrived and much of this book aims to show you how:

- **saving**. It may be too late for you to save much more but you should certainly ensure that the savings you have built up are used in the best possible way. This means making the right decisions at the time you claim your pensions (Chapters 2 to 7), getting the return you want from other savings and investments (Chapters 9 and 10) and considering how investments such as your home might be used to provide extra income (Chapter 11)

- **state support**. The state provides a range of benefits for retired people, in addition to any state pension you've built up. Make sure you claim all the benefits to which you are entitled (Chapters 12 and 13)

- **working**. Working beyond state pension age – perhaps part-time rather than on a full-time basis – is a way of improving your income, not just through the wages you get, but because putting off the start of your pensions can mean a substantial increase in the amount you get once they do begin (Chapters 8 and 2 to 4). Carrying on working has non-financial benefits too – it can provide mental stimulation, physical activity and a social life.

Another important factor in making the most of your money is keeping tax to a minimum. Chapters 14 to 16 explain how tax works and suggest ways to keep the bills down, including guidance on passing your money on tax efficiently.

You might reckon that planning and reviewing your finances is a chore and not how you've chosen to spend your retirement. But checking your position and the options available need not take long and can really pay dividends. For example, shopping around for the best pension at the point of retirement could boost your income this year and every year of your retirement by as much as £500 if you have a £20,000 pension fund[3]. Switching from a high street bank to a best buy savings account could boost your income by nearly £300 a year if you have £10,000 to invest[3]. If your health deteriorates, claiming state benefits that are available to everyone regardless of income could give you over £3,000 a year[5]. So make time to make the most of your money in retirement.

---

[1] Pensions Commission, First Report, 2004.
[2] Department for Work and Pensions, Pensioners Income Series, 2004.
[3] Man aged 65 based on best and worst annuity rates as published in Moneyfacts, Investment Life & Pensions, February 2005.
[4] Based on after-tax return to a basic-rate taxpayer for instant access accounts as published in Moneyfacts, February 2005.
[5] Higher rate of attendance allowance in 2005-6.

Chapter 1

Plan for prosperity

Money does not necessarily create happiness, but a lack of it certainly makes life difficult. This is as true in retirement as at any other time of life.

If you are on the brink of retiring, the decisions you make now may affect your financial well-being throughout the rest of your life. You are probably keen to secure the highest possible income, but it would be a mistake to focus only on today. You also need to take a longer-term view and consider how you will cope financially as retirement progresses.

If you take a snapshot of retired households, older ones tend to have a much lower income than younger households (see Table 1.1). However, this does not mean you should necessarily expect your own income to decline as retirement progresses.

There are some special reasons why the present generation of older retired households is often on low incomes and these might not apply to you:

- older pensioners often have not had the benefit of many years in an occupational pension scheme. These schemes started to become widespread only during the 1960s and 1970s
- women tend to outlive men so make up a high proportion of older pensioners. Women's pensions tend to be lower than men's for a

Table 1.1 Average household income

Type of pensioner household	Before-tax income £ per week
Recently retired	£356
Head of household under 75	£311
Head of household 75 or older	£236

Source: Department for Work and Pensions, *Pensioners' Income Series*, 2002–3.

variety of reasons. Culturally, wives have in the past depended financially on their husbands, often resulting in low incomes on becoming widowed or divorced. Even where women have built up their own pension during their working years, the pension is often low because of broken work patterns and a tendency towards part-time or lower-paid work.

However, you might be affected by another, very important reason why incomes often fall as retirement progresses: inflation. Rising prices eat into the value of a fixed income, as shown in Table 1.2. Sources of

---

Buying power

'Buying power' is literally what you can buy with a given amount of income. For example, if you have £10 and today chocolate bars cost 50 pence each, you can buy 20 bars. If next year the price of chocolate bars has doubled to £1, you will be able to buy only ten bars. The buying power of your money will have halved. In other words, the value of £10 next year – in terms of what you can buy with it – is only the same as £5 today.

CASE HISTORY: PETER AND ELAINE

Peter and Elaine retired in July 1982 on an income made up of £2,733 a year state pension and £3,400 a year from a personal pension. They felt pretty well off. Their total income was over £6,000 a year and broadly two-thirds of the average household income for the nation as a whole. By July 2005, the state pension had more than kept pace with prices and risen to £6,822, but their personal pension remained unchanged at £3,400 a year. Now their income is £10,222 a year in total – only some 40 per cent of national average household incomes. Peter and Elaine are feeling the pinch. Over the past 20 years, prices have risen by nearly 4 per cent a year on average, so their income does not go as far as it used to. Table 1.2 shows that at 4 per cent a year inflation, if £100 of income bought £100 of goods 20 years ago, it now buys only the equivalent of £46 worth of goods.

Table 1.2 How inflation eats into the buying power of your money

After this many years	The buying power of £100 will have fallen to this much if yearly inflation averages							
	2.5%	3%	3.5%	4%	4.5%	5%	7.5%	10%
1	£98	£97	£97	£96	£96	£95	£93	£91
2	£95	£94	£93	£92	£92	£91	£87	£83
3	£93	£92	£90	£89	£88	£86	£80	£75
4	£91	£89	£87	£85	£84	£82	£75	£68
5	£88	£86	£84	£82	£80	£78	£70	£62
6	£86	£84	£81	£79	£77	£75	£65	£56
7	£84	£81	£79	£76	£73	£71	£60	£51
8	£82	£79	£76	£73	£70	£68	£56	£47
9	£80	£77	£73	£70	£67	£64	£52	£42
10	£78	£74	£71	£68	£64	£61	£49	£39
11	£76	£72	£68	£65	£62	£58	£45	£35
12	£74	£70	£66	£62	£59	£56	£42	£32
13	£73	£68	£64	£60	£56	£53	£39	£29
14	£71	£66	£62	£58	£54	£51	£36	£26
15	£69	£64	£60	£56	£52	£48	£34	£24
16	£67	£62	£58	£53	£49	£46	£31	£22
17	£66	£61	£56	£51	£47	£44	£29	£20
18	£64	£59	£54	£49	£45	£42	£27	£18
19	£63	£57	£52	£47	£43	£40	£25	£16
20	£61	£55	£50	£46	£41	£38	£24	£15
21	£60	£54	£49	£44	£40	£36	£22	£14
22	£58	£52	£47	£42	£38	£34	£20	£12
23	£57	£51	£45	£41	£36	£33	£19	£11
24	£55	£49	£44	£39	£35	£31	£18	£10
25	£54	£48	£42	£38	£33	£30	£16	£9
26	£53	£46	£41	£36	£32	£28	£15	£8
27	£51	£45	£40	£35	£30	£27	£14	£8
28	£50	£44	£38	£33	£29	£26	£13	£7
29	£49	£42	£37	£32	£28	£24	£12	£6
30	£48	£41	£36	£31	£27	£23	£11	£6

income such as state pensions and some occupational pensions automatically increase each year in line with inflation to protect the buying power of your income. Other pensions and sources of income often don't, so it is vital that you look ahead and plan now to protect your buying power throughout retirement.

CASE HISTORY: SASHA

Sasha is shortly to retire. She expects to have an income of about £16,000 a year. Roughly £4,000 of this will come from state pensions, which should increase in line with inflation over the years. Sasha wonders what impact inflation might have on the remaining £12,000. Table 1.2 shows that, if inflation averaged 2.5 per cent a year, after ten years each £100 of pension would buy only the same as £78 today. This would be equivalent to living on an income today of £78/£100 × £12,000 = £9,360 plus the state pension of £4,000, making £13,360. So, even this modest rate of inflation would reduce the buying power of her income by about one-sixth in the space of just ten years. After 20 years, her income would have lost nearly a third of its buying power.

Another factor to take into account is any earnings you still have. If you carry on working in early retirement, then your income is likely to fall later on when you cut back or stop work completely. You might want to consider planning your finances to use, say, savings or extra pension to plug the gap when your earnings stop.

You need also to consider how your spending might alter as retirement progresses. A major factor is likely to be your health. If you remain well and active, your spending patterns might not alter significantly. But if you run into difficulties caring for yourself, you may need to earmark significant sums to pay for care, though the state may help.

It is very unlikely that decisions you take at the point of retirement will continue exactly to match your financial needs and circumstances many years ahead. To sustain your financial security, you should review your finances regularly – see Table 1.3. It's a good idea to do this once a year, but even once every five years will help you to stay on track.

Table 1.3 Review your finances

Questions to ask	Action to take
If you have not yet retired, are your pension savings on track for the retirement income you want?	Look at ways of boosting your pension (see Chapters 2 to 7).
Is your income enough to meet your spending?	If no, look at ways of boosting your income (for example, see Chapters 8 to 11) or cutting your spending.
Are you getting the best return from your investments?	Consider switching to investments offering a higher or more tax-efficient return. See Chapters 9 and 10.
Are you paying too much tax?	Check whether there are ways you could cut your tax bills (see Chapters 14 and 15).
Are your circumstances likely to change in future?	If yes, consider whether you need to save extra now to help you cope with the change (see Chapter 9) and check whether you might be eligible for state help (see Chapters 12 and 13).
Have you made a will and is it up to date?	If necessary, get help from a solicitor. Bear in mind that a will is often an important tool in planning away an inheritance tax bill (see Chapter 16).

Part 1

Pension choices

Chapter 2

State pension choices at retirement

Most people build up the right to receive a state pension when they reach state pension age. You do this by paying, or being credited with, National Insurance contributions during your working life. On its own, the state pension is unlikely to finance the lifestyle you want, but it is substantial enough to be a useful core to your retirement income. Moreover, state pensions are increased each year by at least enough to match price inflation, so they maintain their value throughout retirement.

What is the state pension?

The state pension has three elements:

- **basic pension** This is a flat-rate amount. Everyone who has enough National Insurance contributions on their record gets the same amount. If you do not have enough contributions to qualify for the full pension, you may get a reduced amount
- **additional pension** Employees (but not currently people who are self-employed) earning more than a minimum amount can build up this pension. At present, the pension is earnings-related, so different people get different amounts depending on their earnings during their working life. Your additional pension scheme might be made up of State Earnings Related Pension Scheme (SERPS) pension from the scheme that ran from 1978 to 2002 and/or State Second Pension (S2P) which is the current additional state pension

- **graduated pension** Small pensions built up by some employees through this forerunner of the state additional pension scheme.

Details of each of these schemes are given later in this chapter.

When can you get your state pension?

You do not have to stop work to start getting your state pension, but you must have reached state pension age. For all men and for women born on or after 6 March 1955, state pension age is 65. For women born before 6 April 1950, state pension age is 60. See Chart 2.1 if you are a woman born between those dates.

If you are planning early retirement, be aware that you will have to manage without your state pension until you reach state pension age. This might mean coping on a lower income for a while. However, some occupational pension schemes take this into account (see Chapter 3 for further details). You can delay starting

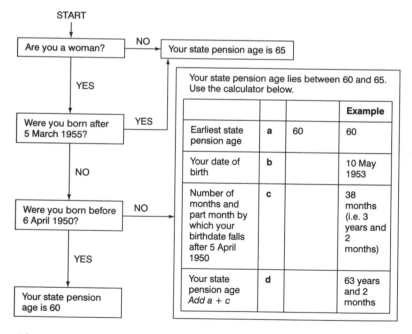

Chart 2.1 Your state pension age

your state pension, in which case you get extra once it does start to be paid (see page 32 for details).

How do you get your pension?

You must actually claim your state pension – it is not paid automatically. About four months before you reach state pension age, you will usually receive a letter from The Pension Service★. This is part of the Department for Work and Pensions (DWP) and is the government agency that deals with all aspects of state pensions. The letter will invite you to call the State Pension Claims Line★, in which case someone will fill in a claim form for you over the phone. Alternatively, you can ask for a form to be posted to you so that you can fill it in yourself.

If you are four months or fewer from retirement and you have not had a letter from The Pension Service, call the State Pension Claims Line★.

How is the state pension paid?

Your state pension must normally be paid into a bank or building society account. Alternatively, you can open a Post Office Card Account (POCA). A POCA is a special account into which your pension and any other state benefits are paid. It cannot accept any other types of payments (such as wages from an employer).You withdraw money from your POCA by using a card and personal identification number (PIN) at post offices. If you cannot operate a bank or building society account or POCA, you may be able to arrange to receive your state pension by weekly girocheque through the post. The Pension Service★ will give you details of these options when you claim your pension.

You choose whether to have your pension paid into your account either at the end of every four-week period or at the end of every thirteen-week period.

How much pension?

The Pension Service will work out how much state pension you qualify for based on its records of your earnings, National Insurance payments and credits. Shortly before the first payment becomes due, the Pension Service should tell you how much you will get. Since state pensions are increased on an annual basis, you will receive a new statement each year letting you know the increased amount.

If you are still some way from retirement, you can ask for a State Pension Forecast*. This will tell you how much state pension you have built up so far and how much you can expect if you carry on contributing until you reach state pension age. If you also belong to an occupational pension scheme or have a personal pension or stakeholder scheme, you might get a 'combined pension statement' from that scheme. This will include the amount of state pension you can expect at state pension age based on your National Insurance record.

In many cases, you can fairly easily work out for yourself how much state basic pension to expect. However, working out any state additional pension is extremely difficult, not least because you need to have kept records of past earnings over many years. Some guidance is given in this chapter, but you are advised to rely on the figures from The Pension Service unless they seem very wide of the mark.

The state basic pension

The basic rules

In 2005–6 the maximum state basic pension is £82.05 a week for a single person. You get the maximum basic pension if you have paid or been credited with National Insurance contributions for roughly nine-tenths of your working life.

PENSION YEARS AND MONTHS

A state pension year is the same as a tax year. It runs from 6 April to the following 5 April. For example, 2005–6 means the year from 6 April 2005 to 5 April 2006. Similarly, a pension month is the same as a tax month and runs from the sixth day of one month to the fifth day of the next.

Each year for which you have enough earnings, contributions of the right type or credits is called a 'qualifying year'. See Table 2.1 for guidance on what counts. Your working life normally runs from the year in which you reached age 16 (regardless of whether you had started work), to the last complete pension year before you reach state pension age.

If your working life is 40 years or longer, the number of qualifying years you need for a full pension is your working life less five years. So, if your state pension age is 65, your working life is normally 49 years and you'll need at least 44 qualifying years for the maximum pension. If your state pension age is 60, your working life is 44 years and you need 39 qualifying years for the maximum pension. (The rule is slightly different for people with working lives that are shorter than 40 years.)

If you are unable to work because you are looking after a child or a sick or disabled person, you might qualify for 'home responsibilities protection' (HRP). Whole years for which you get HRP are deducted from the number of qualifying years you need for the

---

CASE HISTORY: PHIL

Phil was born in November 1942. His state pension age is 65 and his working life runs from 6 April 1958 to 5 April 2007, a period of 49 years. He needs 49 − 5 = 44 qualifying years to get the maximum state basic pension.

CASE HISTORY: MARIE

Marie was born on 10 May 1953 and reached age 16 in May 1969. She uses Chart 2.1 to find that her state pension age will be 63 years and two months. She will reach 63 in the pension month starting 6 May 2016, so adding two months means that she can start to get her pension from 6 July 2016. Her working life runs from 6 April 1969 (the start of the year she reached 16) to 5 April 2016 (the end of the last pension year before she reaches state pension age). This gives her a working life of 47 years. According to the general rule, she needs 47 − 5 = 42 qualifying years in order to get the maximum state pension. However, Marie has two full years of home responsibilities protection when she was off work looking after her children. So 42 − 2 = 40 years will be enough to entitle her to the full basic pension.

Table 2.1 Have you been building up a basic pension?

Your work status	What you pay/paid in National Insurance	Does it count towards the basic pension?
Employee		
Earning less than the lower earnings limit (LEL) – £82 a week in 2005–6	Nothing	No
Earning at least the LEL	Class 1 contributions[1]	Yes
Employed married woman who has opted under pre-April 1977 rules to pay National Insurance at the reduced rate ('small stamp')	Married women's reduced rate Class 1 contributions[2]	No
Self-employed		
Earning less than the small earnings exception (£4,345 in 2005–6) who has opted not to pay contributions	Nothing	No
Married woman who has opted under pre-April 1977 rules not to pay contributions	Nothing[2]	No
Other self-employed	Class 2 contributions	Yes
Self-employed earning at least the lower profit limit (£4,895 in 2005–6)	Class 4 contributions	No
Not working		
Opted to pay voluntary contributions	Class 3 contributions	Yes
Claiming certain state benefits, e.g. Jobseeker's Allowance, maternity allowance or incapacity benefit	Credits	Yes
Under state pension age but aged 60 or over	Credits	Yes
People born after 5 April 1957, years you reached 16, 17 and 18 and were in full-time education	Credits	Yes
People born after 5 April 1957, years you took part in an approved training course (but not university)	Credits	Yes

[1] If you have low earnings at least equal to the LEL but less than the primary threshold (£94 a week in 2005–6), you pay no Class 1 contributions but still build up basic pension.
[2] To check whether it is worth switching to full-rate Class 1 or Class 2 contributions see Inland Revenue leaflet CA13 *National Insurance for Married Women.*

maximum pension. HRP cannot reduce the number of qualifying years you need to fewer than half the number you would have required without HRP, and if you will reach state pension age before 6 April 2010 the number of years required cannot be reduced to fewer than 20.

A reduced pension

If you don't have enough qualifying years to get the maximum state basic pension, you might still be entitled to a reduced amount. But to get any basic pension at all, at least a quarter of the years in your working life must be qualifying ones.

Table 2.2 sets out how much basic pension you can get assuming your working life is between 44 and 49 years.

CASE HISTORY: REBECCA

Rebecca was born on 1 January 1946 and her working life is 44 years long. She reaches state pension age on 1 January 2006 and has 32 qualifying years. Table 2.2 tells her that this entitles her to a basic pension of 83 per cent of the full rate. In 2005–6, she receives 83% × £82.05 = £68.10 a week.

CASE HISTORY: HAMID

Hamid was born on 10 August 1940 and has a working life of 49 years. When he reaches state pension age in August 2005, he has 21 qualifying years. Table 2.2 tells him he will get only 48 per cent of the maximum basic pension, which comes to 48% × £82.05 = £39.38 a week in 2005–6.

State additional pension

The state additional pension is paid on top of any state basic pension you receive. Even if you do not qualify for any basic pension, you might still get some additional pension. However, many employees do not build up additional pension (or build up only a reduced amount) because they are 'contracted out' (see page 26).

Table 2.2 How much state pension you will get

And you have this many qualifying years:	You will get this percentage of the maximum basic pension if your working life is:					
	44 years	45 years	46 years	47 years	48 years	49 years
9 or fewer	0%	0%	0%	0%	0%	0%
10	26%	25%	25%	0%	0%	0%
11	29%	28%	27%	27%	26%	25%
12	31%	30%	30%	29%	28%	28%
13	34%	33%	32%	31%	31%	30%
14	36%	35%	35%	34%	33%	32%
15	39%	38%	37%	36%	35%	35%
16	42%	40%	40%	39%	38%	37%
17	44%	43%	42%	41%	40%	39%
18	47%	45%	44%	43%	42%	41%
19	49%	48%	47%	46%	45%	44%
20	52%	50%	49%	48%	47%	46%
21	54%	53%	52%	50%	49%	48%
22	57%	55%	54%	53%	52%	50%
23	59%	58%	57%	55%	54%	53%
24	62%	60%	59%	58%	56%	55%
25	65%	63%	61%	60%	59%	57%
26	67%	65%	64%	62%	61%	60%
27	70%	68%	66%	65%	63%	62%
28	72%	70%	69%	67%	66%	64%
29	75%	73%	71%	70%	68%	66%
30	77%	75%	74%	72%	70%	69%
31	80%	78%	76%	74%	73%	71%
32	83%	80%	79%	77%	75%	73%
33	85%	83%	81%	79%	77%	75%
34	88%	85%	83%	81%	80%	78%
35	90%	88%	86%	84%	82%	80%
36	93%	90%	88%	86%	84%	82%
37	95%	93%	91%	89%	87%	85%
38	98%	95%	93%	91%	89%	87%
39	100%	98%	96%	93%	91%	89%
40	100%	100%	98%	96%	94%	91%
41	100%	100%	100%	98%	96%	94%
42	100%	100%	100%	100%	98%	96%
43	100%	100%	100%	100%	100%	98%
44 or more	100%	100%	100%	100%	100%	100%

State additional pensions are very complicated and only a brief outline is given here. You do not have to work out your own entitlement. You can get a forecast or statement of your additional pension (see page 20).

State Earnings Related Pension Scheme

If you were an employee, you may have built up a State Earnings Related Pension Scheme (SERPS) pension during the period 6 April 1978 to 5 April 2002. Only employees could belong to SERPS. The scheme was not open to the self-employed or people who could not work.

As the name suggests, the amount of SERPS pension is linked to your earnings. This means that higher-paid employees build up a larger SERPS pension than lower-paid employees.

The pension is a percentage of the average of your earnings over your whole working life if this started on or after 6 April 1978. If your working life started before then, the pension is a percentage of your average earnings over the rest of your working life from that date onwards. The percentage has changed over the years and there are transitional rules, but broadly the SERPS pension will be at least one-fifth of your average earnings over the relevant years.

Only earnings above a certain amount – called the lower earnings limit (LEL) – count towards SERPS. This means employees earning less than the LEL have not built up any SERPS pension. Earnings above an upper earnings limit (UEL) are also ignored. These limits are changed every year, but the LEL for 2005–6 is £82 a week and the UEL is £630 a week. For the purpose of the calculation, the earnings for years when you were not building up SERPS are set to zero. For example, these include any years you were contracted out (see page 26) and all the years from 6 April 2002 onwards, because from then on SERPS has been replaced by the State Second Pension (see overleaf).

The earnings used in the calculation are revalued in line with earnings inflation between the time you earned them and the time you reach state pension age to ensure that the pension maintains its value over the years. Like all state pensions, once a SERPS pension starts to be paid, it is increased each year by at least enough to keep pace with price inflation.

State Second Pension

Fundamentally, the State Second Pension (S2P) works in the same way as SERPS, with your pension being based on the average of your revalued earnings (between certain limits) over your working life or the years since 6 April 1978. But S2P has been introduced to address some of the shortcomings of SERPS.

Like SERPS, S2P is not open to people who are self-employed (but see below) and you are not building up S2P if you are an employee earning less than the LEL. But S2P does provide pensions for people who cannot work because they are caring for young children or an ill or disabled person, and in some cases for people who are themselves ill or disabled.

For now, S2P pensions are also linked to earnings, but low earners, regardless of their actual earnings, and the carers and other groups mentioned above are treated as if they have earnings equal to a low earnings threshold (£12,100 in 2005–6). This has the effect of ensuring the pension they build up is at least a minimum, reasonable amount. Other features of S2P also help people on modest earnings to build up bigger pensions than they would have had under SERPS.

The government has indicated that from a date yet to be confirmed S2P might become a flat-rate scheme. You would then be treated as if you had earnings equal to the low earnings threshold with your pension equal to 40 per cent of earnings between the LEL and the threshold. This would mean lower pensions for higher earners. But people above a certain age – say, 45 – at the time S2P becomes flat-rate are likely to continue building up earnings-related pensions rather than being moved to a flat-rate scheme.

The government has consulted on whether self-employed people should be allowed to volunteer to pay higher National Insurance contributions and in return build up S2P but, at the time of writing, no decision had been announced.

Contracting out

For employees, the state additional pension is based on earnings between the LEL and UEL and, by and large, you pay for your pension rights through the National Insurance contributions made on these earnings. (However, since April 2000, people

---

CASE HISTORY: TIM

Tim was born on 10 March 1942. His working life runs from 6 April 1957 to 5 April 2006, a total of 49 years. Of these, 28 years fall in the period since 6 April 1978. He has been an employee all his life (currently earning around £25,000 a year), and a member of SERPS and S2P since they started.

To work out his SERPS pension, the relevant earnings are taken for each year from 6 April 1978 to 5 April 2002 and revalued in line with earnings inflation. The answer is divided by 26 – in other words by the total years covered by both SERPS and S2P (not just the years covered by SERPS) – and the relevant percentage worked out. Tim's SERPS pension comes to £59.75 a week.

Next his S2P pension is worked out. The relevant earnings are taken for the years he is in S2P (2002–3 to 2005–6). They are revalued in line with earnings inflation. This time the relevant percentage is worked out first and the result is then divided by 26 (the total years in both SERPS and S2P). His S2P pension comes to £12.38 a week.

Tim's total state additional pension is £59.75 + £12.38 = £72.13 a week.

---

earning more than the LEL but less than the 'primary threshold', which is £94 a week in 2005–6, do not pay contributions but still build up state additional pension.) You can give up your state additional pension (or in some cases part of it) and instead build up a pension through an occupational pension scheme, personal pension or stakeholder pension scheme. This is called 'contracting out'.

If you belong to a contracted-out occupational pension scheme, you pay National Insurance contributions at a lower rate. The pension scheme must promise to pay you certain benefits at retirement, or it must invest at least a given amount that will be used to provide retirement benefits (see Chapter 3). Your employer might ask you to make contributions to the scheme to help to pay for these benefits.

If you decide to contract out through a personal pension or stakeholder scheme, part of the National Insurance contributions you have paid are rebated and put direct into your pension plan, where they grow and must be used to provide certain retirement benefits (see Chapter 4).

Graduated pension

The state graduated pension scheme covered only employees and ran from 6 April 1961 to 5 April 1975. Graduated pension is paid on top of any basic pension. You might qualify for graduated pension even if you have no basic pension.

Under the scheme, your National Insurance contributions were converted to units that entitle you to a set amount of pension upon reaching state pension age. Women got fewer units, reflecting the higher cost of providing their pensions because women had an earlier retirement age than men and tend to live longer.

In 2005–6, each unit is worth 9.93 pence a week. The biggest graduated pension a man can have is £8.53 a week and for women the maximum is £7.14 a week. You will get less if you were contracted out of the scheme, which means that you built up pension in an occupational pension scheme instead of earning graduated pension.

Special rules for married couples

Each person in a couple can build up his or her own state pensions as described above. For example, if both qualify for the full basic pension, they would get a maximum of 2 × £82.05 = £164.10 a week between them in 2005–6. However, married – but not unmarried – couples can take advantage of special rules.

Same-sex couples

In 2004 new laws were passed which will give the same rights as married couples to same-sex couples who register their relationship as a civil partnership. Among the new rights, one partner in a civil partnership will be able to claim a state basic pension based on the other partner's record provided the person whose record is being used was born on or after 6 April 1950.

A husband who has reached state pension age and is married to a wife who has not reached her state pension age may be entitled to receive extra basic pension in respect of his dependent wife. The maximum extra pension in 2005–6 is £49.15 a week. This is reduced by the same proportion set out in Table 2.2 if the husband qualifies for less than the maximum basic pension. The extra is not payable if the wife has earnings of more than a certain amount – £56.20 a week in 2005–6 – and it stops when the wife qualifies for her own pension on reaching state pension age. At present, a wife cannot normally claim extra pension for her husband, but women born on or after 6 April 1950 (reaching state pension age on or after 6 April 2010) will be able to do so.

Where husband and wife have both reached state pension age, the wife can claim a basic pension of up to £49.15 a week based on her husband's National Insurance record. This pension is paid direct to the wife rather than to the husband and counts as her own income

---

CASE HISTORY: GILLIAN

Gillian reaches age 60 in November 2005 and qualifies for a pension, based on her own National Insurance record, of £25.44 per week (which is 31 per cent of the maximum basic pension). Her husband Zac has already retired. He too did not have enough contributions for the maximum basic pension and gets £61.54, which is 75 per cent of the full rate. Any pension for Gillian based on his contribution record would also be reduced by the same proportion.

Gillian is entitled to claim a composite pension. This equals the pension of £25.44 based on her own contribution record plus the lower of:

- the amount needed to top up her pension to the maximum wife's rate of £49.15, in other words £49.15 – £25.44 = £23.71, and
- the amount of pension she could otherwise get based on Zac's contribution record, in other words 75% × £49.15 = £36.86.

As £23.71 is lower than £36.86, her composite pension is £25.44 + £23.71 = £49.15.

for tax purposes. A married couple both relying on the husband's record would get a maximum pension of £82.05 + £49.15 = £131.20 a week between them. But, if the husband qualifies only for a reduced pension, the wife's pension is reduced by the same proportion as set out in Table 2.2. At present, a husband cannot claim a similar pension based on his wife's contribution record, but men married to women reaching state pension age on or after 6 April 2010 will be able to do so.

If a wife has built up a reduced-rate basic pension based on her own contribution record and is also entitled to claim a basic pension based on her husband's record, she can have a 'composite pension'. This is made up of:

- her own pension, plus
- the pension based on her husband's record or, if lower, the amount needed to make her pension up to the maximum pension based on a husband's record (£49.15 in 2005–6).

The whole composite pension is paid direct to the wife and counts as her income for tax purposes. Once again, husbands are not currently entitled to a composite pension, but men married to women reaching state pension age on or after 6 April 2010 will be.

A wife may receive additional pension and graduated pension that she has built up in her own right on top of any basic pension based on her husband's National Insurance record.

Special rules for divorced people

If you are divorced, you may have built up your own state basic pension. However, if this would be paid at a reduced rate, you might get a higher basic pension by using special rules that apply to divorced people. These allow a divorced man or woman to substitute for some or all of the years in his or her working life the contributions record of the former wife or husband.

When you ask for a State Pension Forecast or claim your pension, The Pension Service will ask you for details of any former husband or wife whose National Insurance record could be used in calculating your pension entitlement. Ideally, you should keep a note of your former husband's or wife's full name, date of birth and National Insurance number.

On top of any enhanced basic pension, you will also get any additional pension and graduated pension you have built up in your own right.

If your divorce proceedings commenced on or after 1 December 2000, a court can make a pension-sharing order, requiring most retirement pensions (but not the state basic pension) to be split between the couple. Such an order can be applied to state additional pensions. If you are going through a divorce and need advice about this, contact a solicitor★, local Law Centre★ or Citizens Advice Bureau (CAB)★.

Special rules for widows and widowers

If you are widowed either before or after reaching state pension age, you might qualify for extra state retirement pension based on your late husband's or wife's contribution record. The rules are complicated and depend on when you are widowed, your age when widowed, whether your late husband or wife died before or after reaching retirement age, and whether you were entitled to other state benefits before you reached retirement.

When you ask for a State Pension Forecast or claim your pension, The Pension Service will ask for details of a late husband or late wife whose National Insurance record could be used in calculating your pension entitlement. Ideally, you should keep a note of your late spouse's full name, date of birth and National Insurance number.

For more information, see DWP leaflets NP46, *A guide to retirement pensions*, GL14, *Widowed?* and NP45, *A guide to bereavement benefits*, available from social security offices★ and the DWP★ website.

Boosting your state pension
Paying voluntary contributions

If you do not have enough qualifying years to get the maximum basic pension, you may be able to pay voluntary National Insurance contributions to turn a non-qualifying year into a qualifying one. However, you can normally go back only up to six years to fill any gaps.

Married women cannot pay voluntary contributions for years when they had opted to pay Class 1 contributions at the reduced rate or had opted not to pay Class 2 contributions under pre-May 1977 rules. Class 3 contributions are usually payable at the rates shown in Table 2.3. Voluntary contributions boost your basic pension, but not any additional or graduated pension.

Table 2.3   Rate at which you pay Class 3 contributions in 2005–6

Year to which the contribution is being allocated	Weekly rate	Cost for a whole year
2005–6	£7.35	£382.20
2004–5	£7.15	£371.80
2003–4	£6.95	£361.40
2002–3	£7.35	£382.20
2001–2	£7.35	£382.20
2000–1	£7.35	£382.20
1999–2000	£7.35	£382.20

For more information, see leaflet CA08, *National Insurance voluntary contributions*, available from the Inland Revenue★ and social security offices★.

Delaying the start of your state pension to earn extra

Another way to boost the state pension that is open to everyone is to put off starting to receive your pension. This earns an increase in the pension when payment eventually starts. This may be particularly worth doing if you will have other sources of income in early retirement (for example, because you plan to carry on doing some work).

You have to defer your whole state pension – basic, additional and any graduated pension. If you are a married man, and your wife is claiming a pension based on your contribution record (see page 28), she must consent to the deferment because her pension is automatically deferred as well (except any amounts based on her own contribution record). A wife can independently decide to defer her own pension regardless of whether it is based on her own contribution record or that of her husband.

You can take the decision to defer your pension at the date when it would first become payable (in other words on reaching state pension age). Alternatively, if your pension has already started to be paid, you can decide to stop the payments. But you can only defer your pension once.

Where you defer your pension on or after 6 April 2005, you can earn an increase in your pension when it does start of 1/5 per cent for every week you put off the pension (with a minimum overall increase of 1 per cent). This is equivalent to an increase of 10.4 per cent for each whole year. The extra pension, like the rest of your state pension, is taxable (see Chapter 14). You can put off starting your pension for as long as you like.

Alternatively, provided you put off claiming your pension for at least a year, you can earn a one-off lump sum instead of extra pension. The lump sum is equal to the total pension you deferred plus interest at a rate set by the government at roughly 2 per cent above the Bank of England base rate, which can go up and down. (If you defer for less than a year but want a lump sum, you'll get the total pension deferred but without any interest added.) The lump sum is taxable but only at the top rate you were paying before getting the lump sum – in other words, whatever the size of lump sum, it does not take you into a higher tax bracket. You can choose to receive the lump sum either in the year you start your pension or the following year (when your income and tax rate might be lower if, say, you are stopping work).

Different rules applied before 6 April 2005: you earned an increase of 1/7 per cent for each week of deferment (equivalent to 7.4 per cent for each year) and you could not earn a lump sum. If you started to defer your pension before 6 April 2005 and continue to defer it after that date, you earn an increase under the old rules for the period up to 6 April 2005 and then switch to the new rules for the rest of the deferment falling after that date.

Is deferring your pension a good idea? Table 2.4 shows the amount of extra pension you could earn. The extra needs to be paid out for about 9½ years before you have got back as much in extra pension as you gave up while the pension was deferred. If you die, your widow or widower continues to benefit from the increase, so to weigh up whether the deal would be worthwhile, consider the average life expectancy for someone your or your spouse's age. A man aged 75 or less and a woman aged 78 or less can be expected on average to survive at least another 9½ years. If you or your spouse is

Table 2.4 How much state pension increase you can earn

Length of time you defer the pension	Each £1 of your state pension will increase to:
6 months	£1.05
1 year	£1.10
2 years	£1.21
3 years	£1.31
4 years	£1.42
5 years	£1.52
6 years	£1.62
7 years	£1.73
8 years	£1.83
9 years	£1.94
10 years	£2.04

older, deferring and opting for extra pension might not be such a good idea. But bear in mind these are just averages – you personally might live for a longer or shorter period.

If you defer your pension and opt for the lump sum, you need to consider whether you could get a better return by receiving your pension straight away and investing it. At the time of writing, the Bank of England base rate was 4.75 per cent, so deferring your state pension would earn you 6.75 per cent interest before tax. This is equivalent to an after-tax return of 6.1 per cent, 5.4 per cent or 4.1 per cent if you are a starting-rate, basic-rate or higher-rate taxpayer, respectively. You could not at that time get as much from an ordinary bank or building society savings account but a basic- or higher-rate taxpayer could get a better return from a cash individual savings account (ISA) – see Chapter 9.

CASE HISTORY: GRAEME AND JESSIE

Graeme is coming up to age 65 and will qualify for a state basic and additional pension of £103 a week, and Jessie, who is 62, will be able to claim £49.15 a week on Graeme's National Insurance record. This gives them total state pensions of £152.15 a week. But Graeme plans to carry on working for a while and does not really need his state pension yet. He and Jessie agree to defer their state pensions.

Five years later, they decide to start receiving their pensions. Working in today's money, instead of £152.15 a week, they could opt for increased pensions of 1.52 × £152.15 = £231.27. If they prefer a lump sum, they could stick with pensions of £152.15 a week but also receive a lump sum of around £47,000 before tax assuming interest rates stay at the current level.

For more information, contact The Pension Service★ and see DWP leaflet NP46, *A guide to retirement pensions*, available from The Pension Service★ and the DWP★ website.

Deciding whether or not to contract out

You may be able to choose whether or not to contract out (see page 26). Many experts see little advantage in contracting out at any age and most agree that men in their mid-50s and older and women aged 50 and above are probably better off staying in or contracting back into the state scheme. However, if you are in a contracted-out occupational scheme, the only way to contract back in would be to leave the scheme. This is not recommended. You would give up a whole package of benefits and the loss of these would normally far outweigh any gain from contracting back into the state scheme.

For more information, get advice from an independent financial adviser★.

Chapter 3

Occupational pension choices at retirement

For many people, the major source of retirement income is a pension from an occupational pension scheme. If you have worked for several employers during your lifetime, you might be entitled to pensions from more than one scheme.

What are occupational schemes?

An occupational scheme is a pension scheme offered by an employer as part of the benefits of your job.

You can be offered other pension arrangements through your workplace, but the distinguishing feature of an occupational scheme is that your employer normally pays substantial contributions into the scheme on your behalf. In a 'contributory scheme' you also make regular contributions towards the cost of your pension.

Under current rules, you cannot be forced to join an occupational scheme at work, but, if one is on offer, it is usually the best way to save for retirement.

When can you get your occupational pension?

Under the present rules, you cannot start to get a pension from your current employer's occupational scheme until you actually retire, in other words stop working for that employer. In the past, where people have simultaneously worked and drawn a pension, the Inland Revenue has penalised them by taxing any lump sum drawn from the pension scheme. However, the rules are changing and, from 6 April 2006, you will be able to carry on working while drawing a pension from your current employer's scheme.

Under the present rules, you can without a problem work for someone else (another employer, as a self-employed person, doing voluntary work, and so on) while drawing your pension.

Each scheme has a 'normal retirement age', commonly 65, at which your full pension becomes payable. Normal retirement ages are usually in the range 60 to 75 years, but earlier ages are permitted for some occupations, for example 35 for professional footballers and 55 for foreign-exchange brokers.

You can often choose to retire earlier than the normal retirement age, but your pension is then reduced (see page 47). The reduction can be surprisingly large, although it is usually less if you have to retire due to ill health or your employer is trying to encourage voluntary redundancies. The earliest age at which you can draw your pension is usually 50 under current rules, though this is being raised to 55 by 2010.

You might be allowed to put off your retirement beyond the normal retirement age and receive a larger pension when you do finally stop work.

If the occupational scheme is 'contracted out', at least part of the pension it provides is designed to replace pension you would otherwise have received from the state. Under current rules, you cannot start to receive this contracted-out pension before reaching a certain age. The age varies depending on the type of scheme and when you built up the benefits, but will be state pension age, age 60 or the normal retirement age for the scheme. This restriction is particularly important if you are thinking about early retirement, because you may have to manage on a reduced occupational pension until you reach the age at which your contracted-out benefits kick in. Your pension scheme administrator* can tell you what restrictions apply.

From 6 April 2006, the age restrictions on starting to receive contracted-out pensions are being abolished. This will simplify schemes, allowing them to pay all benefits from the same age.

How do you get your pension?

About four months or so before you reach the normal retirement date for a scheme, the scheme administrators should write to you to set in motion arrangements to pay your pension (or to defer your pension if that is your intention). If you are within four months of retiring and have not heard from a scheme, you should make the first move and get in touch.

You may be due a pension not only from a current employer's scheme but also 'preserved pensions' from schemes you belonged to in the past (see box). If you have lost touch with a scheme that owes you a preserved pension, the Pension Schemes Registry* may be able to help you to trace the scheme.

If you are hoping to take early retirement, you should contact all the schemes from which you want to draw a pension early. Ask them for a statement showing the benefits you would get. You will need these to help you to decide whether you can afford early retirement.

Pensions from previous employers' schemes

When you leave a pension scheme before retirement – for example, on changing jobs – provided that you have been a member of the scheme for a minimum period (currently two years, previously five years), you have the right to a preserved pension from the scheme. The pension becomes payable when you reach the normal retirement age for the scheme. You can, if you choose, transfer these rights to another pension scheme or plan. If you do transfer, the old scheme no longer has any obligations to you, nor do you need to keep in touch with the scheme.

Any scheme that is due to pay you a preserved pension at retirement should send you regular benefit statements estimating the amount that pension will be and should contact you shortly before retirement. Take care to send the scheme your new address if you move.

If you leave a pension scheme before you have been a member for two years (previously five), you will usually get a refund of your contributions (less tax). The scheme then has no further obligations to you and you do not need to keep in contact. From 6 April 2006, if you have been in a scheme less than two years but at least six months, you will have the choice of either a refund or a transfer to another scheme or plan.

How are occupational pensions paid?

In most cases, occupational pensions are paid monthly by direct transfer into your bank or building society account.

The pension will be paid through the Pay-As-You-Earn (PAYE) system, so tax will have been deducted from the payment before you receive it. The amount of tax deducted will be based on your income from all sources – for example, including your state pension – not just your occupational pension (see Chapter 14).

How much pension?

In most schemes, the same general rules apply to all members. However, the precise amount of pension you'll receive is personal to you and depends on your particular circumstances, for example how long you have been in the scheme and your pay, or how much has been paid in. What you get will be different from the amount any other employee gets. Your pension is worked out on either:

- a 'defined benefit' basis This means you are promised a pension based on some kind of formula typically linked to your pay near retirement or your average pay while in the scheme. The most common type of defined benefit scheme is a 'final salary scheme' though 'career average schemes' are becoming more widespread, or
- a 'money purchase' (also called 'defined contribution') basis You are not promised any particular level of pension. How much you get depends on the pension fund that has built up by retirement and the amount of pension it can buy.

'Hybrid schemes' work out your pension on both bases and pay you whichever amount is greatest. Details of the main types of schemes are given later in this chapter.

Often, you have the option of giving up part of your pension and instead receiving a tax-free cash sum (see page 50). Some schemes automatically pay a cash sum and so do not offer you the choice.

When you joined the scheme, you should have received a scheme booklet. This will describe the basis on which your pension is worked out and the various rules that apply.

You should receive regular benefit statements (see below) estimating the amount of pension you can expect at retirement. These will help you to see whether you are saving enough for the retirement you want and whether you can afford to retire at your preferred age.

Increases to your pension once it starts to be paid

Any contracted-out salary-related pensions (see page 26) payable at retirement must be increased in line with inflation once they start to be paid, although often only up to a maximum of 5 per cent or 2.5 per cent a year. Depending on the type of contracted-out pension and when you built it up, the increase may be provided partly or wholly by the scheme and added to your occupational pension, or provided partly or wholly by the state and added to your state pension. In some circumstances, the scheme is also obliged to increase non-contracted out pensions in line with inflation up to a maximum.

Schemes used also to be obliged to increase certain money purchase pensions in line with inflation up to a maximum. However, where pensions start to be paid on or after 6 April 2005, this requirement is abolished. It will be up to either the scheme or you to choose whether to make regular increases. Bear in mind that a pension which does not increase regularly is vulnerable to inflation – see Chapter 1.

Schemes are free to make larger pension increases and voluntarily to increase pensions where there is no legal obligation to do so. Public sector schemes (covering teachers, local authority workers, the police, and so on) usually fully index-link pensions in payment, giving complete protection against price inflation. Large private sector schemes also tend to provide generous increases, often on a discretionary basis rather than being contractually bound to do so.

Ask your pension scheme administrator★ for details of the scheme's policy on pension increases. This will help you to plan your income as retirement progresses.

Benefit statements

Once a year you should receive a benefit statement from each scheme that is due to pay you a pension at retirement. If you still belong to the scheme, this tells you how much pension you can expect at retirement if you carry on being a member until you retire. If the statement is from a scheme you have left, it tells you how much preserved pension you can expect at retirement based on the rights you had built up at the time you left.

Often statements also give some indication of the pension you might get from the state. Many benefit statements just quote the maximum basic pension regardless of the actual state pension you personally will qualify for. However, increasingly schemes are being encouraged to issue 'combined benefit statements' (also called 'combined pension forecasts'). These include figures from the Department for Work and Pensions (DWP) based on your National Insurance contribution record to forecast the actual state pension you are expected to get at retirement. If you get combined statements from more than one pension scheme, be careful not to double-count your state pension when totting up the various sources of your expected retirement income.

Benefit statements are important. Although they can only estimate your pension rather than telling you precisely what you will get, they are a useful tool in helping you check whether you are on target for the retirement income you want. If you're not on track, the benefit statements act as a prompt to review your retirement planning. Steps you can take include paying extra towards your pension (see page 54), or delaying your retirement so that you can earn a pension increase (see page 53) or at least have more time in which to build up your savings.

New rules from April 2006

The sections below briefly describe the main types of pension scheme including the current government rules that restrict the benefits you can have. However, from 6 April 2006, all the different rules applying to different types of pension scheme and plans are being swept away and replaced by a single, new, simplified regime. The main features of the new regime are:

- the limits on the amount of pension you can have from an occupational scheme and the earnings cap are abolished
- instead, by retirement, you are allowed to accumulate total pension funds in all your occupational schemes (this chapter) and

personal pensions (see Chapter 4) up to a lifetime allowance. Initially the standard lifetime allowance has been set at £1.5 million and this will be increased each year broadly in line with price inflation – see Table 3.1. A tax charge will be levied on any pension fund in excess of the lifetime allowance. If you are in a salary-related scheme , you convert the pension into an equivalent lump sum (usually by multiplying the pension by 20) in order to compare it against the lifetime allowance

- you can take a quarter of your total pension funds (up to the lifetime allowance) as a tax-free lump sum. The rest must normally be taken as pension.

- but if your total pension funds come to no more than 1 per cent of the lifetime allowance (for example, £15,000 in 2006–7) you can take the whole amount as a lump sum, though only a quarter is tax-free.

- if you 'phase' your retirement – in other words, start part of your pension on one date and part on one or more later dates – you use up part of your lifetime allowance with the first pension to start, and the remaining allowance increased for inflation is carried forward to be used when you start the later tranches of pension

- other rules allow people who have already built up substantial pension savings or tax-free lump sums by April 2006 which are over the permitted limits to protect these from extra tax charges. If this might affect you, there are steps you may need to take before the new rules come into effect so you should urgently seek advice from an independent financial adviser★ specialising in pension planning. But for the vast majority of people the new limits comfortably exceed the amount of pension or other benefits you are likely to build up

Table 3.1 The lifetime and annual allowances

Tax year	Lifetime allowance	Annual allowance
2006–7	£1.5 million	£215,000
2007–8	£1.6 million	£225,000
2008–9	£1.65 million	£235,000
2009–10	£1.75 million	£245,000
2010–11	£1.8 million	£255,000

- the different rules limiting the amount you can pay into different types of pension scheme and plan are abolished and replaced by a single new set of rules applying collectively to all your occupational schemes and personal pensions
- each year, your pension funds and benefits may increase up to an annual allowance. Initially this allowance is set at £215,000 and will increase each year broadly in line with inflation – see Table 3.1. A tax charge is levied on any increase in excess of the annual allowance. To compare additions to a promised pension against the annual allowance, you convert it into an equivalent lump sum (by multiplying the pension by 10)
- the most you can pay into your pension schemes and plans each year is £3,600 or the full amount of your earnings for the year, whichever is greater
- pension schemes and plans continue to attract the same tax reliefs as now, for example you get tax relief on contributions and the invested contributions build up largely tax-free.

Final salary schemes

This is the most common type of defined benefit scheme. You are promised a pension worked out according to a formula based on:

- **your final salary** This is some or all of your pay shortly before retirement. The rules of the scheme will say what is included in 'pensionable salary' (for example, whether overtime is included), and whether it is, say, your pay in the last year, your average pay over the last three years or some other measure
- **how long you have been in the scheme** Usually measured in years and complete months
- **the accrual rate** This is a fraction, often one-sixtieth or one-eightieth. Your pension is this fraction of your final salary for each year you have been in the scheme.

Under current rules (but see *New rules from April 2006* above), the Inland Revenue sets an overall limit on the pension you can have. The limit is usually one-sixtieth of your final salary for each year of membership, up to a maximum pension of two-thirds of your final salary.

For schemes set up on or after 14 March 1989 and schemes you joined on or after 1 June 1989, the earnings used in this calculation are capped. The 'earnings cap' changes each year; it is £105,600 in 2005–6. This means that there is also a cash limit on the maximum pension of $2/3 \times$ £105,600 = £70,400 a year.

In some cases, your pension and lump sum from an occupational scheme may be restricted to take account of benefits you are due from other occupational schemes.

If you left a scheme before retirement, the pension is worked out using your final salary at the time you left the scheme. Where you left on or after 1 January 1986, any pension you built up from 1 January 1985 onwards must be increased between the time you left up to the time you retire in line with price inflation up to a maximum of 5 per cent a year. This prevents the buying power of the preserved pension being eaten away by inflation.

CASE HISTORY: PAUL

Paul has worked for the same employer for 22 years and is shortly to retire. His pay just before retirement is £32,000 and the scheme pays a pension of one-sixtieth of final salary for each year of membership. His pension will be:

$1/60 \times$ £32,000 $\times$ 22 = £11,733.33 a year.

CASE HISTORY: DAPHNE

Daphne is entitled to a preserved pension from a previous employer's occupational scheme. When she left five years ago, she was on £18,000 a year and she had been in the scheme for six years. The scheme pays one-eightieth of final salary for each year of membership, but the preserved pension is also increased in line with inflation up to a maximum of 5 per cent a year between the time Daphne left and her retirement. The preserved pension before inflation-proofing is:

$1/80 \times$ £18,000 $\times$ 6 = £1,350 a year.

Increasing this in line with inflation over the last five years, boosts the pension to £1,507.71 a year.

There is no obligation on schemes to increase pensions (apart from any contracted-out ones) you built up before 1 January 1985. So a pension from the early part of your career might now buy very little. However, many schemes voluntarily increase these pensions.

At least part of your pension from a contracted-out scheme is designed to replace benefits you would otherwise have had from the state (see Chapter 2). The scheme must ensure final salary contracted-out pensions comply with government rules that ensure you get a fair-value replacement for the state benefits you have given up. The precise rules depend on when you were contracted out and are fairly complicated.

Benefit statements from your occupational scheme do not normally separate your contracted-out pension from any additional pension that you will get from the scheme. However, the distinction may become important if you are planning to retire early, because of restrictions under current rules on when contracted-out pensions can be paid.

Money purchase schemes

All money purchase schemes (whether occupational schemes, personal pension or stakeholder schemes) work in broadly the same way. You build up a personal savings pot and the amount of pension you receive depends on:

- the amount paid in
- how well your savings grow
- the amount taken out in charges, and
- the amount of pension you can buy at retirement with the fund that has built up.

In occupational schemes, there is under current rules usually an overall limit on the pension you can receive. Even though money purchase schemes work in a different way, the limit is currently the same as that which applies to final salary schemes. So the maximum pension is generally one-sixtieth of your final salary for each year of membership, up to a maximum pension of two-thirds of your final salary. However, see 'New rules from April 2006' on page 41.

Occupational schemes have an advantage over other types of money purchase scheme because your employer must usually contribute, boosting the amount paid in, and charges for occupational schemes are often low.

Typically, a money purchase scheme hands the pension fund over to professional fund managers to invest, but there is no way of knowing in advance how the investments will perform. The bulk of the money is invested in the stock market. Since share prices can fall as well as rise, gains made one year can be subsequently lost.

Some occupational money purchase schemes let you choose how your fund will be invested. The range of possible options is the same as for personal pensions (see Chapter 4). Being able to choose is particularly useful in the run up to retirement, because you can then progressively switch away from volatile investments like shares into more stable bonds, gilts and money funds. That way, past gains can be preserved and the risk of a fall in the value of your fund just at the time you want to spend it on a pension can be reduced.

The amount of pension you can buy at retirement is considered in detail in Chapters 5 to 7. Chapter 5 includes details of the benefits, called 'protected rights', that must be purchased with the proceeds of a contracted-out occupational money purchase scheme.

You may be due a preserved pension (see box on page 38) from a previous employer's money purchase scheme. Even though nothing more will have been paid into the scheme since you left, the fund you had built up will have remained invested and will have continued growing. Your pension will be whatever the resulting fund can buy at retirement.

CASE HISTORY: EDWARD

Edward is about to retire. He has been a member of an occupational money purchase scheme for ten years. Edward has paid 5 per cent of his salary into the scheme each month and his employer paid in the same. Edward now has a pension fund of £38,900, which is presently enough to buy a pension of around £2,400 a year.

Your pension if you retire early

Retiring in, say, your fifties can seem very tempting, but it puts enormous strain on your retirement savings for two reasons. Firstly, you have cut short the time over which to build up your pension. Secondly, you have increased the length of time over which the pension must be paid. Therefore it is not too surprising that occupational schemes usually provide only a reduced pension if you opt for early retirement.

Some occupational pensions are designed to dovetail closely with the state basic pension scheme. If you retire before state pension age, these schemes may pay you a higher level of pension which then reduces once your state basic pension kicks in. The aim is to provide you with a reasonably stable income from the combined sources. Your pension scheme booklet or pension scheme administrator* can tell you if this arrangement applies to your pension.

There are currently restrictions on when contracted-out pensions (designed to replace some, or all, of your state additional pension) can be paid. If a large part of your occupational pension is contracted-out pension, the scheme may refuse to pay you any early retirement pension at all.

An early retirement pension from a final salary scheme

Your pension will be based on your final salary at the time you retire. This is likely to be lower than your pay would have been if you had waited until normal retirement age, because salaries tend to increase each year and also you might be missing out on promotions you would have had if you had stayed on. The lower final salary feeds through the formula to produce a lower pension.

You will also have been in the scheme for fewer years than if you had stayed on until normal retirement age. Again, this feeds through the formula to produce a lower pension.

However, there may be a further 'actuarial reduction'. This is made because your pension will have to be paid out for more years than if you had waited until normal retirement age. Different schemes have different rules, but a common actuarial reduction is 6 per cent for each year that you retire early. For example, if you retire two years before normal retirement age, the reduction would

CASE HISTORY: BETTY

Betty belongs to a one-sixtieths final salary scheme. If she stays until the normal retirement age of 65, she will have been in the scheme 35 years. Assuming her final salary would then be £40,000 a year, her pension would be:

$1/60 \times £40,000 \times 35 = £23,333$ a year.

However, she is considering retiring now, five years early, at age 60. Her salary is currently £33,000 a year and she has been in the scheme 30 years, so her formula pension is:

$1/60 \times £33,000 \times 30 = £16,500$ a year.

But this is not the end of the story. The scheme would also make an actuarial reduction to her pension because the pension will have to be paid out for more years. The reduction is 6 per cent for each year of early retirement. Retiring five years early means the reduction will be $5 \times 6\% = 30\%$. So Betty's pension will be only:

$70\% \times £16,500 = £11,550$ a year.

Retiring five years early has more than halved the pension Betty will receive throughout retirement.

CASE HISTORY: DENNIS

Dennis develops Parkinson's Disease and has to retire five years early from work. He has belonged to a good final salary scheme for 30 years and currently earns £33,000. The scheme pays one-sixtieth of his final salary for each year of membership. But, in cases of ill health, the pension is based on the years of membership had the person been able to stay until normal retirement age. Therefore Dennis' pension is based on 35 years of membership and comes to:

$1/60 \times £33,000 \times 35 = £19,250$ a year.

The scheme makes no actuarial reduction to ill-health pensions.

be $2 \times 6\% = 12\%$. If you retire five years early, the reduction would be $5 \times 6\% = 30\%$. The actuarial reduction can cause a very large cut in your pension.

The actuarial reduction is not usually applied if you have to retire early because of ill health. An ill-health early pension can also be based on the years you would have had in the scheme had you been able to stay on until normal retirement age.

If your employer is downsizing and looking for voluntary redundancies, you may be offered a good pension deal as an incentive. Typically, the actuarial reduction would be waived in this case.

Some schemes do not apply an actuarial reduction provided that you have built up sufficient years of membership and are not retiring too early. A common rule is the 'rule of 85', which allows you an unreduced pension if your age and years of membership add up to 85 or more.

An early retirement pension from a money purchase scheme

If you retire early from a money purchase scheme, your pension fund will be smaller than if you had carried on until normal retirement age because:

- fewer contributions will have been paid in. You lose the contributions that you and your employer would have paid in between the date of your early retirement and normal retirement age. You also lose the return those contributions would have generated
- your fund will have had less time to grow. You lose the return you would have had during those last few years up to normal retirement age.

Retiring early also means that your pension will have to be paid out for more years and this is reflected in the rate at which you can convert your pension fund into pension. The earlier you retire, the less pension you get for your money. See Chapters 5 to 7 for details.

If you have to retire early due to ill health, some employers have a separate insurance scheme to provide you with income to top up whatever you get from the pension scheme.

CASE HISTORY: JEAN

Jean is currently 60 years old and has been paying into a money purchase pension scheme for the past 20 years. Her employer's and her own contributions to the scheme total 8.5 per cent of her salary and she currently earns about £25,000 a year. By the time she reaches the normal retirement age of 65, she is forecast to have a pension fund of £72,000 in today's money, which would buy a level pension of around £4,790 a year.

If instead Jean retired today at age 60, her pension fund stands at £50,600 and this would buy her a level pension of £3,000 a year.

Retiring five years early would nearly halve her pension. This happens because:

- the fund misses out on £11,000 (in today's money) that would have been paid in contributions by Jean and her employer
- the fund loses £17,500 (in today's money) investment growth on both the fund that had already built up by the early retirement date and the lost contributions
- at age 60, Jean gets just £593 of level pension for each £10,000 of pension fund; at age 65 she gets £665 pension per £10,000 of fund.

Choosing whether to take a lump sum

You can take part of the proceeds from a pension scheme as a tax-free lump sum. Since the rest must be taken as taxable pension, this option is a major reason why pension schemes are a tax-efficient way to save for retirement.

If you opt to take the tax-free cash, your pension is reduced. This swapping of pension for cash is called 'commutation'. The rate at which the swap is made can vary, but typically you might get around £9 of tax-free cash for every £1 of pension you give up.

Under current rules, the maximum lump sum you can have (whether from a money purchase or final salary scheme) is usually three-eightieths of your final salary for each year of membership up to a maximum of one-and-a-half times your final salary. For schemes set up on or after 14 March 1989 and schemes you joined on or after 1 June 1989, the earnings used in this calculation are capped. The 'earnings cap' changes each year and is £105,600 in 2005–6. This means there is also a cash limit on the maximum lump sum of 1½ × £105,600 = £158,400. As mentioned earlier, the maximum pension you can have is usually one-sixtieth of your pay for each year of membership, up to a pension of two-thirds of your final salary. This is the limit before you swap any of the pension for cash, so the maximum pension is less if you take the cash.

Under the new rules from 6 April 2006 (see page 41), you can take a tax-free lump sum equal to one-quarter of your pension fund up to the lifetime limit.

Usually, taking tax-free cash affects only your own pension and does not reduce any pensions that would be payable to your dependants if you died (see overleaf) but check your scheme rules.

On the face of it, deciding how much tax-free cash to take seems to be a decision about whether you can manage on the reduced pension. But, in practice, it is nearly always worth taking the maximum cash even if you then use it to provide extra income. This is because you are swapping taxable pension for tax-free cash. You can invest the cash to provide income which is either tax-free or at least only partially taxed. See Chapter 14 for how this works.

CASE HISTORY: RUBY

In 2005–6 Ruby has a final salary of £13,500 and has built up the maximum permitted pension of $2/3$ × £13,500 = £9,000 a year. Alternatively, she could have a smaller pension plus a tax-free lump sum. The maximum lump sum would be 1½ × £13,500 = £20,250. Her pension is reduced by £1 for every £9 of lump sum, in other words by £20,250 / 9 = £2,250. Taking the maximum lump sum reduces her pension to £6,750, which is half her final salary.

Choices involving dependants

As well as a pension for yourself, an occupational scheme typically provides a pension for your widow or widower if you die first. This is usually compulsory in the case of a contracted-out scheme (though if you are in a contracted-out money purchase scheme and single at the time you retire you can opt to forego the widow/er's pension). From a date yet to be confirmed but expected to be October 2005, schemes will be required to treat in the same way as a widow/er, a same-sex partner if the couple has registered the relationship as a civil partnership.

Most private sector schemes but only around half of public sector schemes (covering, for example, teachers and local authority workers) will pay a pension to an unmarried partner who survives you and who is deemed to be either financially dependent on you or with whom you had mutually dependent financial arrangements. It is now illegal to discriminate in the workplace on the grounds of sexual orientation, so if the scheme does pay pensions to unmarried partners this must apply equally to same-sex partners and opposite-sex partners.

Under current government rules, the maximum pension is two-thirds of the pension to which you were entitled. However the scheme rules might limit the pension to less. Bear in mind too that schemes often change their rules as time goes by. Even if the current survivor's pension is generous, this might be based only on your most recent years of membership. Your widow/er or partner may get less than you expect if part of his or her pension is based on less generous rules that applied during earlier years of your membership. The only way to plan adequately is to check your benefit statement or ask your pension scheme administrator* for a figure estimating the amount your survivor would get in the event of your death.

Some schemes allow you to give up the widow's/widower's/partner's pension at retirement in return for an increase in your own pension. Only do this if you have no partner or if your partner has his or her own income and is in no way financially dependent on you. Be aware that this is a one-way choice. You cannot reverse it if, say, you marry after retiring.

Most schemes also provide pensions for other dependants, such as children, in the event of your death. The total of the pension for your widow/widower/partner and any other dependants under current rules must not come to more than the pension you were entitled to.

The choices if you have dependants to protect remain broadly the same under new rules which apply from 6 April 2006, but see Chapter 5 for additional options.

Divorce

If you divorce and proceedings start on or after 1 December 2000, a court can order that any pension rights that you and your former husband or wife have, including occupational pensions, be shared. Under pension sharing, part of a pension fund or rights under a pension scheme is taken away from one person and allocated to the other. If the pension has already started to be paid, then part of the pension is transferred to the ex-husband or ex-wife.

Another possibility which can apply to divorces started before or after December 2000 is 'earmarking'. The pension fund or pension rights are not transferred, but, once the pension starts to be paid, the earmarked part is paid out to the ex-husband or ex-wife. Earmarking orders are not widely made and their impact can be lessened if the person whose pension has been earmarked stops paying into the earmarked pension scheme and starts up a new one instead.

On the other hand, divorce proceedings need not have affected any pension arrangements directly, but one party may have been awarded extra maintenance income or a bigger share of the non-pension assets to compensate for the loss of pension rights.

From a date yet to be announced, possibly October 2005, the arrangements described above can also apply to same-sex partners who had registered their relationship as a civil partnership but have subsequently dissolved the partnership.

Boosting your occupational pension

Putting off your retirement

At present, not all employers allow you to carry on working beyond normal retirement age. But, where they do, you will usually earn extra pension. This reflects both the extended period over which your pension builds up and the shorter time for which it is likely to be paid. Talk to the pension scheme administrator★ if you want to explore this option. By 2006, the UK must implement a European Union directive outlawing age discrimination.

Consultation on how to implement this is still going on. However, the government has indicated that, for five years at least, it will allow employers to retain the right to insist that an employee retires at age 65. Employees will merely have a right to request later retirement but the request can be turned down if the employer has sound business reasons for doing so.

Making additional voluntary contributions

Under current rules, all occupational pension schemes must offer an in-house additional voluntary contribution (AVC) scheme that allows you to pay in extra contributions. These can be used to boost your pension and other benefits (though often not the tax-free lump sum). Some employers encourage you to make AVCs to an in-house scheme by offering to match what you pay in. In-house AVC schemes work in either of two ways: as 'added years schemes', or on a money purchase basis.

You can also make your own extra contributions to a totally separate free-standing AVC scheme that you arrange yourself. The proceeds of free-standing AVC schemes cannot currently be taken as tax-free cash.

Under current rules, the total of your normal contributions to the occupational scheme plus any AVCs must not exceed 15 per cent of your earnings (which can include the taxable value of any fringe benefits). For schemes set up on or after 14 March 1989 and schemes you joined on or after 1 June 1989, the earnings used in this calculation are capped. The 'earnings cap' changes each year and is £105,600 in 2005–6. This means that there is also a cash limit on the maximum contributions of 15% × £105,600 = £15,840 a year. Anything paid by your employer on your behalf does not count towards the contribution limit.

Under current rules, you cannot increase the pension and other benefits from your occupational scheme beyond the limits set by the Inland Revenue (broadly, a pension of two-thirds of final salary before adjusting for a tax-free lump sum of no more than one-and-a-half times final salary).

The requirements and restrictions described above cease to apply from 6 April 2006 onwards. From then on, the single new regime applies collectively to all your occupational schemes (this chapter) and personal pensions (see Chapter 4). Provided you are within the limits described on page 41, you can contribute what you like to any type of or combination of schemes and plans. Occupational schemes will also cease to be obliged to offer an in-house AVC scheme though many may continue to do so.

Added years schemes

This type of AVC scheme is offered only by final salary schemes, nearly always public sector schemes. In return for your AVCs, you are credited with extra years (or part years) of membership. This works through the pension formula to boost all your benefits (including any tax-free lump sum).

Even if you are near retirement, you can usually still buy extra years, though as you have little time to spread the cost, the amount you must pay will be high. Given the current 15 per cent limit on the amount you can contribute each year, you might not be able to buy many extra years if you are very close to retirement, but this problem will largely disappear under the new rules from 6 April 2006 (see page 41).

The scheme may put restrictions on the number of extra years you can buy.

CASE HISTORY: WADU

Wadu is currently 60 years old and plans to retire at age 65, by which time he will have 15 years' membership in a one-eightieths final salary scheme. Based on his current final salary of £26,000, he can expect a pension of:

$1/80 \times £26,000 \times 15 = £4,875$ a year.

He would like to buy added years to boost his pension. The scheme administrator tells him that he must pay in an extra 4.5 per cent of his final salary from now until retirement for each extra year he wants to buy. Wadu already pays ordinary contributions of 5 per cent of his salary. Without breaching the 15 per cent limit on total contributions, he can afford to buy roughly two extra years. Based on his current salary, this would boost his pension to:

$1/80 \times £26,000 \times 17 = £5,525$ a year.

In-house AVC scheme

This works on a money purchase basis. Your extra contributions are invested to build up a fund which is used to provide extra pension or other benefits at retirement. The closer you are to retirement, the less time your pension fund has to grow.

You can usually choose how your AVCs are invested, though the choice with an in-house scheme is often limited. The kinds of funds available are the same as those for personal pensions (see Chapter 4). Chapters 5 to 7 describe how the pension fund is converted to pension.

AVCs paid into a scheme you started before 8 April 1987 can be used to provide or boost the tax-free lump sum you can take from your occupational scheme. Under current rules, AVCs started on or after that date cannot be taken as a lump sum.

As a government rule, this restriction will cease to apply when the new rules described on page 41 come into force from 6 April 2006. But whether or not you can then take part of the proceeds of any particular scheme as a lump sum will depend on what the scheme provider allows.

You do not have to take the benefits from a money purchase AVC scheme at the same time as you start to draw your pension from the main occupational scheme. You can start your AVC-funded pension at any time between ages 50 (increasing to 55 by 2010) and 75 regardless of whether you are drawing benefits from the main scheme and regardless of whether you have stopped work. But under current rules, starting your AVC pension at a different time from the main scheme restricts your ability to take a lump sum from a pre-April 1987 scheme:

- if you draw the AVC benefits earlier than the main-scheme pension, you can initially have only an income from the AVC scheme and must wait until the main-scheme pension starts before you can draw a lump sum from the AVC scheme
- if you draw the AVC benefits later than the main pension, you cannot have a lump sum from the AVC scheme at all.

Free-standing AVC scheme

These also work on a money purchase basis. Your extra contributions are invested to build up a fund which is used to provide extra pension or other benefits (but not a lump sum under pre-April 2006 rules) at retirement. The closer you are to retirement, the less time your pension fund has to grow.

Note that from 6 April 2006, the government ban on taking a lump sum from this type of scheme is abolished and replaced by the overall rules described on page 41. However, whether you can then take a lump sum from any particular scheme will depend on the rules of the scheme provider.

You choose the free-standing AVC provider and how the AVCs are invested. The kinds of funds available are the same as those for personal pensions (see Chapter 4). Chapters 5 to 7 describe how the pension fund is converted to pension.

You do not have to take the benefits from a free-standing AVC scheme at the same time as you start to draw your pension from the main occupational scheme. You can start your AVC-funded pension at any time between ages 50 (increasing to 55 by 2010) and 75 regardless of whether you are drawing benefits from the main scheme and regardless of whether you have stopped work. If you have more than one free-standing AVC scheme, you can start drawing the benefits from each one at different times if you want to.

Chapter 4

Personal pension choices at retirement

'Personal pension' is used loosely to describe any pension plan that qualifies for special tax treatment, is personal to you and not tied to any particular job. However, because of changes over the years, there are three distinct types of plan:

- **retirement annuity contracts** These are personal pensions started before 1 July 1988. Different rules apply to these plans than to later personal plans, for example retirement annuity contracts cannot be used to contract out of the state additional pension scheme
- **personal pensions** Plans started on or after 1 July 1988
- **stakeholder schemes** Personal pensions available from 6 April 2001 onwards that meet certain conditions (see box opposite) designed to ensure that you get value for money.

At the time of writing, different rules apply to retirement annuity contracts and other types of personal pensions. But from 6 April 2006, a single, new set of simplified rules applies collectively to all occupational schemes (see Chapter 3) and personal pensions (this chapter) that you have. This chapter describes the rules applying up to 5 April 2006. See page 41 for a description of the rules which apply after that date.

When can you get your personal pension?

The pension from personal pensions, including stakeholder schemes (but excluding retirement annuity contracts), can usually be started at any age between 50 and 75 (though the minimum age is being increased to 55 by 2010). However, you cannot currently start the pension from a personal pension or stakeholder scheme used to contract out of the state additional pension (see box on page 60) before age 60.

Stakeholder pension schemes

A personal pension can be called a 'stakeholder scheme' only if it meets the following conditions:

- **low charges** For schemes started on or after 6 April 2005, charges must total no more than 1.5 per cent a year of the value of your pension fund during the first ten years and 1 per cent thereafter. This must cover all the costs of running the scheme and managing your investments. The cost must include information and basic advice. If there is a fee for more detailed advice, this must be set out in a separate contract and charged separately
- **low and flexible contributions** The minimum contribution must be no higher than £20, whether as a one-off payment or a regular contribution. You cannot be required to make contributions at regular intervals. It is up to you when and how often you pay
- **portability** You must be able to transfer out of a stakeholder scheme into another stakeholder scheme or other pension arrangement without penalty. Stakeholder schemes must accept transfers from other stakeholder schemes and other pension arrangements
- **simplicity** The scheme must include a default investment option which determines how your money is invested if you don't want to choose an investment fund for yourself. For schemes started on or after 6 April 2005, the default must be a lifestyle fund (see page 76)
- **keeping you informed** The scheme provider must give you a benefit statement at least once a year showing you in straightforward terms the value of your rights under the scheme. If the scheme's charges alter, you must be informed within one month of the change.

The pension from a retirement annuity contract can normally be paid at any age between 60 (reducing to 55 by 2010) and 75. However, if you wanted to start the pension before age 60, you could transfer your pension fund out of the retirement annuity contract and into a personal pension. In that case, you would be subject to the personal pension rules, including the earlier minimum pension age.

People in some occupations are currently allowed to draw their pension before the normal minimum age – for example, athletes (age 35), divers (40) and flat-racing jockeys (45). Existing rights to draw a pension at these younger ages will be protected when the minimum age rises to 55, but the lifetime allowance (see page 42) applying at these younger ages will be lower than the standard amounts described in Chapter 3.

If you have to retire early because of ill health, you can start your pension immediately whatever your age.

Contracted-out personal pensions and stakeholder schemes

Employees can contract out of the state additional pension scheme (see Chapter 2). They give up some or all of the state pension and instead build up a private pension through either an occupational scheme (see Chapter 3) or a personal pension or stakeholder scheme.

If you are contracted out through a personal pension or stakeholder scheme, the state rebates part of the National Insurance contributions paid by you and your employer, paying the rebate into your stakeholder scheme.

The rebates (together with tax relief on the part representing your National Insurance contributions) are invested and the proceeds must be used to provide a set package of benefits called 'protected rights'. These comprise an index-linked pension for you and usually an index-linked pension for your widow or widower (but not any unmarried partner) on your death. See Chapter 5 for further details. Under current rules, you cannot take any of the pension fund as a tax-free lump sum, but this restriction is being abolished under new rules which take effect from 6 April 2006.

When you started paying into a plan, you may have been asked to select a particular pension age, but this is not usually binding. Provided you are within the limits set out above, you can usually retire earlier or later than the age you originally selected. However, with some schemes (in particular those invested on a with-profits basis; see page 78), there may be a charge deducted from your pension fund if you start your pension either earlier or later than the date originally agreed. The charge can be substantial, so check the position with the provider before changing your retirement date.

How do you get your personal pension?

If you selected a retirement age when you started the plan, the provider will usually contact you a few months before you reach that age. Otherwise, about four months before you want to start drawing your pension, contact the pension provider with whom you have been building up your pension fund to let them know your intention. The provider should send you a statement of the amount of pension that provider can offer, but must also alert you to your 'open-market option' (OMO), which is the right to shop around and transfer your fund to another provider. This is worth doing if a new provider would pay you a higher pension. Further information is given in Chapter 5.

How are personal pensions paid?

The pension provider pays a personal pension, including a stake-holder pension, under the Pay-As-You-Earn (PAYE system). This means that tax has already been deducted from the amount you receive. PAYE may be used to collect tax on other income you have, such as your state pension, as well as tax on the personal pension (see Chapter 14 for details).

The pension from a retirement annuity contract is not paid through PAYE. However, the provider normally deducts tax at the basic rate before handing over each payment. If you are a non-taxpayer you can arrange to receive the income without this deduction. Otherwise, you will usually have to complete a tax return each year and the self assessment system will be used to ensure that you pay the correct amount of tax overall on the pension and any other income on which tax is due.

You can choose how frequently your pension is paid – monthly is common. Normally payment is made by direct transfer to your bank or building society account.

How much pension?

All personal pensions, stakeholder schemes and retirement annuity contracts work on a 'money purchase' basis. This means the pension you get depends on:

- the amount paid in
- the charges deducted by the provider
- how well your pension fund grows
- the amount of pension you can buy with your fund at retirement.

With a retirement annuity contract, the amount paid in is simply whatever contributions you have paid. Other amounts may have been paid into a personal pension or stakeholder scheme. These may be, for example, contributions from an employer, rebates from the Department of Work and Pensions (DWP) if it is a rebate-only plan used to contract out, or contributions from someone else – say, a husband – who pays into the plan on your behalf. Tax relief on some contributions is also added to the plan (see page 75).

Charges vary considerably from one provider to another. To earn the title 'stakeholder scheme', a personal pension must be relatively low-charging (with charges of 1.5 per cent a year of your fund or less). Other personal pensions and retirement annuity contracts often charge more. The higher the charges, the less money is available to invest for your pension.

How well your pension fund grows is usually the most important factor determining how much pension you will receive. You cannot know in advance how your fund will grow, but it will be influenced by your choice of investments (see page 76).

The amount of pension you can buy with your fund at retirement is considered in Chapters 5 to 7.

Pension increases after retirement

It used to be the case that pensions from rebate-only personal pensions and stakeholder schemes had to be increased each year in line with inflation up to a maximum amount. However, this requirement has been abolished for pensions that start to be paid on or after 6 April 2005.

Now, with all personal pensions and stakeholder schemes, it is your decision as to whether or not your pension will increase once it starts to be paid. This decision is considered in Chapter 5.

Annual statements

The provider with whom you build up your pension fund should send you a statement each year. In the past, these usually contained only the details of the contributions paid during the year and the value of your pension fund so far. Since April 2003, statements must also estimate the amount of pension you might get at retirement.

Increasingly, providers are being encouraged to issue 'combined benefit statements'. These include figures from the Department for Work and Pensions (DWP) based on your National Insurance contribution record to forecast the actual state pension you are expected to get at retirement. If you get combined statements from more than one pension plan or scheme, be careful not to double-count your state pension when totting up the various sources of your expected retirement income.

CASE HISTORY: FLORA AND BETTY

Flora and Betty both saved £100 a month for 20 years through a personal pension. Betty retired in mid-2001. Her pension fund amounted to £45,300 and bought her an inflation-proofed pension of £2,002 a year. Flora retired a year later. Despite making the same contributions, her fund was worth only £35,800 largely because of falls in the stock market during the final year before she retired. She was able to buy an inflation-proofed pension of only £1,614 a year. See page 77 for steps that Flora could have taken to help to protect her from falls in the stock market.

Always check your annual statement to see if you are on track for the retirement you want. The value of money purchase schemes is usually linked to the stock market and can fall as well as rise. If retirement is many years away, you can probably ignore a temporary slide in the stock market. But, if retirement is getting near or there is a prolonged downturn in share prices, you might want to consider taking action, for example by increasing the amount you save or by switching the way your pension fund is invested. See page 75 for guidance on pension fund investments.

Early retirement

Provided that you are within the retirement ages described on page 58, there is no legal restriction on starting your pension early. But early retirement reduces the amount of pension you will receive because:

- the period over which you are paying contributions is reduced, so less goes into the plan
- the period over which the pension fund is invested and can grow is reduced

---

CASE HISTORY: ALOUPH

Alouph is 60 and thinking about retiring now, five years earlier than he had originally intended. He has built up a pension fund of £100,000, which would currently buy him a pension that increases in line with inflation of £4,510 a year. That's a good deal less than he had hoped for. If he works on until age 65, his pension is likely to be half as much again, at £6,740 a year in today's money. That's because:

- another five years' contributions will have been paid into the scheme (in Alouph's case a further £11,200 in today's money)
- the pension fund and new contributions will have had extra time to grow (adding, say, another £33,000 in today's money to the fund)
- at age 60, Alouph gets just £451 a year of pension for each £10,000 in his pension fund. At age 65, he gets £516 a year for each £10,000.

Alouph decides he cannot afford to retire early after all.

- with some plans (especially those invested on a with-profits basis – see page 78), a charge may be deducted from your fund
- the period for which the pension must be paid is extended (this causes a reduction in the amount of pension you receive for each £1 in your fund).

Therefore, if you want to retire early, it is essential to plan ahead. To ensure that you have enough pension, you may need to save extra. If you don't, early retirement might simply be unaffordable.

Choosing whether to take a lump sum

With many personal pensions, when you decide to start your pension you can draw part of the fund you have built up as a tax-free lump sum before converting the rest of the fund into taxable pension.

Under current rules, this does not apply to rebate-only personal pensions or stakeholder schemes used to contract out of the state additional pension. How much tax-free cash you can have from other personal pensions depends on the type of plan you have:

- **retirement annuity contracts** The maximum lump sum is three times the remaining pension (or, if the remaining pension will, or can, change each year, three times the initial yearly amount). If you first took out the contract on or after 17 March 1987, there is also an overall cash limit of £150,000. However, this limit applies to each contract, so the restriction was usually avoided by issuing you with a cluster of several contracts instead of just one
- **personal pensions and stakeholder schemes** The maximum lump sum is one quarter of the pension fund (excluding any contracted-out part that must be used to provide protected rights).

From 6 April 2006, these rules will be abolished and a single, simplified limit will apply collectively to all your occupational schemes (see Chapter 3) and personal pensions allowing you to take a quarter of the pension funds you have built up as tax-free cash – see page 41 for details. Whether or not an individual plan allows you to take a lump sum will then depend on the provider's rules.

You do not have to do any sums for yourself. The pension provider will give you a statement showing the maximum tax-free cash you can have and the amount of the remaining pension.

If you transfer your pension fund from a retirement annuity contract to a personal pension – for example, as a result of using your open-market option – the rules for personal pensions then apply, so the maximum lump sum allowable would then be a quarter of your pension fund. At present-day annuity rates (the rates at which you can convert the pension fund into pension), the maximum lump sum from 'a personal pension is nearly always bigger than the maximum you could get from the retirement annuity. But you might get a bigger lump sum from the retirement annuity contract if you are relatively old or in poor health.

CASE HISTORY: STAN

Stan is retiring at age 65. He has built up a pension fund of £80,000 in a retirement annuity contract and wants to take the maximum possible lump sum. Although he sees the sense in having a pension that increases in line with inflation each year, the starting pension is much lower than a pension that remains level throughout retirement. The lower starting pension would inhibit the size of lump sum he could take. Therefore, Stan opts for a level pension. If he used the whole £80,000 fund he could currently buy a pension of £5,616 a year. Alternatively, he can take a tax-free cash sum of £13,917. The remaining fund of £80,000 – £13,917 = £66,083 would be enough to buy him a pension of £4,639. The cash sum is within the rules because it is three times the remaining pension (3 × £4,639 = £13,917). However, Stan could get an even larger lump sum by transferring his pension fund to a personal pension (see case history below).

CASE HISTORY: JOHN

John, who is self-employed, is about to retire at age 65. He has built up a pension fund of £80,000 in a personal pension. He can take $1/4$ × £80,000 = £20,000 of this as a tax-free lump sum. The remaining £60,000 fund is used to buy him a level pension of £4,212 a year.

Although taking a lump sum reduces your remaining pension, it is usually worth taking the largest possible sum. This is because you are turning taxable pension into tax-free cash. You can invest the cash to provide an income which is either tax-free or at least only partly taxable, depending on the investments you choose. See Chapter 14 for more information.

Choices involving dependants

If you have a personal pension or stakeholder scheme used for contracting out of the state additional pension, your pension fund must be used to provide protected rights (see box on page 60). These usually automatically include a pension for your widow or widower if you die after starting your pension (and from a date to be announced will also apply to same-sex partners where the couple's relationship has been registered as a civil partnership). However, if you are single when you start the pension, in respect of protected rights built up since 6 April 1997, you can opt to exclude the widow's or widower's pension, in which case your own retirement pension will be a bit higher.

In the case of other personal pensions, stakeholder schemes and retirement annuity contracts, there is no automatic pension or lump sum for your dependants in the event of your dying after retirement, although you can include such benefits (see Chapters 5 to 7).

Divorce

If you divorce and proceedings start on or after 1 December 2000, a court can order the sharing of any pension rights you and your former husband or wife have, including retirement annuity contracts, personal pensions and stakeholder schemes. Under pension sharing, part of a pension fund or rights under a pension scheme is taken away from one person and allocated to the other. If the pension has already started to be paid, then part of the pension is transferred to the ex-husband or ex-wife.

Another possibility which can apply to divorces started before or after December 2000 is 'earmarking'. The pension fund or pension rights are not transferred, but once the pension starts to be paid the earmarked part is paid out to the ex-husband or ex-wife.

Earmarking orders are not widely made and their impact can be lessened if the person whose pension has been earmarked stops paying into the earmarked pension scheme and starts up a new one instead.

On the other hand, divorce proceedings need not have affected any pension arrangements directly, but one party may have been awarded extra maintenance income or a bigger share of the non-pension assets to compensate for the loss of pension rights.

From a date yet to be announced, possibly October 2005, the arrangements described above can also apply to same-sex partners who had registered their relationship as a civil partnership but have subsequently dissolved the partnership.

Boosting your personal pension
Putting off your retirement

Just as retiring early reduces your pension, deferring your retirement usually means you will get a higher pension because:

- you have time to pay in more contributions
- your pension fund is invested for longer and so has more time to grow

---

CASE HISTORY: ANDREA

Andrea has built up a pension fund of £50,000. When she started her personal pension, she had intended to retire at age 60. Having reached that age, she has now decided to put off her retirement until age 65. This increases her eventual pension by more than half from £2,255 to £3,420 a year in today's money. The increase is due to:

- five more years' contributions being paid in, which come to about £6,500 in today's money
- another five years for the original fund and new contributions to grow, adding about £16,670 to the fund in today's money.

At age 60, Andrea gets just £451 a year of pension for each £10,000 in her pension fund. At age 65, she gets £516 a year for each £10,000.

- your pension is likely to be paid out for a shorter period, which is reflected in an increase in the amount of pension you can buy with each £1 of your pension fund.

However, you cannot put off the start of your pension beyond age 75.

Watch out if your pension fund is invested on a with-profits basis (see page 78), because there might be a charge deducted from your pension fund if you had originally agreed a particular retirement age but then retire later.

Phasing your retirement

Instead of completely putting off the start of your pension, you could defer just part. This might suit you if you want to wind down work gradually, perhaps switching to working part-time. There are several ways to organise a phased retirement:

- if you have several different pension plans, you can simply start drawing a pension from one or two while leaving the rest invested until later
- what you have thought of as a single pension plan might in fact be a cluster of separate plans, making it easy to start a pension from some in the cluster while delaying the pension from others
- since April 2001, personal pensions and stakeholder schemes can have multiple maturity dates. This means you do not have to convert your fund into pension all in one go. Instead, you can start a pension from part of the fund while leaving the rest invested until later
- you could opt for income drawdown (see Chapter 7 for how this works).

If none of the above are possible with your current provider, you could transfer your pension fund to another provider who does offer phased retirement facilities.

Making extra contributions

Once you have converted a pension fund into pension, you can no longer pay contributions into that plan. But there is nothing to stop you continuing to contribute towards any other retirement annuity contract, personal pension or stakeholder scheme that you have, or starting a new personal pension or stakeholder scheme.

Paying into a pension plan after you have retired may seem an odd way to save, but it can be very tax-efficient because you get tax relief on your contributions and part of the proceeds is tax-free.

The main proviso is that you may not make any further contributions after the age of 75. There are also limits on the amount you can pay – though under the new rules from 6 April 2006 (see page 41), most people will have plenty of scope to carry on saving. The current rules applying up to 5 April 2006 are more restrictive and are described below.

Retirement annuity contract

It has not been possible to start a new retirement annuity contract since 30 June 1988, so your extra contributions must be paid into a contract that has been in existence for some time.

You must still be working, because the amount you are allowed to pay into a retirement annuity contract is a percentage of your 'net relevant earnings' (basically, your pay including taxable benefits or your taxable profits). Income from savings, investments and pensions does not count as earnings.

The maximum contributions you can pay each year into all the retirement annuity contracts you have are shown in Table 4.1. However, you can go over the limit if you have not made the maximum possible contributions in all of the last six or seven tax years by taking advantage of the 'carry-forward' and carry-back'

Table 4.1   Maximum contributions to retirement annuity contracts[1]

Age at the start of the tax year (on 6 April)	Maximum contribution as percentage of your earnings	For example, maximum contribution for each £1,000 you earn
Up to 50	17.5%	£175
51 to 55	20.0%	£200
56 to 60	22.5%	£225
61 to 74	27.5%	£275
75 and over	You can no longer contribute	

[1] These limits cease to apply from 6 April 2006 – see page 41.

rules. The carry-back rule lets you opt to have a contribution paid this year treated as if it had been paid in the previous tax year. The carry-forward rule lets you bring forward any unused contribution relief from the previous six years to use up against a contribution made now. Carry-forward and carry-back cease to be available from 6 April 2006.

You get tax relief up to your top rate of tax on contributions to a retirement annuity contract. You make the contributions gross (in other words, without deducting any relief) and claim relief through your tax return. If you do not get a tax return, contact your tax office to claim relief. You continue to get tax relief in the same way under the new regime starting on 6 April 2006.

CASE HISTORY: TOM

Tom is 58. He draws a pension, but also works part-time as a business consultant. His net relevant earnings in 2005–6 are £12,000. He can pay up to 22.5% × £12,000 = £2,700 in 2005–6 into the retirement annuity contract that he started back in 1970 and has not yet turned into pension. Tom pays tax at the basic rate on at least £2,700 of his income, so he gets tax relief of 22% × £2,700 = £594 if he pays the maximum contribution. This reduces the cost of the contribution to £2,700 – £594 = £2,106.

CASE HISTORY: SHEILA

Sheila is 66 and earns £5,000 in 2005–6. She still has a retirement annuity contract and can pay 27.5% × £5,000 = £1,375 into the plan in 2005–6. However, six years ago, before she went into semi-retirement, she earned more but did not make the maximum possible contributions to the contract. She has £3,150 of unused relief to carry forward, which means that the maximum contribution she can make in 2005–6 is £1,375 + £3,150 = £4,525.

Personal pensions and stakeholder schemes

You do not need to have any earnings to be eligible to have a personal pension or stakeholder scheme. Nearly everyone under age 75 can contribute up to £3,600 a year to these schemes (but see box opposite). However, if you do have some earnings, you may be able to contribute even more. In 2005–6, if they come to more than £3,600, you can make contributions up to:

- 25 per cent of your net relevant earnings if you are aged 46 to 50
- 30 per cent if you are aged 51 to 55
- 35 per cent if you are aged 56 to 60
- 40 per cent if you are aged 61 to 74.

(Lower percentages apply below age 46.) You do not have to use the net relevant earnings for the year in which you make the contribution. You can instead use the earnings from any of the previous five tax years as the basis for working out the maximum contributions you make now. For example, if you are paying a contribution in 2005–6, you can use earnings for any year from 2000–01 up to 2005–6 as the basis year. If you want to make the maximum possible contributions it makes sense to choose the year with the highest earnings as your basis year. However, you can only use earnings up to a certain level – the 'earnings cap' – which the government sets each year. The earnings cap for 2005–6 is £105,600. To work out how much you can contribute, you use the earnings cap for the year in which the contribution is paid (or treated as paid if you are using the carry-back rules – see page 73).

CASE HISTORY: SVEN

Looking back over the last five years, Sven's earnings were highest in 2001–2 when he earned £120,000. These exceeded the earnings cap for 2001–2 which was £95,400 but that does not limit the earnings he can use as the basis for contributions in 2005–6. The earnings cap for 2005–6 is £105,600, so by selecting 2001–2 as his basis year, Sven's contributions in 2005–6 can be based on earnings of £105,600.

Who cannot contribute to personal pensions and stakeholder schemes

Under current rules, nearly everyone can pay up to £3,600 a year into personal pensions and stakeholder schemes. This includes people who are also still paying into an occupational pension scheme provided that:

- they earned £30,000 or less in at least one of the last five tax years but not counting any year before 2000–1, and
- they are not a controlling director either in the current tax year or in any of the previous five years but not counting any year before 2000–1. (A controlling director is someone who on his or her own or with family or other associates owns or controls more than 20 per cent of the shares of the company for which he or she works.)

These restrictions cease to apply when new rules come into effect from 6 April 2006 (see page 41). From then you will be able to pay into any combination of pension schemes and plans whatever your circumstances, provided your total contributions to all schemes and plans do not exceed the greater of £3,600 and your whole earnings for the year in which you pay the contribution.

Once chosen, your basis year is fixed for the five years following the basis year unless you elect for a new year to be the basis. For example, if you choose 2000–1 as your basis year, it counts as the basis for contributions in all the years up to 2005–6, unless you make a new election to have a different basis year.

You can elect to have a contribution that was paid in one year treated as if it had been paid in the previous tax year. Tax relief is then given at the tax rates for the earlier year and you can choose a basis year from any of the five years preceding the year to which the contribution is carried back. You must pay the contribution and make the election by 31 January following the year to which you want the contribution carried back. For example, if you make a contribution in 2005–6 and want it carried back to 2004–5, you must make the contribution and election by 31 January 2006, and the contribution limit can be based on earnings for any year from 1999–2000 to 2004–5.

The limits on contributions described above apply to the total of payments made by you, your employer or anyone else on your behalf, but do not include any rebates paid by the DWP because you are contracted out.

All the complicated rules described above cease to apply from 6 April 2006. From that date, the rules described on page 41 apply collectively to your total contributions to all occupational schemes (see Chapter 3) and personal pensions. Under the post-6-April-2006 rules, there are no carry-back arrangements.

Under both the current rules and the post-6-April-2006 regime, whatever you pay into a personal pension or stakeholder scheme

---

CASE HISTORY: HELGA

Helga is 72. She has no earnings, but can pay up to £3,600 a year into stakeholder schemes and personal pensions.

CASE HISTORY: MIKE

Mike is 67. He can make pension contributions up to 40 per cent of his earnings. In 2005–6, he earned only £7,000, but he can elect to base his contributions on earnings from any of the previous five years. His earnings were highest in 2002–3 at £42,000 – this was just before he started to wind down work in preparation for retirement. He elects to have 2002–3 as his basis year, which means he can make contributions in 2005–6 up to 40% × £42,000 = £16,800.

CASE HISTORY: PYARA

In 2004–5, Pyara pays a lump sum of £2,000 into a stakeholder scheme. This is treated as a contribution net of tax relief at the basic rate (22 per cent in 2004–5). The pension provider claims £564 from the Inland Revenue and adds this to the scheme (£564 is 22 per cent of £2,564). Pyara is a higher-rate taxpayer and so qualifies for an extra 40% – 22% = 18% relief on the gross contribution. The extra tax relief comes to 18% × £2,564 = £462. Pyara claims this through his tax return.

(whether for yourself or someone else) is treated as a contribution from which tax relief at the basic rate has already been deducted. The contribution limits discussed above are all gross (before-tax-relief) limits. For example, everyone can make gross contributions up to £3,600 a year. In 2004–5, the basic tax rate is 22 per cent, so the maximum contribution after tax relief is £3,600 × (1 − 22%) = £2,808. The pension provider claims the relief from the Inland Revenue and adds it to your plan. For example, if you pay the maximum of £2,808, the provider claims £792 from the Inland Revenue and adds it to your plan. Therefore, the total paid in is £2,808 + £792 = £3,600. You get this basic-rate tax relief even if you are not a taxpayer or pay tax at less than the basic rate.

If you are a higher-rate taxpayer, you qualify for extra tax relief on contributions you pay into your own personal pension or stake-holder scheme (but not a plan for someone else). Claim the relief through your tax return or, if you don't get a return, by contacting your tax office.

Choosing how to invest your pension fund

With all money purchase pension schemes and plans, the contributions paid into your plan are invested to build up your pension fund. Most plans let you choose how the fund is invested (see the summary in Table 4.2). In making this choice, the three main – and interrelated – factors that have to be taken into account are your attitude towards risk, the length of time until you retire and what other resources you have as a source of retirement income.

Risk, time to retirement and other resources

In an ideal world, most people would choose to invest for a high return without any risk. Unfortunately, in the real world, risk and return go hand in hand. Safer investments offer relatively poor returns. To get higher returns, you have to take on extra risk.

Pension fund investments typically range from relatively safe money funds (which work much like bank or building society savings accounts), where you cannot lose any capital, to shares, where the value of your fund can fall as well as rise, depending on the movement of the stock markets. Over the long term, the low-risk money funds have tended to produce lower returns than the higher-risk shares.

Table 4.2 Summary of how you can invest your pension fund

Type of fund	Description	Risk 1 (low) to 5 (high)
With profits	Your savings grow through addition of yearly bonuses which, once added, cannot usually be taken back. Size of bonuses depends on growth of underlying investments in shares, gilts, property and so on, and the overall profitability of the provider's business. Bonuses are smoothed by keeping back some growth from good years to top up the return in poor years. Extra bonus also added at retirement.	2–3
Actively managed fund	A fund manager decides which shares and other investments to hold and when to buy and sell them. Managers try to 'beat the market' (though many experts do not believe this is consistently possible). Charges include an annual management charge of typically 1.5 per cent a year. Examples include:	Depends on fund you choose
Money fund	An actively managed fund investing in deposits that earn interest. The value of your capital cannot fall.	1
UK gilt or UK corporate bond fund	An actively managed fund investing in government stocks or corporate bonds issued by UK companies	2
Cautious or Balanced managed fund	An actively managed fund that holds a range of assets, such as shares, bonds and property.	2–3
UK all companies	An actively managed fund investing mainly in the shares of UK companies.	4
Lifestyle	Your investments are automatically shifted as you approach retirement from higher-risk/higher-return share-based funds to lower-risk/lower-return gilt, bond and other funds.	Varies over life of investment
Passively managed fund (tracker fund)	The investments are chosen to mimic the performance of a stock market index, for example the FTSE 100. There is no attempt to beat the market and so less buying and selling than in an actively managed fund. Annual charge is usually under 1 per cent a year.	3

If you are many years from retirement, it usually makes sense to opt for share-based investments because you can ride out short-term dips in stock markets. The higher long-term returns that you can expect as a result reduce the amount you need to save to reach your pension target, compared with investing in lower-returning, safer investments.

When you are within five to ten years of retirement, you should consider gradually shifting your pension fund from shares to safer investments, such as good-quality corporate bonds, gilts and money funds. Although you may miss out on higher returns from shares, you also avoid the risk of your pension fund falling in value just at the time you want to use it to buy a pension.

Some providers offer 'lifestyle' pension plans, which automatically shift the balance of your pension fund towards safer investments as retirement approaches.

On top of this general strategy as retirement approaches, you need to consider the level of risk with which you are personally comfortable. Even if you are many years from retirement, you might not like the idea of putting all of your pension fund into shares, especially given the volatile stock markets of recent years.

A sound strategy is to spread your risks by having some of your fund in each of the following classes of assets:

- **cash** (money funds). These are low-risk assets
- **bonds** (good-quality corporate bonds and gilts). These are medium-risk
- **property** Usually considered medium-risk (though more risky than bonds)
- **shares** These are higher-risk.

You can choose your own selection of investments to achieve this split. Alternatively, you can invest on a 'with-profits' basis (see overleaf), or opt for a 'balanced' fund (see opposite), which give you a ready-made split. There are no hard and fast rules about the appropriate split between the different asset classes, but the more risk-averse you are, the higher the proportion of your pension fund you should consider having in bonds and cash.

If your pension is relatively small and you will be heavily dependent on it for your retirement income, you cannot afford to take big risks with your money and should consider a cautious approach to investing your pension fund with a fairly high proportion in bonds and cash. On the other hand, if you have other sources of retirement income – say a good occupational scheme and other investments – your pension fund might be just the icing on the cake and money you can afford to take a few risks with. In that case, even in the run-up to retirement you could consider having a higher proportion in shares and less in bonds and cash.

An independent financial adviser* can help you choose the appropriate asset split for your circumstances.

Investing on a with-profits basis

In the past, investing on a with-profits basis has been a popular medium-risk choice. It allows you to participate in stock market returns but with some cushioning against the risk of falling share prices. However, recent experience has shown that with-profits funds do not protect you from the effects of a prolonged stock market downturn. This has come as a shock to many investors, who now perceive with-profits to be riskier than they had previously thought.

With-profits policies aim to reduce stock market risk by:

- investing in a range of different assets including cash, gilts, corporate bonds and property as well as shares
- smoothing the returns you get by keeping back in reserve some of the gains from good years to top up your return in poor years.

Your return is in the form of 'reversionary bonuses', which are added to your pension fund each year, plus a further 'terminal bonus' paid when your policy matures (which generally happens when you reach a pre-selected retirement age; however, depending on the terms of the pension plan, you might still get the terminal bonus if you retire earlier or later).

Some providers tell you each year the amount of terminal bonus that has built up so far, but this is a non-guaranteed bonus that can subsequently be cut.

Provided that you keep your pension plan until it matures, the reversionary bonuses once added cannot be taken away, so they are sometimes called 'guaranteed' bonuses. But there is no guarantee about the bonuses you will get in future – they vary from year to year. The provider sets each year's bonus level in the light of investment returns, the cost of running its business and a host of other factors. The provider tries to keep bonuses reasonably consistent from year to year by using the smoothing process described above.

If you do not keep your plan until maturity, for example you transfer your fund to another provider, the original provider may deduct a 'market-value reduction' (MVR) – also called a 'market-value adjuster' (MVA) – from your pension fund. The aim of the MVR is to ensure that you do not take out more than your fair share of the with-profits fund, leaving too little to be shared amongst the remaining with-profits holders (see Chart 4.1 below). This could happen if past annual bonuses have been high but the investments in the with-profits funds have subsequently made losses.

Most providers do not usually levy an MVR if you are converting your pension fund to pension. However, some have been known to charge an MVR if you take your pension at an age other than the originally selected retirement age and you exercise your open-market option to buy your pension from another provider.

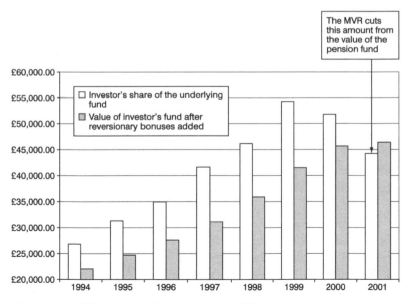

Chart 4.1 With-profits funds and the MVR

In Chart 4.1:

- the dark columns show how an investor's pension fund grows steadily as reversionary bonuses are added
- the white columns show the value of the underlying with-profits fund divided by the total number of investors. In effect, this is a single investor's actual share of the underlying fund. The value of the underlying fund goes up and down, reflecting stock market performance
- in most years, the value of the pension fund is less than the investor's actual share of the fund. This is because some of the profits made by the fund are not paid out in bonuses. Instead, they are held in reserve to top up bonuses in the bad years
- in 2000 and 2001, the value of the underlying fund fell because of big falls in the stock market
- by 2001, the investor's share of the underlying fund has fallen below the value of his pension fund. If the investor transferred his pension fund then, an MVR would be deducted from the value of his pension fund to reduce it to the same amount as his share of the underlying fund.

Investing on a unit-linked basis

The main alternative to the with-profits basis is to invest on a unit-linked basis. The value of your pension fund moves up and down directly with the value of one or more underlying investment funds. You choose the investment funds – they range from money funds, gilts, other bonds, UK shares, international shares, shares in specific countries, smaller companies, and so on. Table 4.2 gives a few examples. By choosing several different funds you can achieve the asset allocation that matches the level of risk you want to take (see page 77).

Managed funds are either actively or passively managed. A passively managed fund – also called a 'tracker fund' – is made up of investments that have been chosen to mimic the performance of a particular stock market index such as the FTSE 100. Tracker funds tend to have low charges because there is relatively little buying and selling of investments and less work for the fund manager. In an actively managed fund, a manager uses a variety of research techniques to try to select investments that he or she thinks will perform well in future. Charges for actively managed funds tend to be higher in order to pay for the fund management and finance a higher volume of investment sales and purchases.

Academic research suggests that many actively managed funds in fact try to achieve returns that are close to a chosen benchmark index, such as the FTSE 100 or the FTSE All Share Index. In effect, these are closet tracker funds, so you may be paying extra for active management but getting the same performance as a tracker fund.

Charges are important. They can reduce the overall return you get on your pension fund by a surprisingly large amount. It is worth paying extra only if you believe you stand a good chance of getting a superior return.

Chapter 5

Choosing an annuity

With all money purchase pension schemes and plans you build up a pension fund that is eventually used to provide your pension. This is the case with:

- occupational money purchase schemes
- in-house additional voluntary contribution (AVC) schemes, except added years schemes
- free-standing AVC schemes
- retirement annuity contracts
- personal pensions, and
- stakeholder pension schemes.

In some large money purchase schemes, your pension is paid direct from the fund that has built up, though under new rules coming in from 6 April 2006 you must be offered the option of buying an annuity instead if you want to. With many money purchase schemes you also have the option to draw a pension direct from your pension fund; this is called 'income drawdown' (see Chapter 7). But, with the vast majority of money purchase schemes and plans, the pension fund is used to buy an annuity.

What is an annuity?

An annuity is a type of investment where you exchange a lump sum for income. In the case of pension schemes, you usually exchange your pension fund (the lump sum) for an income payable for the rest of your life. Pension annuities are often called 'compulsory purchase annuities'. Once you have bought an annuity, you cannot get your money back as a lump sum.

A pension annuity is in effect insurance against living too long. The annuity provider can offer you an income for life because the risk of your living too long is pooled with lots of other people's risk. The people who die young cross-subsidise the cost of providing an income for people who live longer than average.

'Annuity rates' describe the amount of income you get in return for your lump sum. They are usually expressed as a number of £s of income a year for each £10,000 of lump sum. For example, an annuity rate of £600 would mean you could get £600 of income each year for each £10,000 you invest.

Your right to choose an annuity

The annuity rate at the time you swap your pension fund for an annuity usually determines your income for the rest of your life. So it is very important to shop around for the best annuity rate you can get. The difference between the best and worst rates can be large, for example 15 per cent or more for someone in average health. In other words, shopping around for a good rate can easily boost your income throughout retirement by around a sixth or more. And, if you are in poor health, shopping around could boost your income by 50 per cent.

If you have a contracted-out money purchase scheme or plan, a personal pension, stakeholder scheme or free-standing AVC scheme, you automatically have an 'open-market option' (OMO). This means that when you want to start your pension you have a right to shop around and transfer your pension fund to another provider if you want to. This is worth doing if another provider can offer you a better annuity rate. Some providers specialise in annuity business while others do not, so it would be a coincidence if the provider with whom you had built up your fund also happened to be the one offering the best annuity rate. The provider with whom you have built up your pension fund must draw your attention to your OMO.

If you have a retirement annuity contract, you will not necessarily have an OMO – it depends on the terms of your particular contract. Bear in mind that, if you do transfer your pension fund from a retirement annuity contract, the new plan you transfer into will be a personal pension or stakeholder scheme. You will then be subject to the personal pension and stakeholder scheme rules, for example concerning the age at which you retire (see page 58) and the amount you can have as a tax-free lump sum (see page 65).

If you belong to a money purchase occupational scheme or have an in-house AVC scheme, the scheme trustees rather than you might be responsible for arranging the purchase of an annuity. They have a duty to get you a good deal. Don't be afraid to ask what steps they have taken to check the annuity market to secure the best rate.

Using your OMO to shop around is usually a good idea. However, if your provider just happens to offer one of the best annuity rates on the market, it makes sense to stay. Some providers with whom you have built up a fund offer you a guaranteed annuity rate if you stay with them. The guaranteed rate might be higher than the rate you can get elsewhere.

Watch out for transfer charges levied by the old provider if you exercise your OMO. In general, you should not be charged if you transfer your pension fund at the age you originally selected as your retirement age. But there have been incidents of providers making charges if you exercise your OMO at an earlier or even a later age.

What influences the annuity rate?

Annuities are sold by insurance companies; these companies set the rates they offer. Rates are influenced by a variety of different factors.

Your age

A pension annuity pays an income for the rest of your life. The younger you are when you start an annuity, the greater the number of years on average that the insurance company will probably have to pay out the income. Paying out for longer makes the annuity more expensive, so the younger you are at the time of purchase, the lower the annuity rate you will be offered.

Your sex

On average, women tend to live longer than men. Therefore, if you take a man and a woman of the same age, on average it will cost more to provide the woman with an income for life because the income will have to be paid out for longer. For this reason, women are usually offered lower annuity rates than men of the same age.

An exception is where you are buying a pension using a contracted-out scheme or plan (see page 60). In that case, the law requires men and women to be offered the same annuity rates (called 'unisex rates').

Your health

If you know in advance that your life is likely to be shorter than average, it can seem unfair that you have to buy an annuity geared up for the average person. Some insurance companies recognise this and offer better-than-average annuity rates for people who have poorer-than-average life expectancy. These annuities are often called 'impaired life annuities' or 'enhanced annuities' and are available to people with health problems or lifestyles that reduce their life expectancy. For example, you might qualify if:

- you have severe health problems, such as a history of heart attacks or cancer
- you have a chronic health condition, such as diabetes
- you smoke heavily
- you are obese
- you live in a postcode area or have worked in an industry, such as construction, that is statistically associated with reduced life expectancy.

Investment returns

The insurance company pays annuity income out of a fund made up of the lump sum paid by customers for their annuity plus the return from investing the lump sums.

The insurance company is usually committed to paying out a known amount of annuity income each year. The company wants to make sure it has the money available to make these payments, so it cannot afford to take too much risk with the investments it chooses. In general, the company will tend to invest in gilts and sometimes high-quality corporate bonds.

The upshot is that the annuity rates you are offered are closely linked to the return available on long-term gilts. A fall in the yield from gilts over the last decade or so is one reason why annuity rates have been falling (see Chart 5.1 overleaf).

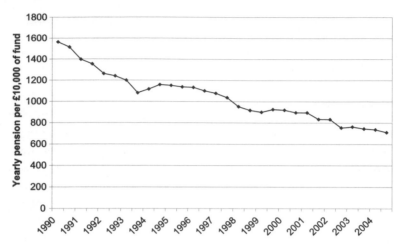

Chart 5.1 How annuity rates have been falling

The size of your pension fund

Some annuity providers offer better rates to people with pension funds over a set size, such as £20,000, £40,000 or even more.

Life expectancy in the nation as a whole

Life expectancy for people in the UK is increasing (see Table 5.1). While living longer is surely good news, it does make providing pensions more expensive if retirement ages stay the same, because on average a pension has to be paid out for more years. For this

Table 5.1 How life expectancy is changing in the UK

Life expectancy at age 65 in:	Men (years)	Women (years)
1928	11.5	13.3
1960	12.1	15.3
2002	16.0	19.0
2025	18.3	21.1
2050	19.0	21.7

Source: Government Actuary's Department.

reason, increasing longevity tends to drive annuity rates down and is an important reason why the annuity rates being offered today are a good deal lower than rates, say, ten years ago (see Chart 5.1).

Where to get information and advice

The decisions you make about your pension fund at the point of retirement could be the most important of your life. It is worth taking the time and trouble to make the right choice and to secure the best rate. Chapters 6 and 7 outline the main options.

If you need help deciding on the best course of action, contact an independent financial adviser (IFA)★. Some IFAs specialise in annuities and income drawdown★. The adviser may be paid by commission from the annuity provider; alternatively, you might have to pay a fee direct to the adviser. By 1 June 2005, any adviser describing themself as 'independent' must give you the option of paying by fee.

If you want to do your own research, there are many published sources of annuity rates that can help you compare your options and shop around for the best rates:

- personal finance pages of many newspapers
- specialist magazines, such as *Money Management*, which are available through larger newsagents
- specialist magazines, such as *Moneyfacts Life and Pensions*, which are available only on subscription but might be available in larger public reference libraries
- faxback services, such as Moneyfacts★
- websites, including:
  www.fsa.co.uk/tables
  www.moneyfacts.co.uk
  www.annuity-bureau.co.uk
  www.annuitydirect.co.uk
  www.williamburrows.com

Chapter 6

Types of annuity

When you are ready to start your pension, your open-market option (see Chapter 5) lets you shop around for the provider offering the best annuity rates. But that is not the only choice you face. Most importantly, you need to decide what type of annuity would be suitable for you – and whether income drawdown (see Chapter 7) would be a better option. The major concern will be how much income you can get, but other factors to consider are:

- how you will deal with inflation during retirement
- how much risk you are happy to take
- whether anyone else is financially dependent on you
- how much flexibility you require to be able to alter your pension once it has started to be paid
- how much control you want to have over your investment
- what charges you will need to pay
- whether you want to provide an inheritance for your survivors.

Table 6.1 summarises the main options open to you and how they rate against these factors. The rest of this chapter looks at the various types of annuity currently available and new annuity developments. The next chapter looks at the pros and cons of income drawdown.

Whatever choice you make when your pension starts, the government currently insists that you use any remaining pension to buy an annuity by age 75. From 6 April 2006 onwards, a restricted form of income drawdown will be available after age 75 – see Chapter 7.

When you start to take a pension from most occupational money purchase schemes, stakeholder schemes, other personal pensions and retirement annuity contracts, you can take part of your pension fund as a tax-free lump sum before using the rest to provide a

Table 6.1 Your main options at retirement

Type of arrangement	Some protection against inflation	Low risk	Protection for a dependant	Flexibility after pension starts	Investment control	Low charges	Inheritance for your survivors
Level annuity	No	Yes	Yes[1]	No	No	Yes	No[3]
Escalating annuity	Yes	Yes	Yes[1]	No	No	Yes	No[3]
LPI-linked annuity	Yes	Yes	Yes[1]	No	No	Yes	No[3]
RPI-linked annuity	Yes (full protection)	Yes	Yes[1]	No	No	Yes	No[3]
With-profits annuity	Possibly	No	Yes[1]	No	No	No	No[3]
Unit-linked annuity	Possibly	No	Yes[1]	Not usually	Yes	No	No[3]
Phased retirement	Possibly	No	Yes[2]	Yes	Yes	No	Yes, up to age 75
Income drawdown (see Chapter 7)	Possibly	No	Yes[2]	Yes	Yes	No	Yes, up to age 75

[1]Yes, provided you choose a joint-life last survivor annuity; otherwise, no.
[2]Dependants can benefit from remaining pension fund up to you reaching age 75, but this element diminishes over time. Protection then depends on whether you use the fund to buy a joint-life last survivor annuity.
[3]Inheritance for a limited period if you choose an annuity with a guarantee period.

pension (see Chapters 3 and 4). In effect, you are giving up taxable pension in exchange for tax-free cash. Even if you need the largest possible income, it is still worth taking the maximum lump sum and investing it to produce income – for example, by buying a purchased life annuity – because the tax-free status of the lump sum ensures that you usually end up with a larger after-tax income than the taxable pension would have provided (see Chapter 14). All the examples in the current chapter assume that a pension is being purchased with what remains of the pension fund after taking the maximum tax-free lump sum.

Level annuity

The most basic type of annuity is a level annuity (also called a flat annuity). It pays out the same income year after year throughout retirement.

Level annuities are the most popular choice, accounting for around four-fifths of all pension annuities sold. The reason for this popularity is probably because level annuities offer the highest starting income. On the downside, level annuities are vulnerable to inflation. As Chapter 1 discussed, rising prices reduce the buying power of a flat income. If the income is to be paid over many years, even at low rates of inflation, the reduction can be severe.

However, if you choose an annuity with some built-in protection against inflation (see below), you have to accept a lower starting income. Although your income generally increases over time, it might be many years before it catches up with the income from a level annuity and even more years before you have received the same amount of income in total (see Table 6.6 on page 97). Therefore, choosing a level annuity might be a sensible option, provided you take other steps to protect yourself against inflation – for example, by setting aside savings in early retirement to boost your income later on.

If you are not prepared to take other steps to protect yourself against future inflation, a level annuity is not suitable. Retirement can easily last two decades or more. Even at low rates of inflation, prices can rise by a surprisingly large amount over such a long period, which means a level income loses much of its buying power. See Chapter 1 for examples of how inflation eats away the value of your income.

CASE HISTORY: AMRAN

Amran is 70 and single. He has a pension fund of £32,000 with which to buy an annuity. The provider with whom he built up the fund is offering a level annuity rate of £840 per £10,000. This means Amran could have a pension of £840 / £10,000 × £32,000 = £2,688 a year. Since this is a level annuity, Amran would receive £2,688 each year throughout retirement.

However, Amran has diabetes. Some providers offer enhanced annuities (see Chapter 5) for people with this condition. By using his open-market option, Amran can switch his fund to a provider offering an enhanced level annuity rate of £1,061. At that rate, Amran can get a pension of £1,061 / £10,000 × £32,000 = £3,395 a year. Again, because this is a level annuity, Amran will receive the same sum throughout his retirement.

Joint-life last survivor annuities

All types of annuity come in both single-life and joint-life last survivor versions.

A single-life annuity pays you an income until you die. If you are in a couple and you died first, your partner could be left short of money if your income stopped with you. You can guard against this by choosing a joint-life last survivor annuity: the income is still in the first place paid just to you, but if you die the income switches to your partner and continues to be paid until he or she dies.

In effect, by choosing a joint-life last survivor annuity, you are providing for a widow's or widower's pension, but you and your partner do not have to be married to benefit. This type of annuity can be arranged for same-sex couples, though the annuity rates shown in this chapter assume the couple comprises a man and a woman.

Of course, nothing in life is free, so a joint-life last survivor annuity is more expensive than a single-life annuity, which means the starting income is lower. With the most expensive version, on the first death, the income continues to be paid out at the same level. An annuity where the income falls by a third or a half on the first death is a bit cheaper. See Table 6.2 for examples of joint-life and single-life level annuities.

Table 6.2 Comparison of joint-life last survivor level annuities and single-life level annuities

Type of annuity	Average income from a level annuity bought at age:				
Age of person	**55**	**60**	**65**	**70**	**75**
Single-life annuity for a man	£569	£633	£734	£875	£1,096
Single-life annuity for a woman	£545	£597	£671	£784	£948
Age of man/woman	**60/55**	**60/60**	**65/60**	**70/65**	**75/70**
Joint-life last survivor. No reduction in income on first death.	£504	£531	£545	£603	£687
Joint-life last survivor. Income reduces by one-third on man's death	£541	£561	£594	£669	£777

Source: *Moneyfacts Life & Pensions*, December 2004. Rates show yearly income for each £10,000 of pension fund.

CASE HISTORY: HAMISH AND RALPH

Hamish and Ralph, both married, retire at 65 with identical pension funds of £47,000.

Hamish opts to buy a joint-life last survivor annuity, with the pension reducing by a third if he dies first. His wife Suzie is five years younger than him and, at an annuity rate of £594, Hamish gets a pension of £594 / £10,000 × £47,000 = £2,793 a year. Five years later, Hamish dies, but the pension, at a reduced rate of $^2/_3$ × £2,793 = £1,861 a year, continues to be paid to Suzie.

Ralph, not wishing to contemplate morbid topics like death, opts for a single-life annuity at a rate of £734. His pension is £734 / £10,000 × £47,000 = £3,450 a year. Six years later, Ralph dies, and the pension stops with him. His wife, Clare, now has to struggle to make ends meet.

Annuities with a guarantee period

With pension annuities you hand over a lump sum and in return get an income for life. You cannot normally get your original investment back as a lump sum and there is generally no lump sum for your heirs to inherit when you die. However, a guarantee period is an option with most annuities.

Where an annuity has a guarantee period, the income is paid out for at least a set period, usually five or ten years, even if you die during that time. If you do die during the guarantee period, the payments may continue as an income to your survivor(s) for the remainder of the period, or, sometimes, can be rolled up into a lump sum.

An annuity with a guarantee period is sometimes viewed as a way of providing for a dependant. But a moment's thought shows that it does not really fit the bill. If you died within the guarantee period, your survivor would continue to get an income but only for a limited period, after which it would stop. If you died after the guarantee period, your survivor would get nothing at all.

CASE HISTORY: GEORGE

George, 65, uses his £24,000 pension fund to buy a level annuity without guarantee. The rate is £734 and the pension is £734 / £10,000 × £24,000 = £1,762 a year. Two years later, George dies. In return for his £24,000 lump sum, he had back just 2 × £1,762 = £3,524. Not a very good deal.

If George had bought an annuity with a ten-year guarantee, he would have had a lower pension of £693 / £10,000 × £24,000 = £1,663 a year. But, after his death, the annuity would have continued to pay out to his heirs for a further eight years. In total, the annuity would have paid out 10 × £1,663 = £16,632. This is still less than the £24,000 he paid for the annuity, but represents a better deal than the annuity without guarantee.

Of course, George did not know when he would die. If he had survived ten years, the annuity without guarantee would, with hindsight, have proved the better deal. His choice of annuity at the start of retirement depended largely on whether he was concerned about leaving something to his heirs in the event of early death.

The main purpose of a guarantee period is to guard against getting a very poor deal from the annuity should you die soon after buying it.

Opting for a guarantee period reduces the starting income you get from an annuity (see Table 6.3). The reduction is greater the older you are (because of the greater risk of dying within the guarantee period).

Do not confuse an annuity with a guarantee period with a 'guaranteed annuity' which pays you income at a pre-set annuity rate regardless of annuity rates generally at the time you start your pension.

Escalating annuities

Escalating annuities increase by a fixed percentage every year, often 5 per cent. If inflation is low, this can be more than enough to protect a pension's buying power; conversely, if inflation exceeds 5 per cent a year, some of the pension's buying power would be lost.

The penalty you pay for an escalating annuity is a lower starting pension, as shown in Table 6.4. Because inflation is currently running at much less than 5 per cent a year, a 5 per cent escalating

Table 6.3 Comparison of single-life level annuities with and without guarantee periods

Type of annuity	Average income from a level annuity bought at age:				
	55	60	65	70	75
Level annuity without a guarantee for a man	£569	£633	£734	£875	£1096
Level annuity with five-year guarantee for a man	£568	£630	£725	£853	£1033
Level annuity with ten-year guarantee for a man	£559	£615	£693	£787	£894
Level annuity without a guarantee for a woman	£545	£597	£671	£784	£948
Level annuity with five-year guarantee for a woman	£544	£594	£666	£772	£915
Level annuity with ten-year guarantee for a woman	£538	£585	£649	£735	£833

Source: *Moneyfacts Life & Pensions*, December 2004. Rates show yearly income for each £10,000 of pension fund.

Table 6.4 Comparison of the starting income from single-life escalating and level annuities without guarantee

Type of annuity	Average income from an annuity bought at age:				
	55	60	65	70	75
Level annuity for a man	£569	£633	£734	£875	£1096
5% a year escalating annuity for a man	£287	£348	£444	£576	£779
Level annuity for a woman	£545	£597	£671	£784	£948
5% a year escalating annuity for a woman	£260	£310	£382	£490	£641

Source: *Moneyfacts Life & Pensions*, December 2004. Rates show yearly income for each £10,000 of pension fund.

annuity is expensive, so there is a big drop in starting income. The drop is proportionately larger at younger ages, because the increases will, on average, have to be made over a longer period.

CASE HISTORY: GILL

Gill has a pension fund of £60,000 and opts to buy an annuity escalating at 5 per cent a year. She is 65.

At an annuity rate of £382, her starting pension is £382 / £10,000 × £60,000 = £2,292. In the second year, the income increases to 105% × £2,292 = £2,407. In the third year, the income increases to 105% × £2,407 = £2,527. The income continues to increase by 5 per cent every year throughout her retirement.

After ten years, the pension has increased to £3,557. Over the ten years, inflation has averaged 2.5 per cent. The pension would have needed to increase to only £2,862 to keep pace with inflation, so Gill has seen a real increase in her income over the ten years and can afford to buy more now than she could at the start of retirement.

RPI-linked annuities

'RPI' stands for Retail Prices Index, which is a government measure of the general price level in the UK. Changes in the RPI are a measure of price inflation. With an RPI-linked annuity, your income increases (or falls) each year in line with changes in the RPI, thus protecting the buying power of your pension.

Unlike an escalating annuity, the income from an RPI-linked annuity could fall if there was a fall in the RPI. Since this would signify a fall in the general price level in the UK, the buying power of your pension would still be preserved.

The starting pension from an RPI-linked pension is lower than the starting pension from a level annuity (see Table 6.5).

Since retirement can easily last two decades or more, you would be unwise to ignore the impact that inflation could have on the buying power of your income. Buying an RPI-linked annuity relieves you of any need to plan how you would cope with inflation – your income will automatically change as required. On the other hand, you have to accept a sizeable drop in your starting income and it may be many years before you 'catch up' with the income you would have had from a level annuity. Table 6.6 shows how a

Table 6.5 Comparison of the starting income from single-life RPI-linked and level annuities without guarantee

Type of annuity	Average income from an annuity bought at age:				
	55	60	65	70	75
Level annuity without a guarantee for a man	£569	£633	£734	£875	£1096
RPI-linked annuity without a guarantee for a man	£354	£425	£518	£655	£863
Level annuity without a guarantee for a woman	£545	£597	£671	£784	£948
RPI-linked annuity without a guarantee for a woman	£325	£382	£462	£571	£726

Source: *Moneyfacts Life & Pensions*, December 2004. Rates show yearly income for each £10,000 of pension fund.

Table 6.6 RPI and level annuity without guarantee compared for a man aged 65 as retirement progresses

| Year of retirement | Level annuity | | RPI-linked annuity Yearly inflation of: | | | | | |
| | | | 2.50% | | 5% | | 7.50% | |
	Yearly income	Total income received	Yearly income	Total income received	Yearly income	Total income received	Yearly income	Total income received
Year retirement starts	£734	£734	£518	£518	£518	£518	£518	£518
1	£734	£1,468	£531	£1,049	£544	£1,062	£557	£1,075
2	£734	£2,202	£544	£1,593	£571	£1,633	£599	£1,673
3	£734	£2,936	£558	£2,151	£600	£2,233	£644	£2,317
4	£734	£3,670	£572	£2,723	£630	£2,862	£692	£3,009
5	£734	£4,404	£586	£3,309	£661	£3,523	**£744**	£3,752
6	£734	£5,138	£601	£3,910	£694	£4,218	£799	£4,552
7	£734	£5,872	£616	£4,525	£729	£4,946	£859	£5,411
8	£734	£6,606	£631	£5,156	**£765**	£5,712	£924	£6,335
9	£734	£7,340	£647	£5,803	£804	£6,515	£993	£7,328
10	£734	£8,074	£663	£6,466	£844	£7,359	£1,068	**£8,396**
11	£734	£8,808	£680	£7,146	£886	£8,245	£1,148	£9,543
12	£734	£9,542	£697	£7,843	£930	£9,175	£1,234	£10,777
13	£734	£10,276	£714	£8,557	£977	£10,152	£1,326	£12,104
14	£734	£11,010	£732	£9,289	£1,026	**£11,178**	£1,426	£13,529
15	£734	£11,744	**£750**	£10,039	£1,077	£12,255	£1,533	£15,062
16	£734	£12,478	£769	£10,808	£1,131	£13,385	£1,648	£16,710
17	£734	£13,212	£788	£11,596	£1,187	£14,573	£1,771	£18,481
18	£734	£13,946	£808	£12,404	£1,247	£15,819	£1,904	£20,385
19	£734	£14,680	£828	£13,232	£1,309	£17,128	£2,047	£22,432
20	£734	£15,414	£849	£14,081	£1,374	£18,503	£2,200	£24,632
21	£734	£16,148	£870	£14,951	£1,443	£19,946	£2,365	£26,998
22	£734	£16,882	£892	£15,843	£1,515	£21,461	£2,543	£29,540
23	£734	£17,616	£914	£16,757	£1,591	£23,052	£2,734	£32,274
24	£734	£18,350	£937	£17,694	£1,671	£24,723	£2,939	£35,213
25	£734	£19,084	£960	£18,654	£1,754	£26,477	£3,159	£38,371
26	£734	£19,818	£984	£19,638	£1,842	£28,319	£3,396	£41,767
27	£734	£20,552	£1,009	**£20,647**	£1,934	£30,253	£3,651	£45,418

Based on annuity rates in December 2004.

level annuity and an RPI-linked annuity bought by a 65-year-old man would fare as retirement progresses if inflation averaged different rates. The level annuity pays out the same income year after year. The RPI-linked annuity increases each year. If inflation averaged just 2.5 per cent a year, it would take 15 years before the

RPI-linked income matched the income from the level annuity and 27 years before both annuities had paid out the same amount of £s in total. At higher rates of inflation, the break-even points would be earlier (see Table 6.6). So whether an RPI-linked annuity looks a good deal depends on how you expect inflation to turn out. Nobody has a crystal ball, so this can only be guesswork. It is perhaps salutary to look back over the last 25 years and note that inflation has ranged from as low as 0.7 per cent a year in December 2001 up to 21.9 per cent a year in May 1980.

If you decide not to buy an RPI-linked annuity, make sure you have other plans for coping with inflation as retirement progresses.

CASE HISTORY: PHIL

Phil, 65, has a pension fund of £39,000. At an annuity rate of £518, he can buy an RPI-linked pension starting at £518 / £10,000 × £39,000 = £2,020 in the first year. After one year, prices as measured by the Retail Prices Index have risen by 1.3 per cent. So, his income increases to 101.3% × £2,020 = £2,081 in the second year. At the end of that year, prices have risen by 8 per cent. So, his income increases to 108% × £2,081 = £2,247 in the third year. Because his income has increased by the same amount as prices, the buying power of his pension remains the same. So each year he can buy just the same amount of things as he could with £2,020 in the first year.

LPI-linked annuities

'LPI' stands for 'limited price indexation'. With an LPI-linked annuity, your income increases each year in line with inflation but only up to a maximum amount, say, 2.5, 3 or 5 per cent. You used to be required to buy an LPI-linked annuity with the fund built up in a contracted-out money purchase pension scheme or plan, but this requirement is abolished for pensions that start to be paid from 6 April 2005 onwards.

The problem with conventional annuities

All the annuities discussed so far are examples of 'conventional annuities' – in other words, annuities where you hand over your pension fund and in return get either a fixed income or one that changes in a predictable way during your retirement.

With a conventional annuity, the provider takes the pension fund you hand over and invests it in long-term gilts and similar investments to ensure that it can pay the annuity income. Gilts provide a low-risk, predictable income that is well-matched to the income due under a conventional annuity contract.

However, the return on long-term gilts has been falling over the last decade or so and, as a result, the income from conventional annuities has also been falling (see Chapter 5). People are increasingly unhappy at having to buy an annuity with their pension fund. Why should they have to surrender the fund and be locked into a poor income for the rest of their life? While their pension funds were building up, they were able to invest in shares and share-based investments, which, over the long-term, have tended to produce much higher returns than investments like gilts. So, why should people not be able to invest in shares during the period when they are drawing their pension? To address these criticisms, new types of annuity (such as investment-linked annuities) and alternatives to annuity purchase (namely, income drawdown – see Chapter 7) have been appearing on the market. But they are not a painless alternative to conventional annuities. They offer the potential for a higher income than you can get from a conventional annuity, but they also expose you to the risk of an income that can fall as well as rise.

Investment-linked annuities

With an investment-linked annuity, you hand over your pension fund and, as usual, get an income for the rest of your life. However, the amount of income varies from year to year depending on the performance of an underlying fund of investments. The income may be linked to a with-profits fund (a with-profits annuity), or an investment fund (a unit-linked annuity). Below is an outline of how each of these might work, though different providers operate their investment-linked annuities in different ways.

Most investment-linked annuities give you the option to switch later to a conventional annuity. With some, it is compulsory to switch on or before reaching a particular age, such as 85, or if your income falls below a certain level (in order to counter the effect of 'mortality drag' – see Chapter 7 for an explanation of this). Invariably the switch is to a conventional annuity from the same provider – you cannot shop around and there is no requirement on the provider to give you an open-market option, because you are assumed already to have had that option (if available) at the time you first took out the investment-linked annuity.

While investment-linked annuities aim to solve one of the problems of conventional annuities – being locked into a low income – you still surrender your pension fund when you buy the annuity. This means you cannot leave any of your pension fund to your heirs (beyond whatever they might get if you opt for a joint-life annuity or an annuity with a guarantee period – see pages 91 and 93).

With-profits annuity

With a with-profits annuity, the amount of income you get depends on bonuses declared on a with-profits fund. The size of bonus is influenced by the performance of the investments in the fund, which comprise shares, gilts, property, and so on. But the bonuses are smoothed, meaning that some of the return from the fund in good years is held back in reserve to top up the bonus rate in poor years. In this way, the bonuses should not fluctuate too wildly, although smoothing cannot protect you from very large or prolonged falls in investment returns.

You cannot know in advance how the with-profits fund will grow and what bonuses will be declared. So, when first taking out the annuity, you have to choose an 'assumed bonus rate' (ABR), usually between 0 and 5 per cent. If, in any year, the actual bonus declared equals your selected ABR, your income should be basically the same as in the previous year. (In practice, it will usually fall slightly because of the deduction of charges.) If the actual bonus exceeds the ABR, your income will rise. If the actual bonus is less than the ABR, your income will fall. The example on page 103 shows one way in which this might work.

If you choose a low ABR at the outset, there is a strong chance that actual bonuses will exceed the ABR and so you can expect your income to rise from year to year. However, this scenario is not guaranteed. Bonuses could be unexpectedly low and, in that case, your income would fail to grow as expected and, except where you have chosen an ABR of 0 per cent, might even fall.

The main drawback of choosing a low ABR is that your starting income is low. At the time of writing, choosing a with-profits annuity with a 0 per cent ABR would produce a starting income of about half that available from a conventional level annuity. A low starting income need not be a problem if you have income from other sources, say, part-time work. In fact, a with-profits annuity with a low ABR could be a very good way of organising a pension that increases as retirement progresses to replace income that is falling as you gradually wind down the amount of work you do.

If you choose a high ABR, your starting income is higher but there is a much bigger risk that actual bonuses will fall short of the ABR and the income will then fall. You should generally consider a with-profits annuity with a high ABR only if you can cope with a fluctuating income – if, say, the bulk of your retirement income comes from another source. You should also consider whether income drawdown (see Chapter 7) would not be a more suitable option, especially if you are concerned about leaving something for your heirs. At the time of writing, the maximum ABR allowed was 5 per cent and, at this level, the starting income was slightly lower than you could get from a conventional level annuity.

At one time, you were committed to the ABR you chose at the start of the annuity for the whole life of the annuity. But, with the with-profits annuities available these days, it is usually possible to alter the ABR. For example, you might start with a low ABR (and low income) in early retirement when you still have some income from work and switch to a higher ABR when you want the income to increase.

Unit-linked annuity

Many unit-linked annuities work in a broadly similar way to a with-profits annuity, but your income is linked directly to the performance of an investment fund. You can normally choose from several funds. Some providers let you select your own investments (an option usually called 'self-investment'). At the outset, you select an 'assumed growth rate' (AGR). If the fund actually grows by the same amount as the AGR, your income stays level (or, in practice, declines slightly because of the deduction of charges). If the actual growth rate is higher than the AGR, your income grows. If the actual growth rate is lower than the AGR, your income falls.

Choose a low AGR and the starting income is low, but there is a good chance that the income will grow. Choose a high AGR and the starting income is higher, but there is a bigger risk of the income falling.

With a with-profits annuity, usually the worst case is an actual bonus rate of 0 per cent, but with a unit-linked annuity actual growth can be less than 0 per cent and there is no smoothing to protect you from the effects of falling investment values. So unit-linked annuities are more risky than with-profits annuities even if you choose a low AGR. They are suitable only if you can cope with a fluctuating income. Again, you could consider income drawdown as an alternative, especially if you want to leave something to your heirs (see Chapter 7).

Limited-period annuities

To address the complaint that people are locked into an annuity from the date they retire even if that annuity turns out to be poor value, under new rules from 6 April 2006 you will be able to use part of your pension fund to buy a limited-period annuity.

A limited-period annuity provides an income for a maximum of five years and must end before you reach age 75. When the limited-period annuity ends, you can either use another slice of your pension fund to buy a further limited-period annuity or use the remaining fund to buy a lifetime annuity or for income drawdown (see Chapter 7).

The advantage of a limited-period annuity is that you are not locked in for life. When the limited period ends, investment conditions might have improved and you get another chance to shop around for a better deal. The drawbacks are that investment conditions may have worsened and, in any case, you are exposed to 'mortality drag' – see Chapter 7.

Capital-protection annuities

Also from 6 April 2006, capital-protection annuities will become available. These are annuities where, if you die before age 75, the balance of what you paid for the annuity less the sum of the pension payments already paid out can be paid to your heirs as a lump sum. This ensures that the annuity pays out in total as much as it cost, but the price of this protection will be a lower starting income.

As with annuities with a guarantee period (see page 93), capital-protection annuities are not an adequate way of providing for a dependant. They are simply a way of avoiding a very poor return from your investment.

CASE HISTORY: KARL

Karl, 65, gets a pension from an occupational scheme but has also built up a pension fund of £65,000 in a personal pension. He could buy a conventional level annuity at a rate of £734, which would give him a pension of £4,771 a year throughout retirement.

Another option is to choose a with-profits annuity. He can select an ABR between 0 per cent and 5 per cent. At 0 per cent, the starting income would be £2,576. At 5 per cent, the income would be £4,580. The income would vary each year depending on the actual bonuses declared by the provider.

Table 6.7 shows how the income might change during the first few years, assuming various levels of declared bonus. If Karl opted for a 0 per cent ABR, the income would increase provided any bonus at all were declared. At the 5 per cent ABR, the income increases only if the declared bonus is more than 5 per cent. If the bonus is less, the income falls. Even if the declared bonus is exactly 5 per cent, there is a small fall in income because of the impact of charges deducted by the provider for administering the investments.

Karl opts for the highest ABR of 5 per cent because the starting income is high, he is optimistic about future bonuses, and can easily cope with the risk of the income falling because he relies mainly on the pension from his occupational scheme.

Table 6.7   Income Karl might get from a with-profits annuity

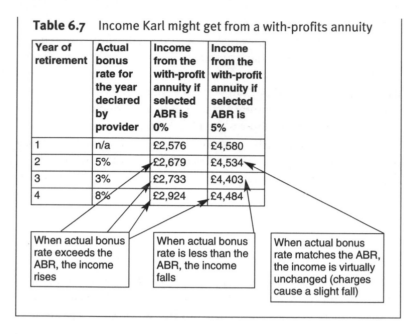

Year of retirement	Actual bonus rate for the year declared by provider	Income from the with-profit annuity if selected ABR is 0%	Income from the with-profit annuity if selected ABR is 5%
1	n/a	£2,576	£4,580
2	5%	£2,679	£4,534
3	3%	£2,733	£4,403
4	8%	£2,924	£4,484

When actual bonus rate exceeds the ABR, the income rises

When actual bonus rate is less than the ABR, the income falls

When actual bonus rate matches the ABR, the income is virtually unchanged (charges cause a slight fall)

Phased retirement

Phased retirement is another way to use a pension fund to buy an income that increases throughout retirement. This is achieved by initially converting just part of the fund into an annuity, while leaving the rest of the fund invested. (You can choose any type of annuity.) Later on, you convert another tranche of the fund into annuity, leaving the remainder invested. Later, you convert another tranche, and so on. But the whole of the fund must have been converted by age 75.

When you first started saving, you may have taken out a pension scheme or plan that was automatically divided into many segments, with each segment being in fact a separate mini-plan. This arrangement makes phased retirement simple, because you just convert some of the segments at any one time into annuities. Since April 2001, personal pensions and stakeholder schemes have been allowed to offer multiple annuity dates, which achieves the same effect. If your plan or scheme does not offer a phased retirement option, you can usually transfer your pension fund to one that does.

The main differences between phased retirement and using your whole fund at the outset to buy some type of increasing annuity are:

- **flexibility** With phased retirement, you have more control over how your income increases. You can also manipulate pension increases to reflect changes in your circumstances, for example by choosing not to make an increase some years, or by bringing forward an increase if your income unexpectedly drops
- **the tax-free lump sum** With phased retirement, you take part of each tranche of pension fund as a lump sum at the time you buy an annuity, so you get a series of small lump sums spread across the retirement years, instead of a single larger lump sum at the outset of retirement
- **cost** While part of your pension fund remains invested, you continue to incur charges for managing your investments
- **leaving something to your heirs** If you die before converting the whole of your pension fund into annuities, the part of the fund that remains invested can be passed to your survivors.

In general, you need a reasonably large pension fund to make phased retirement worthwhile. You should be aware that putting off the time at which you convert part of your pension fund into pension exposes you to 'mortality drag' (explained in Chapter 7). You might want to consider income drawdown (see Chapter 7) as an alternative to phased retirement.

Chapter 7

Income drawdown

When you want to start receiving a pension from a money purchase scheme or plan, you usually use the fund to buy an annuity as described in Chapters 5 and 6. Income drawdown is an alternative way of receiving a pension from your fund.

The basics of income drawdown

Before age 75

With income drawdown, you take an income direct from your pension fund while leaving the fund invested. The advantages of income drawdown are:

- flexibility – under current rules, you choose how much income to take subject to a minimum and a maximum amount. From 6 April 2006 onwards, there will be no minimum limit
- if you die during the income drawdown period, your heirs can inherit the remaining pension fund (after deducting tax)
- control over how your fund is invested
- the ability to put off the date you purchase an annuity, which could be useful if you think annuity rates are temporarily low.

The drawbacks are:

- the maximum pension you are allowed to have can fall, so you must be able to cope with a fluctuating income
- your pension fund may be eroded if investment returns are poor, a problem which is exacerbated if you draw a high pension
- when you eventually buy an annuity you may get a low income because of a general fall in annuity rates

- you are exposed to mortality drag (see page 110), which means you must be prepared to take some risk investing your pension fund
- your fund needs to be invested appropriately and monitored closely, which inevitably involves charges.

After age 75

Under current rules, you can use income drawdown only up to age 75. At that point you must use your remaining pension fund to buy an annuity.

This changes from 6 April 2006. By age 75, you must either buy an annuity or arrange an 'alternatively-secured pension' (ASP). ASP is income drawdown subject to the following restrictions:

- the maximum income you can draw each year is lower than the most you could draw before age 75
- on your death, your survivor(s) cannot inherit any of the remaining fund as a lump sum but only as a pension. However, you can nominate one or more charities to receive your remaining fund as a lump sum.

Is income drawdown an option for you?

You may choose income drawdown if you have a stakeholder scheme or other personal pension (even if it is being used to contract out of the state additional pension – see page 60). Income drawdown is not an option with a retirement annuity contract, though you could transfer your pension fund from such a contract to a stakeholder scheme or personal pension in order to take advantage of income drawdown.

Income drawdown may also be an option with an occupational money purchase scheme, in-house additional voluntary contribution (AVC) scheme (other than an added years scheme) or free-standing AVC scheme, but not in respect of any contracted-out rights from any of these schemes. But there are complications and, in practice, you may find the only way to access income drawdown is to transfer your pension fund to a stakeholder scheme or personal pension.

Even if income drawdown is technically an option, it will not necessarily be appropriate for you. The risks and charges involved

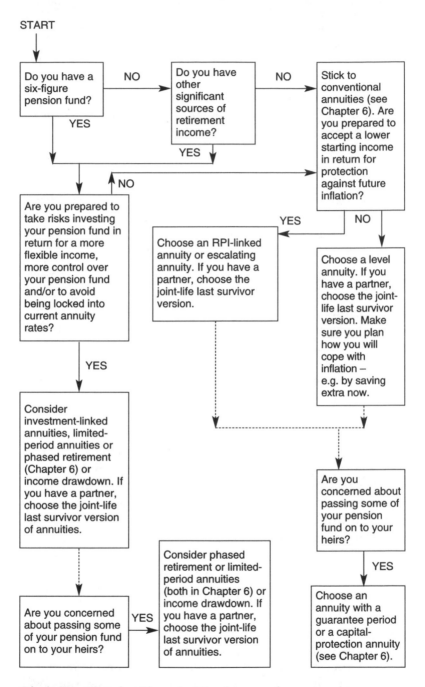

Chart 7.1 Broad guide to deciding how to take your pension

mean that income drawdown is generally suitable only in conjunction with a six-figure pension fund or other sources of retirement income and if you are comfortable with the risks. The decision is complicated, so get advice from an independent financial adviser★ before going down this route. Chart 7.1 gives a broad guide to your options (but excludes contracted-out pensions, which are subject to special rules).

Mortality drag

Any arrangement – such as investment-linked annuities, phased retirement or income drawdown – which involves putting off the date at which you use some or all of your pension fund to buy a conventional annuity exposes you to 'mortality drag'.

What is mortality drag?

Mortality drag occurs for the reasons explained below and means the extra return you need from your invested pension fund when you delay buying an annuity. Essentially, the later you buy an annuity, the worse the deal you get. The pension fund you have invested must work ever harder to compensate for this. Unless you choose relatively high-risk, high-return investments, it is unlikely that the return from investing your pension fund will be good enough to outweigh the mortality drag.

Taking relatively high risks with your pension fund is appropriate only if you have a very large fund to invest or you have other sources of retirement income to fall back on. Therefore any pension arrangement that exposes you to mortality drag is usually not suitable if you have only a small pension fund or if it is your main source of retirement income.

Why does mortality drag occur?

Annuities are a sort of reverse insurance, where you are insuring against living too long. Like all insurance, the risk is managed by pooling you with lots of other people facing the same or similar risks.

If you had to provide your pension on your own, you would have to invest your pension fund and either just live on the income it produced (a cautious and costly approach) or gradually run down

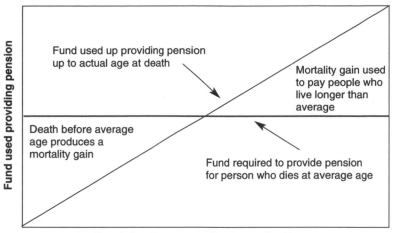

Chart 7.2 How people who die early cross-subsidise the pensions of people who die later than average

the capital as well (cheaper but more risky). If you knew how long you would live, you could time it exactly so that your capital ran out on the day you died. In practice, you don't know when you will die. If you lived longer than expected, your capital would run out and you would have nothing left to live on.

An insurance company can provide pensions by running down capital, so long as it does so for a large pool of people. It works on the basis of the average life expectancy of the people in the pool. Although some people live longer than average, their pension does not need to run out, because other people die sooner than average. The unused part of the pension fund of the people who die early produces a 'mortality gain', which is used to subsidise the pensions of the people who live longer than average (see Chart 7.2). The existence of this cross-subsidy means that annuity rates can be higher than they would otherwise be.

However, the amount of cross-subsidy dwindles the later you leave buying an annuity. An annuity rate is based only on the life expectancy of people who have reached a particular age. For example, if you buy an annuity at age 65, the rate is based on the life expectancy of people who are now aged 65. It does not take into account anyone who died before that age, so you do not get any

---

CASE HISTORY: JACK

Jack, aged 60, has a pension fund of £100,000. He could use it to buy an immediate level annuity of £6,330 a year. Alternatively, he could opt for income drawdown. In early 2005, the minimum and maximum incomes he could draw from his pension fund would be £2,660 and £7,600, respectively. Suppose he draws £6,330 a year – the same as he would have had from the annuity – and is able to continue with the same income until age 75. At age 75, he can get an annuity rate of £1,096 for every £10,000 in his remaining pension fund. To continue drawing an income of £6,330, he will need a remaining pension fund of £6,330 / £1,096 × £10,000 = £57,755. This is possible provided his invested pension fund grows by around 4.8 per cent a year (after charges have been paid), which could be equivalent to, say, 6 per cent a year before charges. In early 2005, the return from deposits or gilts was around 1 to 1.5 per cent a year, implying that Jack needs to invest his pension fund in shares or similar investments, which although higher risk, offer the chance of a better return.

---

cross-subsidy from anyone who died before then. The later you leave buying an annuity, the smaller the pool of people on whom the annuity rate is based and the smaller the cross-subsidy. In the extreme, if you could leave buying an annuity to, say, age 105, you might be the only person in the pool and there could then be no cross-subsidy at all.

The result is: annuities become poorer value the later you buy them. If you are to be no worse off than you would have been buying an annuity straight away, your invested pension fund needs to grow by an extra amount equal to the decline in the value of the cross-subsidy. The amount of extra growth you need increases the older you are when you decide to defer annuity purchase and the older you are when you finally do buy an annuity. The Institute of Actuaries has estimated that the extra return you need is generally in the region of 1 to 3 per cent a year, provided that you buy an annuity by age 75.

When you seek advice about income drawdown, the financial adviser will normally work out a 'critical yield' showing the return your invested pension fund needs to earn if you are to be no worse off opting for income drawdown than if you had bought an annuity straight away.

Income drawdown in detail

Your tax-free lump sum

If you choose income drawdown, you still have the usual option to take part of your pension fund as a tax-free lump sum (see Chapters 3 and 4). The lump sum is taken in full at the time you enter the drawdown contract. (You do not get any further lump sums, for example when eventually purchasing an annuity.)

Your pension

With income drawdown, the provider arranges to pay you a pension direct from your pension fund. Payment is made and tax deducted in the normal way as described in Chapters 3 and 4.

Under current rules, you must receive at least one pension payment a year. The pension must be at least a minimum amount and it must not exceed a maximum amount. The minimum and maximum are worked out according to a formula specified by the government and depend among other things on the return from long-term gilts. The maximum is broadly in line with the income you could get from a single-life level annuity. The minimum is 35 per cent of the maximum.

Under the drawdown rules, the minimum and maximum income must be recalculated every three years to ensure that your pension fund is not being run down too rapidly. As a result of this review, you may find you have to reduce or increase the income you take. Although not compulsory, it is sensible for you or your adviser to make this check more frequently – say, once a year.

At any time before age 75, you can decide to use your remaining pension fund to buy an annuity. (You can choose any type of annuity, for example level, RPI-linked, investment-linked – see Chapter 6). If you have not already done so, under current rules you must switch the remaining fund to an annuity at age 75.

From 6 April 2006 onwards, you can continue income drawdown after age 75 by opting for an alternatively secured pension (see page 108).

Your pension fund

Because of mortality drag and charges, your invested pension fund is going to have to produce a healthy return. Therefore, it is very important to think carefully about how you invest it. Sticking to lower-risk investments, such as deposits and gilts, is unlikely to produce a high enough return. On the other hand, putting all your money into a share-based fund could go badly wrong if share prices fall. The most sensible course is likely to be a spread of different assets carefully chosen to give the necessary risk-return profile. Some people choose income drawdown specifically because they enjoy making their own investment decisions and want to continue deciding how their pension fund will be invested. If you are not confident making these choices for yourself, get advice from an independent financial adviser*.

Since February 2001, you have been allowed to switch your pension fund from one provider to another during the drawdown period. You can only make one switch within any 12-month period. This facility can be useful if, for example, your fund is invested with a provider that is producing disappointing returns, but watch out for extra charges on switching.

What happens if you die during the income drawdown period?

One of the reasons income drawdown is attractive is that you avoid the risk inherent in annuities of losing all your pension fund for little return if you die soon after retirement. With income drawdown, the unused part of your pension fund can be passed on to your survivors. The rules can be complicated, but in general the pension fund can be passed on in the following ways:

- a survivor (or more than one) can continue to receive an income direct from the fund using drawdown. If the survivor is your husband or wife, they can continue using drawdown until they reach age 75, or, if earlier, the date on which you would have reached 75. If more than one survivor draws an income, the sum of the incomes must not be more than the maximum you could have had
- a survivor (or more than one) can use the fund to buy an annuity. If this applies to more than one survivor, the sum of the incomes from the annuities must not exceed the maximum annuity income you could have had
- the survivor(s) can receive the pension fund as a lump sum after tax at a special rate of 35 per cent has been deducted. To be

eligible, the survivor(s) must have been financially dependent on you (which can include sharing household expenses with you). You should arrange for the lump sum to be paid to your survivors through a trust, otherwise it will count as part of your estate and so could be subject to inheritance tax.

If the survivor(s) opt for income drawdown or an annuity, they will receive an income for the rest of their life. However, the pension fund might be larger than needed to provide this income. In that case (as with any annuity), the excess is retained by the scheme. Therefore, if the pension fund looks larger than needed to provide the maximum possible annuity or drawdown income, your survivors might be better off taking the fund as a lump sum.

The Inland Revenue, the government department responsible for pensions and income drawdown, is very sensitive about pension schemes being used as intended to provide retirement income. Income drawdown opens the door to using a pension scheme as a tax-efficient way of passing on wealth to your heirs. To deter this, there are some tax-evasion rules. The pension fund could be subject to inheritance tax if it seems you chose income drawdown primarily for inheritance purposes. However, provided you survive for at least two years after opting for drawdown and you are not known to be in poor health, there is unlikely to be a tax charge. Similarly, there might be inheritance tax on the fund should you discover you are seriously ill and, in consequence, reduce the income you draw from the fund.

From 6 April 2006 onwards, you can continue income drawdown after age 75 by opting for an alternatively secured pension (see page 108). On your death on or after age 75, your survivors will be entitled to a pension either by buying an annuity or via continuing drawdown. However, they will not have the option of receiving a lump sum. You can specify that your remaining fund is paid as a lump sum to charity.

Points to bear in mind if you choose income drawdown

The brief outline of income drawdown in this chapter should be enough to convince you that this is a relatively high-risk way of providing yourself with retirement income.

If your prime concern is to provide yourself with a secure income of the maximum possible amount, in most cases buying an annuity immediately will be the best option. If you are worried about losing your pension fund if you were to die soon after retirement, choose an annuity with a guarantee period (see page 93) or a capital-protection annuity (see page 103). If your worries are due to your poor health, bear in mind that you may be eligible for an enhanced annuity (see page 85).

Only consider income drawdown if you have a large pension fund (a six-figure sum), or you have other substantial sources of retirement income. Your ability to draw the level of income you want during the drawdown period and when you eventually buy an annuity will depend crucially on how your invested pension fund grows. The stock market slump of the early 2000s has vividly brought home the reality of risk and the impact that falling share prices can have on your finances – see the case history overleaf. You will be especially vulnerable if you are drawing a high income from your pension fund

---

CASE HISTORY: PAULA

In November 1999, Paula, then aged 55, started an income drawdown arrangement. After taking a tax-free lump sum, she had a pension fund of £180,000 to invest. If she had bought an annuity, she could have had a level income of £11,500 a year. With drawdown, she could take an income between £4,410 and £12,600 a year. She decided to draw the maximum £12,600 a year. She invested the bulk of her pension fund in the UK stock market.

In November 2002, her drawdown arrangement was reviewed. Unfortunately, with the high income withdrawals and a large slump in the stock market, Paula's pension fund had shrunk alarmingly to £96,750. The return on gilts and annuity rates had also fallen over the three years. When the minimum and maximum drawdown incomes were recalculated based on the new gilts return and pension fund, they came to £2,235 and £6,385 a year. Paula had to accept a very large cut in the income she could draw from the fund.

Paula considered whether she should buy an annuity with the remaining fund, but she would get only £6,153 a year. This was a lot less than she could have bought three years earlier.

during the drawdown period. The lower the income, the more you leave in the fund and the better you may be able to withstand shocks. Income drawdown may look attractive if you think annuity rates are temporarily low but could increase in the future. However, as Chapter 5 explained, there are some fundamental factors depressing annuity rates – for example, increasing longevity and continued downward pressure on the return from gilts. It is unlikely that the position will improve in the immediate future and it could become worse. If annuity rates fall during the drawdown period, your pension fund will buy even less income when you finally swap it for an annuity.

Where to get advice

You are strongly advised to get advice from an independent financial adviser (IFA)★ before deciding on income drawdown instead of annuity purchase. Most IFAs specialising in annuities★ can also advise on income drawdown. The Personal Finance Society (PFS)★ can provide contact details of those members who specialise in pension planning. All PFS members have advanced qualifications that make them an appropriate choice to handle complex financial decisions like drawdown.

Part 2

Other sources of retirement income

Chapter 8

Carrying on working

Retirement does not have to be a distinct point in time. For many people, gradually easing out of work is a more attractive option. A few people shun retirement altogether and prefer to carry on working without any concession to age.

Your right to carry on working

In general terms, you can work as long as you like regardless of your age. It is easy to continue working if you run your own business – you just carry on as normal. But you may run into problems if you are an employee.

At present, if there is a normal retirement age for your job, your employer can dismiss you if you have reached or passed that age. It does not count as unfair dismissal and you have no rights to challenge the decision (unless the dismissal was primarily related to your being a member of a trade union). You may be able to work on after reaching the normal retirement age at the employer's discretion. From October 2006 new legislation is due to come into effect which will outlaw age discrimination. The government is still consulting on the detail but has proposed that there will be a default age of 65 below which you cannot be forced to retire. However, from 65 onwards you would not have an automatic right to work. Instead, the government is proposing that you have the right to ask to stay on after age 65 but your employer will be able to turn down your request if he or she has sound business reasons for doing so. Under current rules you have no right to redundancy pay if you lose your job after age 65 (or the normal retirement age for the job if lower). Under the new legislation, the government is proposing that redundancy pay will be payable to workers over 65.

If you cannot continue working for your current employer, there is nothing to stop you looking for a job elsewhere, though some employers currently do not give serious consideration to older applicants.

The UK has until 2006 to implement measures in the European Employment Directive on Equal Treatment prohibiting direct or indirect discrimination at work on the grounds of age. The directive covers all aspects of work and training, including recruitment. Some areas are specifically excluded from its scope, including occupational pension schemes, and other areas may be excluded if the government can show that age discrimination would be justified (for example, on safety grounds).

In the meantime, the Department of Work and Pensions (DWP), a government department, has introduced a voluntary *Code of practice on age diversity in employment*. This encourages employers to avoid direct or indirect discrimination in recruitment, selection, promotion, training and development, redundancy and retirement. About one-third of employers are now aware of the code, which was introduced in 1999. You can find out more by contacting the DWP's Age Positive Campaign*.

Older workers

- Just over 6 million of the 9 million people aged 50 up to state pension age are working.
- One person in ten over state pension age is working.
- Older people tend to have fewer formal qualifications than younger people.
- Older workers have on average spent 13 years in their current job. The average for younger workers is just seven years.
- Older workers are more likely to work part-time or be self-employed.
- Personnel professionals believe older workers are more efficient and take less time off sick than younger workers.
- A quarter of personnel professionals feel their organisation discriminates against older workers.

Sources: Age Positive Campaign, Age Concern, *Personnel Today* magazine.

Changing the law is one thing, changing social attitudes quite another. While racism and, increasingly, sexism are generally viewed as unacceptable, ageism is often not even recognised as discrimination. Many employers see no problem in advertising for new graduates, passing over older people when it comes to training or promotion, or automatically selecting older workers for redundancy. Yet people over age 50 already make up 40 per cent of the population and will account for half the population by 2011. If they are to avoid skills shortages, employers will as time goes on have to recognise the value of older workers.

Work and pensions

State pensions

State pensions are not payable before state pension age (see page 18). Having reached state pension age, you do not have to stop work to claim your pension. If you do not need your state pension, you can defer it, which earns you an increase in the state pension once it does start to be paid (see page 32).

Occupational pensions

In the case of an occupational scheme from your current employer, at present different rules apply depending on when the scheme started and/or when you joined it:

- **post-1989 scheme** This means a scheme that started on or after 14 March 1989 or you joined on or after 1 June 1989. Under present Inland Revenue rules, you cannot start to draw a pension from the scheme while you are still an employee working for the employer who provides the scheme. However, this restriction is being abolished from 6 April 2006 onwards
- **pre-1989 scheme** A scheme started before 14 March 1989 that you joined before 1 June 1989 and that has not voluntarily been switched to the post-1989 regime. You can continue working beyond the normal retirement age for the scheme even if you have started to draw your pension.

Where you are allowed to work beyond normal retirement age and you put off drawing your pension until later, you might qualify for some increase in your pension. The rules are complicated, so check the position with your pension scheme administrator★.

You can continue working for your current employer while drawing a pension from a previous employer's occupational scheme.

Personal pensions

You do not have to stop work to draw a pension from a stakeholder scheme, other personal pension or retirement annuity contract.

Various options, such as investment-linked annuities, phased retirement (see Chapter 6) and income drawdown (see Chapter 7), give you flexibility, so, for example, you could start off with a low pension while you are still earning and increase the pension later on as you reduce the amount that you work.

Tax and National Insurance

Income tax

If you continue working, you continue to be taxed in the normal way. However, once you reach age 65, you qualify for a higher tax allowance, so you could then see a reduction in your income tax bill. But you lose some or all of the extra allowance if your income from all sources (work, pensions, savings, and so on) exceeds a certain limit (£19,500 in 2005–6). See Chapter 14 for details.

National Insurance contributions

If you are under state pension age, you carry on paying National Insurance contributions in the normal way.

Once you reach state pension age (see page 18), you no longer pay National Insurance contributions. This can cause a large and welcome increase in your take-home pay or profits. There are a couple of points you should note:

- employees' Class 1 contributions stop from the date you reach state pension age. But the employer continues to pay employers' National Insurance on your pay and benefits whatever your age. You should bear this in mind if you run your own business as a company and pay yourself a salary, since your company (as your employer) will still have National Insurance to pay

- if you are self-employed, Class 2 (flat-rate) contributions stop when you reach your sixty-fifth birthday, but Class 4 (profit-related) contributions stop only if you are state pension age or over during the whole of the tax year. In other words, unless your birthday falls on 6 April, you normally pay Class 4 contributions for the whole of the year in which you reach state pension age.

If you are an employee, shortly before you reach state pension age you should apply to your tax office for a certificate of age exception to hand to your employer. (If you have already filled in a claim form for your state pension and said on that form you will continue working, you should automatically receive a certificate.)

If you are self-employed or a partner, the Inland Revenue should already have information about your age and automatically stop charging you Class 2 and 4 contributions. If you work out your own tax bill through the self-assessment system, do not include any Class 4 payment.

Employment rights and older workers

Bear in mind that you are entitled to receive at least a minimum amount of pay. From 1 October 2004, the national minimum wage is £4.85 an hour.

You are entitled to the same rights as any other employee, except that some rights do not apply to the over-65s, for example:

- you have no right to statutory sick pay
- in most cases, you have no right to claim unfair dismissal
- you currently have no right to statutory redundancy pay (but see page 121).

For a summary of your rights as an employee, see Department of Trade and Industry (DTI) leaflet PL176, *Individual rights of employees – a guide for employers and employees*, available from the DTI*.

Volunteering

Paid work is not the only option. If money is not the motivation, there are plenty of opportunities to turn your skills to unpaid, voluntary work. There are endless possibilities, including becoming a Citizens Advice Bureau (CAB)★ adviser, helping to run an animal sanctuary, serving in a charity shop, becoming a local councillor, helping out at a tourist information centre, providing company and odd jobs for elderly or disabled people, being a volunteer driver, helping to run a charity, becoming a school governor, getting involved with a hospital trust, and so on. See 'Volunteering' in the Addresses section for a list of organisations that can help you to find a voluntary job that suits you.

By their nature, voluntary jobs are unpaid. However, you might get an expenses allowance or have your costs reimbursed. These are tax-free provided that they are genuinely to cover your expenses and not a hidden form of pay for your services.

Chapter 9

Savings and investments

Managing your savings and investments to give you the best and most appropriate return is often a very important aspect of retirement. This chapter looks at the broad process of choosing suitable investments and describes the main products available. Chapter 10 considers a number of specific goals that are common in retirement and suggests how they might be met.

How to choose your savings and investments

Chart 9.1 summarises the main factors that are likely to influence which broad types of investment are suitable for you.

Your goals

You may have many reasons for saving or investing, but essentially they boil down to three broad objectives:

- **growth** Increasing the amount of capital you have
- **income** Generating income now, for example to supplement your pension
- **future income** Generating an income that will start at a later date, for example when your earnings stop completely.

Different products are usually suitable for each of these goals. Sometimes the same product used in different ways can help you to meet different goals.

Often objectives are interrelated, for example if you need extra income starting now, in order to ensure that you maintain a comparable income in future you will usually need to invest at least some of your money for growth as well.

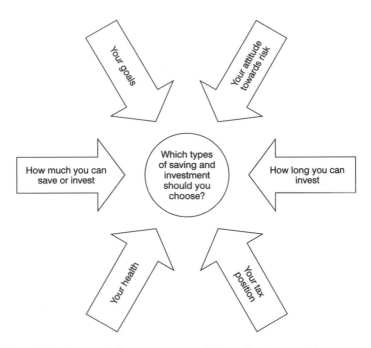

Chart 9.1   Factors influencing your choice of savings and investments

Your attitude towards risk

When you think of investment risk, you probably think of losing part of your original investment because, say, the stock market has fallen. This is called 'capital risk', but it is not the only risk you need to consider. Table 9.1 summarises the main risks you might face.

Unfortunately, there is no way simultaneously to avoid all the risks outlined in Table 9.1. You have to strike a balance between them. In particular, over the long term there is a very strong relationship between capital risk and return. Investments where the value of your capital cannot fall, such as bank and building society accounts, over periods of five years or more have tended to produce much lower returns than investments such as shares where the value of your capital can rise and fall. Understandably, many retired people are cautious with their savings and investments and reluctant to take capital risks, because, once your earnings have stopped it may be very hard or impossible to make good any losses made on your investments. However, although sticking to bank and building

Table 9.1 Savings and investment risks

Type of risk	Description	How to reduce or avoid the risk
Capital risk	Amount of your original investment (your capital) falls, for example because the price of the investment falls, you have to pay large surrender charges, or the provider fails to repay the investment as promised.	Choose investments where the price cannot fall (for example, bank and building society accounts); avoid investments with surrender charges; stick to financially secure providers such as the government.
Inflation risk	The buying power of your income or capital falls because it does not grow fast enough to keep pace with inflation.	Choose index-linked investments; invest some of your money for growth to replace the lost buying power; choose investments offering higher returns.
Shortfall risk	You cannot meet a goal because the return on your investments is too low.	Choose investments offering a higher return; reduce your goal.
Interest-rate risk	If you choose a variable interest rate, the risk is that the rate may fall. If you choose a fixed rate of interest, the risk is that competing interest rates rise, leaving you locked into a low return.	If you could not cope with a fall in interest rates, consider investments with fixed returns. If you think interest rates are likely to rise, avoid fixed returns.

society accounts reduces your capital risk, it increases the shortfall and inflation risks. Acting in a way that minimises capital risk but ignores other risks is sometimes aptly referred to as 'reckless caution'.

If you are saving or investing only for the short- to medium-term (up to five years or so), it is usually not appropriate to take capital risks. To manage capital risks, you need the ability to ride out short-term dips in the value of your investments. This is not possible if you will need your money back at short notice or at a specific time.

How long you can invest

As discussed above, the length of time over which you can save or invest will determine how much capital risk you can take and will thus influence your choice of investments.

How long you can invest influences your choice in other ways too. For example, some savings products offer a higher return if you can invest for, say, five years or give 90 days' notice when you want to withdraw money. Some investments, such as some insurance policies, have hefty early surrender charges that mean you have to commit yourself to long-term saving in order to get a reasonable return. Other investments, like pensions, do not let you get your money back before a certain age or time, and so are totally unsuitable if you might need your money back earlier.

How much you can save or invest

Many products have a minimum investment or savings limit which may put them out of reach if you have only a small amount to invest. Some others have high charges that make investing or saving small sums uneconomic.

If, in total, you have only small amounts to invest, you should avoid taking large risks with your money.

Some investments, for example some National Savings & Investments (NS&I) products, have a maximum limit. Sometimes tax rules – say, for individual savings accounts (ISAs) and pensions – limit the amount you can save or invest.

Your tax position

Different types of savings and investments are taxed in different ways. This can have a big impact on the after-tax return you get. Depending on your income tax or capital gains tax (CGT) position, some investments will give you more tax-efficient returns than others.

Chapters 14 and 15 explain how income tax and CGT work and should help you to identify your own tax position, and the descriptions of investments later in this chapter include details of how each product is taxed. Here are a few general guidelines:

- if you are a non-taxpayer, avoid investments where tax has already been paid and cannot be reclaimed, for example shares and most life-insurance products
- if you are a non-taxpayer and you have savings income (for example, from a bank or building society account), arrange to have the income paid to you gross (in other words, without any tax deducted) or, failing that, make sure you reclaim the tax
- if you are a starting-rate taxpayer and you have savings income, make sure you reclaim part of the tax
- if you are aged 65 or over and your income is in, or close to, the range where you lose age allowance, be wary of cashing in a life-insurance bond or plan. The proceeds count as part of your income for the year and could cause you to lose age allowance
- if you do not usually pay CGT (see Chapter 15), avoid investments where gains have already been taxed and you cannot reclaim the tax. This is a problem with many life-insurance investments
- if you are a taxpayer, try to make use of annual allowances that let you have tax-free returns, for example your ISA allowance and pension contribution limits. (But the return from those ISAs investing in shares and share-based investment funds is not completely tax free – see page 150)
- if you are a higher-rate taxpayer, life insurance investments can be very tax-efficient
- if you pay income tax but no CGT, consider investments that produce gains rather than income.

Your health

With many types of savings and investments, your health is not relevant. However, it will be important with:

- **insurance-based investments** If there is more than token life cover included, you will pay more if you are in poor health, because of the higher probability that the insurance might have to pay out

- **annuities** If your health is poor, some providers will offer you better-than-average annuity rates, reflecting the likelihood that the annuity might have to pay out for a shorter-than-average time (see Chapter 5)
- **long-term investments** If your health is poor and you are considering an investment that locks you in, or is designed to run, for a long period, check what would happen if you were to die during that period.

The main types of savings and investments

In broadly ascending order of capital risk, this section outlines the main types of savings and investments that may be particularly useful during the retirement years. Chapter 10 shows how they can be put to work meeting two of the most common goals.

For each investment, there is an indication of the goals for which it might be particularly suitable. In addition, all the savings and investments might be useful as part of a balanced 'asset allocation' designed to spread your risks (see Chapter 10).

Bank and building society instant access and easy access accounts

Description/suitable for Savings accounts that let you withdraw your money at any time without notice or penalty. Especially suitable for a 'rainy-day fund' that you can call on in emergencies, general money management (for example, setting aside money to pay bills) and short-term saving (for holidays, Christmas, and so on).

Return and charges Interest on the amount in the account. No explicit charges. Interest is often tiered with higher rates paid on larger balances.

Risk No capital risk (see box).

How long you invest No set period.

Minimum investment Often £1, sometimes more.

Maximum investment Usually none.

Tax Interest is usually paid with income tax at the savings rate already deducted. Higher-rate taxpayers have extra to pay. Starting-rate taxpayers can reclaim some tax. Non-taxpayers should either reclaim the tax or arrange to be paid gross interest.

How to invest Contact relevant bank or building society.

Capital risk

In this section, unless specifically mentioned, we have assumed that the risk of your losing capital because the provider goes bust is minimal. In the event it did happen, you might be eligible for compensation from the Financial Services Compensation Scheme*. The compensation limits are shown in Table 9.2.

Table 9.2 Financial Services Compensation Scheme limits on compensation

Type of savings or investment	Level of cover	Maximum payout
Deposits (e.g. bank and building society accounts)	100% of the first £2,000 90% of next £33,000 0% of anything more	£31,700
Non-insurance investments (e.g. unit trusts and oeics) and bad investment advice	100% of first £30,000 90% of next £20,000 0% of anything more	£48,000
Insurance-based investments (e.g. insurance bonds, personal pensions)	100% of first £2,000 Up to 90% of remainder	Unlimited

Bank and building society notice accounts

Description/suitable for Savings accounts that require you to give notice in advance of withdrawing your money. If you cannot give notice, you forfeit some interest instead. Suitable for short- to medium-term saving where you can predict when you will want your money (for example, saving for holidays, family celebrations, and so on).

Return and charges Interest on the amount in the account. No explicit charges. Expect to get higher interest than you would from an instant access account.

Risk No capital risk (see box above).

How long you invest No set period, but the notice period is typically 30 days, 60 days or 90 days.

Minimum investment Varies from, say, £500 upwards.
Maximum investment Usually none.
Tax As for instant access accounts (see page 132).
How to invest Contact relevant bank or building society.

Bank and building society term accounts and bonds

Description/suitable for You invest a lump sum for a set period. Often you cannot get your money back early. Useful as a way of investing for growth with no capital risk.
Return and charges Interest, which may be fixed or variable, on the amount invested. No explicit charges.
Risk No capital risk (see box on page 133).
How long you invest The specified term, for example one year, two years, five years.
Minimum investment Varies from, say, £2,500 upwards.
Maximum investment Usually none.
Tax As for instant access accounts (see page 132). Check whether interest is credited yearly or only when the term is up. If yearly, you are taxed when the interest is credited even though you might have no access until later.
How to invest Contact relevant bank or building society.

Bank and building society monthly income accounts

Description/suitable for Interest is paid out monthly instead of accumulating in the account. Useful as a way of investing for income with no capital risk.
Return and charges Interest, which is usually variable, on the amount in the account. No explicit charges.
Risk No capital risk (see box on page 133). If you are drawing out all the interest as income, your capital is particularly vulnerable to inflation risk. If interest is variable and you are reliant on the income, interest-rate risk is a problem.
How long you invest Usually no set term, but you may need to give notice to withdraw your capital.
Minimum investment Varies from, say, £500 upwards.
Maximum investment Usually none.
Tax As for instant access accounts (see page 132).
How to invest Contact relevant bank or building society.

Bank and building society guaranteed equity bonds

Description/suitable for You invest a lump sum for a set period. Usually you cannot get your money back early. The amount of interest you earn is worked out according to a formula based on stock market performance. A way of benefiting from stock market growth without any capital risk.

Return and charges Interest on the amount invested. Amount of interest varies in line with performance of a stock market index (such as FTSE 100) or basket of shares. Generally no explicit charges, but with some bonds there is an arrangement fee.

Risk No capital risk (see box on page 133). But do not confuse this type of guaranteed equity bond with much higher-risk products bearing the same name offered by life insurance companies and unit trusts.

How long you invest The specified term, for example one year, two years, five years.

Minimum investment Often £1,000 or more.

Maximum investment Usually none, but £3,000 if the bond is available as a cash ISA (see page 139).

Tax As for instant access accounts (see page 132). Usually interest is credited and taxable only when the term is up. Interest is tax-free if the bond is arranged as an ISA (see page 139).

How to invest Contact relevant bank or building society. NS&I⋆ also offer these bonds.

NS&I easy access savings account

Description/suitable for Savings account that lets you instantly withdraw to up to £300 a day from post offices and cash machines. Especially suitable for an emergency fund.

Return and charges Interest on the amount in the account. No explicit charges. Interest tiered with higher rates on larger balances.

Risk No capital risk. NS&I issues investments on behalf of the government which is very unlikely to default.

How long you invest No set period.

Minimum investment £100.

Maximum investment £2 million.

Tax Interest is taxable but paid without any tax deducted.

How to invest NS&I⋆ or through post offices.

NS&I investment account

Description/suitable for Savings account. Suitable for short- to medium-term saving with no capital risk.

Return and charges Interest, which is variable, on amount invested. Tiered account, so that you earn higher interest if your balance exceeds various levels.

Risk No capital risk. NS&I issues investments on behalf of the government, which is very unlikely to default.

How long you invest No set period, but you must give one month's notice to withdraw money or lose 30 days' interest.

Minimum investment £20.

Maximum investment £100,000.

Tax Interest is taxable as savings income (see Chapter 14), but paid without any tax deducted.

How to invest NS&I* or through post offices.

NS&I certificates

Description/suitable for Bonds offering a fixed return over a set period. Useful for growth without capital risk. Also available in an index-linked version which protects you against inflation risk.

Return and charges Interest is credited and paid out when the bond matures.

Risk No capital risk. NS&I issues investments on behalf of the government, which is very unlikely to default. Locking into a fixed return means that you would miss out if competing interest rates rise.

How long you invest You can choose a two-year or five-year term (or three and five for index-linked version). You can get your money back early, but interest is then lost.

Minimum investment £100.

Maximum investment £15,000 per issue.

Tax Tax-free return.

How to invest NS&I* or through post offices.

NS&I fixed-rate savings bonds

Description/suitable for Bonds offering a fixed return over a set period. Useful for growth or income without capital risk.

Return and charges Interest is credited and either paid out when the bond matures or paid out regularly as income.

Risk No capital risk. NS&I issues investments on behalf of the government, which is very unlikely to default. If you draw all the interest as income, your capital is vulnerable to inflation risk. Because return is fixed, any income will not fluctuate. But locking into a fixed return means that you would miss out if competing interest rates rise.

How long you invest You can choose a one-year, three-year or five-year term. You can get your money back early, but interest is then lost.

Minimum investment £500.

Maximum investment £1 million.

Tax Interest is paid with income tax at the savings rate already deducted. Higher-rate taxpayers have extra to pay. Starting-rate taxpayers and non-taxpayers can reclaim some or all of the tax.

How to invest NS&I★ or through post offices.

NS&I capital bonds

Description/suitable for Bonds offering a fixed return over a set period. Useful for growth or income without capital risk.

Return and charges Interest is credited and paid out when the bond matures.

Risk No capital risk. NS&I issues investments on behalf of the government which is very unlikely to default. Locking into a fixed return means you would miss out if competing interest rates rise.

How long you invest Five-year term. You can get your money back early, but you then lose interest.

Minimum investment £100.

Maximum investment £1 million.

Tax Interest is taxable as savings income (see Chapter 14) but paid without any tax deducted. Note that interest is credited each year, so you must pay tax yearly even though you do not receive the interest until the bond matures.

How to invest NS&I★ or through post offices.

NS&I pensioners bonds

Description/suitable for Bonds offering a fixed return over a set period. Available only to people aged 60 and over. Useful for income without capital risk.

Return and charges You earn a fixed rate of interest paid out monthly.

Risk No capital risk. NS&I issues investments on behalf of the government which is very unlikely to default. Drawing out all the interest as income means your capital is particularly vulnerable to inflation risk. Locking into a fixed return means you would miss out if competing interest rates rise.

How long you invest You choose a one-year, two-year or five-year term. You can get your money back early, but you then lose interest.

Minimum investment £500.

Maximum investment £1 million.

Tax Interest is taxable as savings income (see Chapter 14), but paid without any tax deducted.

How to invest NS&I* or through post offices.

NS&I income bonds

Description/suitable for Bonds offering a variable return. Useful for income without capital risk.

Return and charges You earn a variable rate of interest paid out monthly.

Risk No capital risk. NS&I issues investments on behalf of the government, which is very unlikely to default. If you are drawing out all the interest as income, your capital is particularly vulnerable to inflation risk. Your income varies as interest rates change so, if you are reliant on the income, interest-rate risk is a problem.

How long you invest No set period, but you must give six weeks' notice to withdraw your capital or lose six weeks' interest.

Minimum investment £500.

Maximum investment £1 million.

Tax Interest is taxable as savings income (see Chapter 14), but paid without any tax deducted.

How to invest NS&I* or through post offices.

NS&I premium bonds

Description/suitable for Bonds that give you the chance to win prizes by, in effect, gambling with the interest you would otherwise have earned. Way of keeping a lump sum accessible while giving yourself a (remote) chance of winning a life-changing sum.

Return and charges Prizes ranging from £50 up to £1 million. Random prize draw is held every month. Each £1 invested counts as a separate bond and has a chance to win. In early 2005, the yearly prize fund as a percentage of the total invested was 3.2 per cent. No explicit charges.

Risk No capital risk. NS&I issues investments on behalf of the government, which is very unlikely to default. In early 2005, the chance of winning any prize with a single bond was 1 in 24,000 each month. If winnings are not reinvested, or winnings are small, your capital is vulnerable to inflation risk.

How long you invest No set period.

Minimum investment £100.

Maximum investment £30,000 plus reinvested prizes.

Tax Prizes are tax-free. The size of the yearly prize fund as a percentage of the total invested was, in early 2005, less than the after-tax return most people could get from, say, an instant access savings account. But it was comparable to the after-tax return a higher-rate taxpayer could get from a savings account.

How to invest NS&I* or through post offices.

Mini-cash ISA

Description/suitable for Savings account that pays tax-free interest. Many are instant access accounts. Whenever a savings account would be useful in meeting your goals, it often makes sense to choose a cash ISA for at least part of those savings.

Return and charges Interest on the amount invested. This is often variable, but occasionally fixed. Interest rates may be tiered with higher rates paid on larger balances. No explicit charges.

Risk No capital risk. Other risks as for instant access accounts (see page 132) if the ISA is an instant access account or other types of account (see above) as appropriate.

How long you invest If it is an instant access account, no set period. For other types of account, check the conditions.

Minimum investment Often £1.

Maximum investment £3,000 – this is the limit set in the tax rules (see box overleaf).

Tax Tax-free interest.

How to invest Contact provider, which may be a bank, building society or NS&I*.

Gilts

Description/suitable for In effect, you lend money to the government. The loan is usually repayable on a set date (the redemption date) and in the meantime you receive interest. You do not have to wait until redemption, because you can buy and sell gilts

---

Individual savings accounts (ISAs)

Under the tax rules, adults have a yearly ISA allowance. This lets you invest in a range of savings and investments and receive the return completely or partly tax-free.

Each year you can choose whether to have a 'maxi-ISA' or up to two 'mini-ISAs' (three before 6 April 2005). Each ISA is run by an ISA manager. You can have different managers for each mini-ISA.

A maxi-ISA must have a stocks and shares component, which means it invests in things like shares, gilts, corporate bonds, unit trusts, investment trusts and/or investment-type life insurance. It can also have a cash component, meaning deposit-type investments like savings accounts. The most you can invest in a maxi-ISA is £7,000 a year. You can put all of that into the stocks and shares component if you like. If you use part of the £7,000 to invest in cash, the limit is £3,000 a year in cash.

If instead you opt for mini-ISAs, you can put up to £3,000 a year into a mini-cash ISA (a savings account) and up to £4,000 in a mini-stocks-and-shares ISA (investing in, say, unit trusts, investment trusts or investment-type life insurance).

Capital gains from investments held in an ISA are tax-free. The interest from either a cash ISA or a stocks-and-shares ISA invested in gilts or bonds or bond-based investment funds is tax-free. But the dividends from a stocks-and-shares ISA invested in shares or share-based investment funds are paid with the equivalent of tax at 10 per cent already deducted. Unless you are a higher-rate taxpayer, this is the same rate of tax you would pay had you invested in shares and share-based investment funds without using an ISA, so there might be little or no advantage to you in using this type of ISA.

---

on the stock market. These are very flexible investments. They can be used for growth or income and, depending on how you use them, have different levels of risk.

Return and charges Interest at a fixed rate is usually paid out every six months. If you sell at a profit or get back more at redemption than you paid, you make a profit (called a capital gain). You incur dealing charges if you buy and sell on the stock market. There are no dealing charges if you buy newly issued gilts or when you receive repayment on redemption.

Risk The government is very unlikely to default, so there is little risk that you would not get the promised interest and redemption payment. In other respects, risk varies depending on how you use the gilts. If you hold them until redemption, you know at the time you buy exactly what return you will get. If the price you bought at was less than the redemption value, you will make a gain and so there is no capital risk. But, if the price you paid was higher than the redemption value, you will lose some of your capital. If you sell on the stock market, you cannot know in advance whether you will make a gain or loss. Because gilts pay a fixed income, you might miss out if competing interest rates rise, though depending on stock market prices it might be viable to switch to other investments. Over the long term, the return on gilts has trailed behind the return from shares and share-based investments, so if you rely solely on gilts for growth, you are exposed to shortfall risk. With ordinary gilts, the interest and your capital are exposed to inflation risk, but you can avoid this by choosing index-linked gilts where both interest and the redemption value are increased in line with the Retail Prices Index.

How long you invest If you do not hold until redemption, no set period. If you hold until redemption, you do invest for a set period, which varies depending on the gilts you choose. Short-dated gilts have redemption dates within the next five years, medium-dated gilts have five to 15 years until redemption, and long-dated gilts have 15 years or more to go.

Minimum investment No set minimum, but dealing charges make investments of, say, less than £1,000 uneconomic.

Maximum investment None.

Tax Interest is taxable as savings income (see Chapter 14), but normally paid without any tax deducted. However, you can request to

receive income with tax at the savings rate already deducted. Capital gains are tax-free (and losses cannot be set off against other gains).
How to invest Through Debt Management Office's Purchase and Sales Service. or through a stockbroker*. To buy new issues, go through a stockbroker or the government's Debt Management Office*.

Corporate bonds

Description/suitable for In effect, you lend money to a company. The loan is often repayable on a set date (the redemption date) and in the meantime you usually receive interest. You do not have to wait until redemption, because you can buy and sell corporate bonds on the stock market. These are very flexible investments. They can be used for growth or income and have different levels of risk.
Return and charges Interest is usually paid at a fixed rate. If you sell at a profit or get back more at redemption than you paid, you make a profit (called a capital gain). You incur dealing charges when you buy and sell. There are no dealing charges when you receive repayment on redemption.
Risk You need to consider the risk of the company defaulting, in other words failing to pay the interest and/or redemption payment. Large, established, 'blue chip' companies are generally thought unlikely to default and the bonds of these companies are often referred to as 'investment-grade'. Bonds in smaller and newer companies generally carry a much higher risk of default and their prices may move in a very similar way to the company's shares. To compensate you for this higher risk, such bonds should offer a higher return. In other respects, risks are similar to those for gilts (see page 141).
How long you invest If you do not hold until redemption, no set period. If you hold until redemption, you do invest for a set period, which varies depending on the bonds you choose.
Minimum investment No set minimum, but dealing charges make investments of, say, less than £1,000 uneconomic.
Maximum investment None.
Tax Interest is taxable as savings income (see Chapter 14), but since 1 April 2001 is usually paid without any tax deducted. Capital gains are usually tax-free (and losses cannot be set off against other gains).
How to invest Through a stockbroker*.

Bond-based unit trusts and open-ended investment companies (oeics)

Description/suitable for You buy 'units' in a unit trust (or shares in an oeic), which give you a stake in an investment fund. The fund is a ready-made portfolio of many different gilts and/or corporate bonds. Useful if you are seeking income or as a medium-risk way of investing for growth.

Return and charges Although gilts and bonds usually offer a fixed return, a trust investing in a range of gilts and bonds produces a variable return because the underlying investments in the fund are being bought and sold on the stock market rather than necessarily being held to redemption. Your return takes the form of distributions usually paid every six months and, if you sell your units for more than you paid, a capital gain. If you want automatically to reinvest the income, choose 'accumulation units'. Explicit charges are usually an initial charge (generally up to 5 per cent), plus an annual management charge (usually around 1 to 1.5 per cent a year of the value of your investment). Other charges are deducted direct from the investment fund.

Risk Investing in a spread of different gilts and bonds reduces the risk of any one provider defaulting. You are exposed to capital risk and inflation risk, although these are reduced if you opt for the distributions to be reinvested. In general, the higher the income paid out from the trust, the greater the risk of losing some of your capital and the greater your exposure to inflation risk. Since the income is variable, it can fall, which could be a problem if you are reliant on the income. Over the long term, the return on bond-based investment funds has tended to be lower than the return from share-based funds, so if you rely solely on bond-based funds for growth, you are exposed to shortfall risk.

How long you invest No set period, but, because the value of the investment fund can fall as well as rise, you should normally aim to invest for the medium term (say, five years) or longer.

Minimum investment Varies from, say, £500 or more as a lump sum and £50 per month for regular savings.

Maximum investment None, unless you opt to invest through a stocks and shares ISA. The maximum for a mini-ISA is £4,000 and, for a maxi-ISA, £7,000 (see box on page 149).

Tax Distributions are paid with tax at the savings rate (see Chapter 14) already deducted. Higher-rate taxpayers have extra to pay. Starting-rate taxpayers and non-taxpayers can reclaim some or all of the tax. Capital gains are taxable, though if you have unused allowance, there may be no tax to pay (see Chapter 15). If you invest through an ISA both distributions and gains are tax-free.

How to invest You can go to the provider direct, but you will often pay less in charges if you go to a discount broker★ or fund supermarket★. You can also invest through most independent financial advisers (IFAs)★ and many stockbrokers★.

Purchased life annuities

Description/suitable for In return for giving up a lump sum, you get an income either payable for life (a 'permanent annuity') or for a set period of time (a 'temporary annuity'). Useful if you need an income and do not mind giving up your capital.

Return and charges You get an income for life or the set period. You can usually choose how often to receive the income, for example monthly, quarterly, twice a year or annually. An initial charge (up to, say, 5 per cent) may be deducted from your lump sum before the annuity is purchased.

Risk Capital risk, in the sense that you cannot get your capital back as a lump sum, though you can guard against getting a very poor deal by choosing an annuity with a guarantee period. If the annuity provides a level income, you are vulnerable to inflation. However, you can guard against this by choosing an annuity where the income increases. The income or pattern of income is determined by annuity rates at the time you invest, so you would miss out if annuity rates improved in future. The information about different types of pension annuity in Chapter 6 generally applies to purchased life annuities too.

How long you invest For life in the case of a permanent annuity. For a set period in the case of a temporary annuity. Once purchased, you cannot surrender an annuity.

Minimum investment Varies, but may be as low as £1,000.

Maximum investment None.

Tax Part of the income counts as the return of your capital and this part is tax-free. The remainder is taxed as savings income (see Chapter 14) and is usually paid with tax at the savings rate already deducted. Higher-rate taxpayers have extra to pay. Starting-rate taxpayers can reclaim some of the tax. Non-taxpayers may be able to arrange to receive the income without any tax deducted; otherwise, they can reclaim all the tax. (Note that taxation of purchased life annuities is different from the taxation of pension annuities.)

How to invest Direct with providers who are insurance companies or through an IFA★. Some IFAs specialise in annuities★.

Shares

Description/suitable for When you buy its shares you become a part-owner of a company along with all the other shareholders. Depending on the shares you choose, they can be useful to provide growth and/or income.

Return and charges The shares of large, established companies usually pay out dividends twice a year. With 'ordinary shares', the amount of dividends is neither fixed nor guaranteed and depends on the profitability of the company, its policy on distributing profits, and so on. 'Preference shares' often pay a fixed rate of dividend, provided that the company decides to pay any dividend at all. The shares of newer and smaller companies often pay no dividends at all. If you sell your shares for more than you paid, you make a capital gain. You normally pay dealing costs when you buy and sell. There is also stamp duty on purchases.

Risk The price of shares can fall as well as rise, so you are exposed to capital risk. If the company goes bust, you could lose all your original investment. Share prices tend to reflect the profitability of the company and this, in turn, tends to be linked to the general state of the economy. Therefore, over the long-term, share prices tend to rise at least in line with inflation and in line with the growth of the economy as a whole, so share-based investments are used to reduce your exposure to inflation risk and shortfall risk. The dividends from shares can vary, which may be a problem if you are reliant on them for income.

How long you invest No set period, but, because of the capital risk, you should normally aim to invest for the long term (more than five years).

Minimum investment No set minimum, but dealing costs make purchases of less than, say, £1,000 to £1,500 uneconomic.

Maximum investment None.

Tax Dividends are paid with tax at 10 per cent already deducted. Non-taxpayers cannot reclaim this tax. There is no further tax for

Table 9.3   Examples of investment funds

Sector	Description
Funds principally for supplying an immediate income	
UK gilts	Funds that invest mainly in gilts.
UK corporate bond	Funds that invest mainly in £-denominated bonds.
UK equity and bond	Funds that invest in a mix of UK gilts, corporate bonds and equities.
Funds principally for supplying a growing income	
UK equity income	Funds that invest mainly in UK equities and aim to produce a mix of income and growth.
Funds principally targeting capital growth	
UK all companies	Funds that invest mainly in UK equities and have a primary objective of achieving capital growth.
UK smaller companies	Funds that invest mainly in UK equities of relatively small companies.
Japan	Funds that invest mainly in Japanese equities.
North America	Funds that invest mainly in North American equities.
Europe excluding the UK	Funds that invest mainly in European equities and exclude UK equities.
Cautious managed	Funds that offer investment in a range of assets, with the maximum equity exposure restricted to, say, 60 per cent of the fund.
Balanced managed	Funds that offer investment in a range of assets, with the maximum equity exposure restricted to, say, 85 per cent of the fund.
Global growth	Funds that invest mainly in equities with at least some being non-UK assets.
Property	Funds that invest mainly in property securities or directly in property itself.
Funds principally targeting capital protection	
Money market	Funds that invest most of their assets in money market instruments (i.e. cash and near cash, such as bank deposits etc.).
Protected/guaranteed funds	Funds, other than money market funds, that principally aim to provide a return of a set amount of capital back to the investor.

starting-rate and basic-rate taxpayers to pay. Higher-rate taxpayers must pay extra (see Chapter 14).

How to invest Through a stockbroker*.

Share-based unit trusts and oeics

Description/suitable for You buy 'units' in a unit trust (or shares in an oeic),which give you a stake in an investment fund. The fund is a ready-made portfolio of many different shares – see Table 9.3. Can be used for income and/or growth.

Return and charges Your return takes the form of distributions usually paid every six months, and, if you sell your units for more than you paid, a capital gain. If you want automatically to reinvest the income, choose 'accumulation units'. There is an annual management charge (usually around 1 to 1.5 per cent a year of the value of your investment). Other charges are deducted direct from the investment fund.

Risk The price of your units can fall as well as rise, so you are exposed to capital risk. However, investing in a broad spread of different shares lessens risk by reducing your exposure to the misfortunes of any one company. Over the long term, share-based investments have tended to rise at least in line with inflation and in line with the growth of the economy as a whole, so share-based unit trusts are used to reduce your exposure to inflation risk and shortfall risk. The distributions can vary, which may be a problem if you are reliant on them for income.

How long you invest No set period, but, because the value of the investment fund can fall as well as rise, you should normally aim to invest for the long term (more than five years).

Minimum investment Varies from, say, £500 or more as a lump sum and £50 per month for regular savings.

Maximum investment None, unless you opt to invest through a stocks and shares ISA. The maximum for a mini-ISA is £4,000 and, for a maxi-ISA, £7,000 (see box on page 140).

Tax Distributions are paid with tax at 10 per cent already deducted. Non-taxpayers cannot reclaim this tax. There is no further tax for starting-rate and basic-rate taxpayers to pay. Higher-rate taxpayers must pay extra (see Chapter 14). Capital gains are taxable, although, if you have unused allowance, there may be no tax to pay (see Chapter 15). If you invest through an ISA gains are tax-free and there is no tax or no further tax on distributions.

How to invest You can go to the provider direct, but you'll often pay less in charges if you go to a discount broker★ or fund supermarket★. You can also invest through most IFAs★ and many stockbrokers★.

Investment trusts

Description/suitable for These give you a stake in an investment fund similar to those in Table 9.3 and so are an alternative to investing in unit trusts or oeics. However, they work in a different way. An investment trust is a company whose business is running an investment fund. The fund might specialise in shares, gilts, bonds, property, and so on. You invest indirectly in the fund by buying the shares of the investment trust company. The share price is heavily influenced by the value of the investments in the trust, but is also affected by other factors, such as whether the company has large borrowings and the balance of supply and demand for the company's shares.

Return and charges In a conventional investment trust, your return is in the form of dividends, usually paid out twice a year and, if you sell the shares for more than you paid, a capital gain. A 'split capital trust' is different. It has a set date on which the company will be wound up. There are two main types of shares: 'capital shares', which receive no income but get most of the proceeds of selling the investment fund at wind-up; and 'income shares', which receive all the income from the fund in the form of dividends and only a small share of the fund at wind-up. You incur dealing costs when you buy and sell investment trust shares. There is stamp duty to pay on purchases. The trust company levies an explicit annual management charge, often in the region of 1 per cent of the value of the fund. Other charges are deducted from the fund.

Risk The price of your shares can fall as well as rise, so you are exposed to capital risk. However, the broad spread of different shares in the investment fund lessens risk by reducing your exposure to the misfortunes of any one company. Over the long term, share-based investments have tended to rise at least in line with inflation and in line with the growth of the economy as a whole, so share-based unit trusts are used to reduce your exposure to inflation risk and shortfall risk. The distributions can vary, which may be a problem if you are reliant on them for income. The potential returns and also the risks increase if the trust borrows money to invest (a process called 'gearing'). Some, but not all, investment trusts have invested in each other's shares. This practice increases risk, because, if one investment trust performs badly, this also affects the performance of the other trusts that have bought its shares. It is important to check the extent of borrowing and cross-holdings before you invest.

How long you invest No set period but, because the value of the investment fund can fall as well as rise, you should normally aim to invest for the long term (more than five years).

Minimum investment Most investment trusts run their own savings schemes, through which you can invest, say, £500 or more as a lump sum or £50 or more a month as regular savings. If instead you buy shares through a broker, dealing costs make transactions below, say, £1,000 to £1,500 uneconomic.

Maximum investment None, unless you opt to invest through a stocks and shares ISA. The maximum for a mini-ISA is £4,000 and, for a maxi-ISA, £7,000 (see box on page 140).

Tax Dividends are paid with tax at 10 per cent already deducted. Non-taxpayers cannot reclaim this tax. There is no further tax for starting-rate and basic-rate taxpayers to pay. Higher-rate taxpayers must pay extra (see Chapter 14). Capital gains are taxable, although, if you have unused allowance, there may be no tax to pay (see Chapter 15). If you invest through an ISA gains are tax-free and there is no further tax on the income.

How to invest Through the trust company's own savings scheme or a stockbroker*. Some fund supermarkets* offer investment trusts, which can be a relatively cheap way to invest.

Stocks-and-shares ISAs

Description/suitable for ISAs are not really investments in their own right. They are tax-free arrangements you can use to invest in other investments. For example, you could have a 'self-select ISA', into which you put your own choice of shares, gilts, corporate bonds, unit trusts, and so on. More commonly, you take out a ready-made ISA containing one or more unit trusts, oeics or investment trusts.

Return and charges As for the underlying investments. If you are investing in a unit trust, oeic or investment trust, often there will be no extra charges for the ISA arrangement. But, if you have a self-select ISA, there will often be extra charges.

Risk As for the underlying investments.

How long you invest As for the underlying investments.

Minimum investment As for the underlying investments.

Maximum investment £4,000 for a mini-stocks-and-shares ISA and £7,000 for a maxi-ISA (see box on page 140).

Tax Capital gains are tax-free. Taxation of income depends on the investments held within the ISA. Interest from gilts and bonds is tax-free. Dividends from shares and distributions from share-based investment funds have the equivalent of tax at 10 per cent deducted and this cannot be reclaimed.

How to invest From the investment provider: unit trusts, oeic and investment trust providers often offer their investments in a choice of direct investment or ISA investment. Fund supermarkets* offer a cheaper way to buy these investments and also allow you to mix and match different unit trusts, oeics and sometimes investment trusts within the same ISA. Stockbrokers* are the main source of self-select ISAs.

Regular-premium insurance plans

Description/suitable for Some types of life insurance build up a cash-in value, which makes them suitable as investments. Endowment policies pay out after a set number of years. Whole-life policies run until death, but can be cashed in before then. Generally, regular premium plans are used to build up a lump sum. Policies can be written in trust, so that the lump sum is paid out to someone else, which makes policies useful as a way of making gifts and for inheritance tax planning (see Chapter 16).

Return and charges The plan usually pays out a lump sum after a set number of years, for example ten years, or when cashed in. Usually, there is an administration fee when you invest. If the plan is invested on a unit-linked basis, there is normally an initial charge (up to, say, 5 per cent) and an annual management charge (for example, 1.5 per cent a year of the value of the investment fund), with other costs charged direct to the fund. If the plan is invested on a with-profits basis, charges influence the level of bonuses.

Risk Capital risk as for other types of unit-linked or with-profits investments (see pages 78 to 81). See Table 9.3 for examples of the sort of investment funds you might choose if investing on a unit-linked basis.

How long you invest With an endowment policy, you should aim to invest for the set term, which is usually at least ten years. With a whole-life policy, you may need to commit yourself to investing for even longer. If you cash in your investment early, surrender charges reduce the amount you get back – perhaps even to less than you had invested.

Minimum investment Varies.

Maximum investment None.

Tax The insurance company has already paid tax on income and gains from the underlying investments. Usually, there is no further tax for you to pay. Where a policy is cashed in earlier, there could be tax to pay, but only if you are a higher-rate taxpayer (see Chapter 14).

How to invest Direct through insurance companies or via an IFA★.

Single premium insurance bonds

Description/suitable for Some types of life insurance build up a cash-in value, which makes them suitable as investments. With single premium policies, you invest a lump sum. Such policies can be used for capital growth, but are also popular as a way of providing income because of the special tax treatment they get (see overleaf). A popular example is the 'with-profits bond', but bonds can be invested on a unit-linked basis as well. See pages 78 to 81 for details of the with-profits and unit-linked bases of investing. See Table 9.3 for examples of the sort of investment funds you might choose when investing on a unit-linked basis.

Return and charges The plan either pays out a lump sum, normally after a set number of years, for example five years, or can be used to draw an income. Usually, there is an administration fee when you invest. If the plan is invested on a unit-linked basis, there is usually an initial charge (up to, say, 5 per cent) and an annual management charge (for example, 1.5 per cent a year of the value of the investment fund), with other costs charged direct to the fund. If the plan is invested on a with-profits basis, charges influence the level of bonuses.

Risk Capital risk as for unit-linked or with-profits investments (see pages 78 to 81 and page 164). If you are drawing an income, the larger the income, the greater the risk that you will get back less capital than you invested.

How long you invest With an endowment policy, you should aim to invest for the set term, or usually at least five years. With a whole-life policy, you may need to commit yourself to investing for even longer. If you cash in your investment early, surrender charges reduce the amount you get back – perhaps even to less than you had invested.

Minimum investment Varies.

Maximum investment None.

Tax The insurance company has already paid tax on income and gains from the underlying investments. There is no further tax for you to pay unless you are a higher-rate taxpayer. In that case, there could be tax to pay, but you may be able to claim top-slicing relief (see Chapter 14). However, a special facility lets you draw an income each year up to one-twentieth (5 per cent) of the premium(s) you have paid without any tax being due at the time; tax is deferred until the bond is cashed in and is then charged with reference to your tax rate at the time. If you are 65 or over, bear in mind that the proceeds of a maturing bond count as income and could cause you to lose age allowance (see Chapter 14).

How to invest Direct through insurance companies or via an IFA★.

Stakeholder products

From April 2005, a range of 'stakeholder products' is due to become available. These are savings and investment products which meet certain conditions set by the government aimed at ensuring the products are straightforward, good value and not unduly risky. The conditions vary according to the type of product and include for example, a cap on charges and ban on extra charges if you want to transfer to another product. There are five stakeholder products in all:

* **deposit product** – a savings account that can be offered in non-ISA or cash ISA versions. Conditions include linking the interest rate to the Bank of England base rate and no restriction on withdrawals
* **medium-term investment product (MTIP)**. This can be set up as a unit trust (see pages 143 and 147) or similar investment or as a unit-linked insurance policy (see pages 150-1). It must be invested in a broad spread of investments, of which no more than three-fifths are shares and property and the rest are bonds, deposits and so on. The value of your investment will go up and down with the stock market, but because of the wide spread of investments you should normally be shielded from

very large swings in value. The MTIP can be set up as a stocks-and-shares ISA

- **smoothed MTIP** This is invested as already described for the MTIP but some of the return in good years is put into a 'smoothing fund' which is used to top up the return in bad years – in a similar way to a with-profits fund (see page 000)
- **stakeholder pension** This is based on the existing stakeholder pension which has been available since 2001 (see Chapter 3) with the following changes for new schemes: charges are capped at 1.5 per cent during the first ten years, falling to 1 per cent thereafter; the default fund must be a lifestyle fund and, even if you choose another type of fund, it must be lifestyled so that you are automatically shifted into lower-risk bonds and deposits in the last few (probably five) years before you reach the selected retirement age
- **child trust fund** An investment fund for every child born on or after 1 September 2002. Parents set up the fund using vouchers from the government but anyone, including grand-parents, can add to the child's fund. The maximum addition each year from all sources (other than the government vouchers) is £1,200. There is a choice of investments that can be

---

Consumer protection and investments

Firms selling or advising you about most types of investments (including personal pensions and annuities) are regulated by the Financial Services Authority (FSA)*. They must by law abide by detailed FSA rules governing, for example, how they advertise and the information they give you about products. If giving advice, they must ensure any recommendations are suitable for you given your needs and circumstances. If something goes wrong, you have access to an independent complaints body (the Financial Ombudsman Service*) and you may be eligible for redress from a compensation scheme. It is illegal for an investment firm to operate in the UK without being 'authorised' by the FSA. Before doing business, you should check whether the firm is authorised by contacting the FSA*.

held within the fund and they are taxed in the same way as investments held in ISAs (see page 000 and 000).

Where to get advice

If you need help in choosing suitable investments to meet your goals or in deciding which provider to invest with, consult an independent financial adviser (IFA)★.

Stakeholder products can be sold through a new 'basic advice' regime. A basic adviser uses filter questions and a ready-prepared script to check whether a stakeholder product is suitable for you based on limited information about you. The adviser can offer you only one each – that is, not a choice – of providers, of each stakeholder product. The adviser must be competent but does not need to hold the financial advice qualifications an IFA must have.

For information about identifying your goals and building a holistic financial plan to meet them, see *Be Your Own Financial Adviser* from Which? Books★.

Chapter 10

Common investment goals

This chapter looks at two of the most common goals that people in retirement often have and suggests possible ways to meet them. For an explanation of the different types of savings and investments mentioned in this chapter, refer to Chapter 9. For help working out a strategy for meeting your own goals, consult an independent financial adviser (IFA).*

Getting the best rate on your savings accounts

Many retired people are cautious with their money and do not like the thought of taking stock market risks in order to chase higher returns. Since risk and reward go hand in hand, choosing investments with low capital risk means accepting lower returns over the long term than you would probably get from, say, share-based investments.

Is a low-risk strategy right for you?

As described in Chapter 9, sticking to bank and building society savings accounts can be reckless if you intend to rely on these sources for income over a span of many years, because you will be allowing yourself little or no protection against inflation. However, if your main sources of income are protected against rising prices – for example, you have an occupational pension that is increased each year at least in line with prices – you can perhaps afford to take lower risks with your savings.

Where the savings form your emergency fund or short-term savings for, say, holidays, low-risk investments are the appropriate choice.

Be prepared to shop around

Committing yourself to a low-risk, low-return strategy makes it all the more important that you get the best return possible on your savings. Interest rates vary over time with the general state of the economy, but providers do not all act in unison. Therefore, it is a good idea to shop around, say, once a year, to check that you are getting a good interest rate and be prepared to switch if you are not.

All too often people stick with the same savings accounts year after year, either because they do not get around to switching or out of loyalty to an institution where they have been customers for decades. But many of the best interest rates are offered on accounts from relatively new providers operating, for example, phone-based or Internet accounts (see Table 10.1).

Table 10.1 shows that, on average, the best returns are from accounts operated over the Internet, followed by accounts operated by phone and post. On average, the worst rates are offered by branch-based accounts. However, if you look at the worst and best rates, you can see that, whichever type of account you want, there is a big variation in the rates available, so shopping around can be very worthwhile. A handful of branch-based accounts offer rates that match (or in one case beat) the best available from the Internet-based and other accounts, though usually there are restrictions – for example, you might be limited to a maximum number of with-drawals a year.

Table 10.1 shows instant access accounts, but there are other options. If you will not need your money back immediately, consider a notice account where you have to give 30, 60 or 90 days' notice before you withdraw your money (or lose so many days' interest if you fail to give notice). You should expect to receive a higher rate of interest in return for accepting a restriction on access to your money.

Don't forget your ISA allowance

Bear in mind that if you are a taxpayer and not already using your annual individual savings account (ISA) allowance to invest in a maxi-ISA, it makes sense to put at least part of your low-risk savings in a mini-cash ISA. That way, you receive the interest tax-free. Even if you are a non-taxpayer, check the ISA rates available, because

Table 10.1 Before-tax return from instant access savings accounts on a balance of £1,000

	Branch-based accounts	Accounts operated by post	Accounts operated by phone and post	Accounts operated by phone	Accounts operated by Internet
Average rate	2.25%	3.07%	3.26%	3.64%	4.72%
Worst rate	0.10%	1.00%	0.55%	1.28%	3.20%
Best rate	5.50%	4.50%	5.05%	4.85%	5.50%

Source: *Moneyfacts*, January 2005

sometimes they are higher than the return you can get on non-ISA accounts.

How to check out the best rates

It is easy to check out the best rates available on savings accounts. Comparison tables are published in the personal finance sections of daily and weekend newspapers, in personal finance magazines and in *Which?*. They are available on television text services★, through the *Moneyfacts*★ faxback service and from many personal finance websites, such as www.ftyourmoney.com, www.moneyextra.com and www.moneyfacts.co.uk.

CASE HISTORY: LEN

Len has always had a current account with a particular High Street bank. He trusts the bank and so, when he was looking for a home for the £10,000 tax-free lump sum he received on retirement, it seemed natural to turn to his bank for advice. The bank recommended a 60-day notice account paying interest in early 2005 at 3.35 per cent a year. Len pays tax on this at the savings rate (20 per cent in 2004–5) and the after-tax return he gets is $(1 - 0.20) \times 3.35\% = 2.8\%$, or £280 a year on £10,000.

Len realises that he might be able to get a better rate if he switched to another provider. He checks the personal finance section in his newspaper and finds that:

- if he sticks with a 60-day notice account but switches to another provider, he can get 5.19 per cent a year from an account operated by phone and post. After tax this comes to 4.2 per cent, or £415 a year interest on a £10,000 balance, which is £135 more than he is getting at present
- he can get an even better rate of 5.5 per cent with an instant access account
- he can get 5.35 per cent tax-free on a mini-cash ISA.

Len decides to switch £3,000 of his savings to a mini-cash ISA. This provides a tax-free 5.35% × £3,000 = £161 over a year. The remaining £7,000 he puts in an instant access account at 5.5 per cent before tax, which gives him £308 after tax over the year.

As a result of switching, Len gets an extra £469 – £280 = £189 a year.

Investing for income

If you are using your savings to supplement your retirement income, you are likely to have several aims:

- to maximise your income now
- to ensure that the income continues throughout retirement
- to ensure that the income does not lose its buying power as retirement progresses
- to minimise the risk of losing your savings.

These aims are not all compatible and, in practice, you will usually have to strike a balance between them. In particular, you need to accept some capital risk to ensure that your income maintains its buying power in the future, and you may need to accept a lower income now to protect your capital and the future income it will produce.

Why savings accounts are not the whole answer

It may be tempting to put all your money into savings accounts and live off the interest they produce. Most banks and building societies offer accounts especially designed to pay out the interest as income either monthly or less frequently. National Savings & Investments (NS&I)* also has similar products, such as income bonds and pensioners income bonds. However, this strategy provides no protection against inflation and may result in your becoming progressively worse off as time goes by.

Table 10.2 shows how the buying power of your income would fall over time if interest rates stayed at their 2005 level and inflation averaged 2.5 per cent a year. For example, after five years, although you would still receive the same income in £s (£1,032), it would only buy the same as £935 would have done in 2005. After 20 years, the position is far worse, with the £1,032 income buying only the same as £646 would have done in 2005. The loss of buying power is due to inflation over the intervening years. Of course, interest rates might rise, in which case your income would rise. But, if interest rates rise, it is likely that inflation will have risen too, in which case your buying power will have been further eroded.

One way to tackle the problem would be to draw only part of the interest as income and leave the rest in the account so that the capital grows. Assuming unchanged interest rates, this means that the amount of interest earned by the account would increase each year. You could take part of the increase as income, for example just enough to ensure your income keeps pace with inflation. You would be sacrificing some income now to protect your future income. Table 10.3 shows how this might work using the same interest rate and inflation rate as in Table 10.2.

A fundamental problem with savings accounts is that, being investments with low capital risk, the return tends to be low compared with investments that involve some capital risk. Therefore the price of your capital security is a lower income both now and in future. If you have a lot of capital, you may be able to pay that price. But, if your capital is limited, you might need to give up a degree of security in order to secure a higher income.

What about annuities?

Another idea that can be gleaned from Tables 10.2 and 10.3 is how inefficient living off interest can be. In order to receive a steady stream of interest, you need to have a large sum of capital invested. You need an income for life, but when you die the capital still remains.

Table 10.2   How the buying power of income from a savings account might fall

Year	Balance in your savings account	After-tax interest paid as income during year assuming before-tax return of 5.16% a year	Equivalent income in 2005 money with the same buying power
2005	£25,000	£1,032	£1,032
2006	£25,000	£1,032	£1,007
2007	£25,000	£1,032	£982
2008	£25,000	£1,032	£958
2009	£25,000	£1,032	£935
2010	£25,000	£1,032	£912
2011	£25,000	£1,032	£890
2012	£25,000	£1,032	£868
2013	£25,000	£1,032	£847
2014	£25,000	£1,032	£826
2015	£25,000	£1,032	£806
2016	£25,000	£1,032	£787
2017	£25,000	£1,032	£767
2018	£25,000	£1,032	£749
2019	£25,000	£1,032	£730
2020	£25,000	£1,032	£713
2021	£25,000	£1,032	£695
2022	£25,000	£1,032	£678
2023	£25,000	£1,032	£662
2024	£25,000	£1,032	£646

If you could draw both the interest and some of the capital bit by bit, you could have a much higher income. The flaw in this approach is that you do not know for how long you will need the income. For example, you could arrange to run down your capital completely over a period of exactly 20 years. At the end of 20 years, all the capital would be gone and the income would stop. But what

Table 10.3 Protecting the buying power of income from a savings account by reinvesting part of the interest

Year	Balance in your savings account	After-tax interest earned	Interest reinvested	Interest paid out as income	Equivalent income in 2005 money with the same buying power
2005	£25,000	£1,032	£392	£640	£640
2006	£25,392	£1,048	£392	£656	£640
2007	£25,784	£1,064	£392	£672	£640
2008	£26,176	£1,081	£391	£689	£640
2009	£26,567	£1,097	£390	£706	£640
2010	£26,958	£1,113	£389	£724	£640
2011	£27,346	£1,129	£387	£742	£640
2012	£27,733	£1,145	£384	£761	£640
2013	£28,117	£1,161	£381	£780	£640
2014	£28,498	£1,176	£377	£799	£640
2015	£28,875	£1,192	£373	£819	£640
2016	£29,248	£1,207	£368	£840	£640
2017	£29,616	£1,223	£362	£861	£640
2018	£29,977	£1,237	£355	£882	£640
2019	£30,333	£1,252	£348	£904	£640
2020	£30,680	£1,266	£340	£927	£640
2021	£31,020	£1,281	£330	£950	£640
2022	£31,350	£1,294	£320	£974	£640
2023	£31,671	£1,307	£309	£998	£640
2024	£31,980	£1,320	£297	£1,023	£640

if you lived longer than 20 years? You would suddenly have no income.

This is where annuities step in. An annuity is an investment which converts a lump sum into an income. The income is made up partly of interest earned by investing the lump sum and partly by returning your capital bit by bit. But annuities also have an insurance element: they guarantee to pay you an income for life regardless of how long you live. They do this because you are pooled with lots of other people. The people who die soon after buying an annuity help to pay the income of people who survive longer than expected.

The type of annuity you choose to buy with your own money is called a purchased life annuity (see page 144), but the principle is the same for annuities you buy with a pension fund (see Chapters 5 and 6). With both, you can choose annuities that provide a level income, ones which increase with inflation, and various other options as described in Chapter 6.

The advantage of an annuity is that it can provide you with a secure income for life. The drawback is that it is a one-way decision. You give up your capital and cannot change your mind later on. There is no scope for switching to other investments later, and you give up the possibility of leaving capital to your heirs. Before buying an annuity, make very sure that it is what you really want to do.

With-profits bonds

With-profits bonds are often recommended as a way of getting a better return than from a building society without taking on much extra risk. But these bonds are not always as secure as they are made out to be and cynics sometimes suggest their popularity has more to do with the commission earned by the salesperson or adviser who sells the bonds rather than their suitability for the client.

A with-profits bond is an investment-type insurance policy. You invest a lump sum and the aim is usually to return your capital in full provided you invest for at least a minimum period, usually five years.

Special tax rules apply to these bonds, so there is no tax for you to pay on the income at the time you draw it. Each year for a maximum of 20 years, you can draw an income from the bond of up to 5 per cent of the lump sum you invested. When the bond is cashed in, the income is included in working out whether there is any gain and income tax may then be due, although only if you are a higher-rate taxpayer.

The bond is designed to provide you with the chosen income plus the return of your capital so long as the value of the bond grows by at least an assumed rate. The bond grows through the addition of bonuses (see page 78 for a description of how with-profits invest-ments work). The level of bonuses is not guaranteed and depends largely on the performance of an underlying fund, which invests in shares and a spread of other assets in order to keep the risks at a medium level.

When stock markets were doing well, with-profits bonds delivered the income and return of capital as intended. But the prolonged stock market downturn in the early 2000s highlighted the risks inherent in the bonds. As bonus rates were cut, the return on many bonds fell below the level at which the income could be sustained and capital returned in full. Investors have been faced with the difficult choice of cutting their income or accepting that they will probably not get back all of their capital when they cash in the bond. This has come as a shock to those investors who had been misled into believing that with-profits bonds carried little more risk than a building society account.

A further aspect of with-profits bonds that is often poorly under-stood is the tax treatment. Investors, unless they are higher-rate taxpayers, do not have any tax to pay on the return from these bonds. But that does not mean the bonds are tax-free. The reason you pay no tax is because tax has already been paid by the insurance company. The insurance company pays the tax at broadly the equivalent of the savings rate (20 per cent in 2004–5), but it pays this tax on both income and gains from the underlying investments. Regardless of your own personal tax position, you cannot reclaim any of the tax paid by the company. Since many people have unused capital gains tax allowance, it is likely that the investments would have been taxed more lightly if held by you than in the hands of the company. For this reason, it is usually more tax-efficient for all but higher-rate taxpayers to invest in, say, unit trusts and open-ended investment companies (oeics), rather than insurance-based investment funds.

On the other hand, if you consider with-profits bonds as an alter-native to a bank or building society account, there can be an immediate tax advantage. Provided the income you draw from the bond falls within the 5 per cent limit, there is no tax on it at the time and it also does not count as income for the purpose of calculating age allowance. Therefore, if you are 65 or over and your income is in the region where you are losing allowance, switching from a savings account to a with-profits bond can lead to an increase in your allowance and so save you tax. But note that when you cash in the bond, any gain, including the income previously taken, counts as income for that tax year and may well then cause you to lose age allowance for that year (see Chapter 14).

The asset allocation approach to providing income

The advantage of with-profits bonds is that they give you access to a ready-made medium-risk investment fund made up of a spread of different assets that can be used to provide a mixture of income and growth. However, if you have a reasonable sum to invest, you can build your own portfolio of investments with the same characteristics, using an asset allocation strategy.

The fundamental building blocks are the different asset classes:

- **cash** – meaning deposits, such as bank and building society accounts
- **bonds** – gilts and corporate bonds, or investments such as unit trusts investing in these
- **property** – either direct investment in property, the shares of property companies, or investments such as unit trusts investing in either or both of these
- **equities** – shares and share-based investments such as unit trusts.

The aim is to put together a collection of assets that will provide you with income and also give you a reasonable chance of some capital growth. The capital growth should ensure that you continue to receive an income in future which has a good chance of retaining its buying power.

Academic research suggests that when you put together a portfolio, the asset allocation (the spread between cash, bonds, property and equities) accounts for about 90 per cent of the return. The precise choice of investments (the particular shares, accounts or bonds) has relatively little impact on the overall return.

You are likely to need help from an independent financial adviser (IFA)* when choosing the appropriate mix of assets, though there are a few websites, mainly American, that have calculators or charts to help you choose, for example, www.smartmoney.com and www.asset-analysis.com. However, here are a few general guidelines:

CASE HISTORY: LOUISE

Louise had only her state pension and a small occupational pension to live on, but in 2002 she inherited £150,000 from her late mother. Louise wanted to invest the money to provide extra income. As her resources were limited, she wanted to be fairly cautious with her investments, but accepted that she would need some capital growth over the years. To achieve that, she was prepared to take some modest risks. In 2002, investment conditions were particularly difficult for income investors, because interest rates were low and the stock market had yet to recover from steep falls in the previous two years. Louise visited an IFA, who recommended the asset allocation shown in Chart 10.1. The precise investments are shown in Table 10.4.

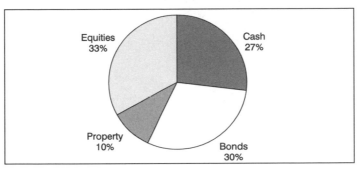

Chart 10.1   Louise's asset allocation

Table 10.4   Louise's investments

Investment	Amount invested	Expected yearly income before tax in 2002
CASH to provide income		
Building society mini-cash ISA	£3,000	£140
Other building society accounts	£37,000	£1,647
BONDS to provide mix of income and growth		
Bond-based unit trust through a stocks-and-shares mini-ISA	£3,000	£237
Other bond-based unit trusts	£42,000	£2,478
PROPERTY mainly for growth but also some income		
Property unit trust	£15,000	£555
EQUITIES to provide mix of growth and income		
Cautious managed unit trust	£35,000	£1,190
UK equity income unit trust	£15,000	£645
TOTAL	**£150,000**	**£6,892**

- if you are seeking income with no more than medium risk, a high proportion of your investments should normally be cash and bonds
- the more risk-averse you are, the higher the proportion that should be allocated to cash and bonds
- cash is mainly targeted at providing you with income
- bonds can be used to provide a combination of income and growth
- for additional growth, some of your money should be allocated to property and equities
- equities and property can provide income as well as growth.

See the case history on page 165 for how the asset allocation strategy might work in practice.

Chapter 11

Income from your home

Your home need not just be a place to live; there are several ways in which it can also be a source of income, for example:

- equity release schemes (see below)
- taking in lodgers (see page 181)
- selling part of your garden (see page 182).

Equity release: turning the capital locked in your home into income

If you own your home, you may be asset-rich even if you are income poor. Wouldn't life be easier if you could turn the capital tied up in your home into income? One option would be to sell your home and buy somewhere cheaper. You could then invest the surplus proceeds to provide you with extra income. But you might not want to move, and, if your home is already fairly bijou, trading down might not be an option. An 'equity release scheme' could be the answer.

Equity release schemes let you use the capital in your home while retaining the right to carry on living in it. They come in two basic forms:

- **home reversion scheme** You sell part of your home. You are paid immediately and can use the money raised to provide income, a lump sum, or both. But you retain the right to carry on living in your home until you die
- **lifetime mortgage** You borrow against the value of your home. You can use the loan to provide income, a lump sum, or both. The loan does not have to be repaid until you die.

Lifetime mortgages used to provide income are often called 'home income plans' (HIPs).

Income or cash?

This chapter looks particularly at sources of income in retirement. Therefore, the various equity release schemes are considered mainly in terms of the income they could provide.

If an equity release scheme is designed to provide income, this is usually done by using the money raised to buy a purchased life annuity (see page 144). A few lifetime mortgages release the loan in instalments to mimic an income.

Some equity release schemes do not pay out an income, but provide only a cash lump sum. If you need income, see Chapter 10 for some examples of how you might invest a lump sum to provide income.

Bear in mind that a level income is vulnerable to inflation. If the scheme provides an annuity, consider opting for an RPI-linked or escalating annuity (see Chapter 6) if available. If you are investing a lump sum to provide income, think how you will cope with inflation (see Chapter 10).

Some equity release schemes are specifically designed to pay care home fees – see Chapter 12.

Who can use equity release schemes?

In general, you need to be at least 65 to make use of lifetime mortgages or home reversion schemes. Some types are viable only if you are a good deal older. A few are available from younger ages, such as 55 or 60 and upwards.

Couples can take out an equity release scheme, in which case the home does not have to be sold or the mortgage repaid until the second of the couple dies. To be eligible, the couple's collective ages may have to meet a minimum number of years such as 145 and/or both must have reached a minimum age. If one spouse is a lot younger than the other, a couple in this situation might not be eligible.

You must usually own your own home outright with no mortgage. Some providers will consider only freehold properties; others will accept properties with a long lease. Houses and bungalows are usually eligible, but flats and maisonettes may not be.

Your home must be worth at least a minimum amount, typically around £40,000.

Costs

Taking out an equity release scheme involves various expenses. Your home will have to be valued, which is likely to cost in the region of £150. Some scheme providers cover the cost for you. In the case of a lifetime mortgage, the cost can usually be added to the outstanding loan.

You are strongly advised to engage a solicitor to check the terms of the equity release scheme for you. Some scheme providers will pay your legal fees for you, possibly only up to a set limit, say, £150.

There may be an arrangement fee, which is often in the region of £600. In the case of a lifetime mortgage, this can usually be added to the outstanding loan. Some or all of this fee may be used to pay commission to any financial adviser who helps you to take out the scheme.

If you pay off a lifetime mortgage within a few years of taking it out, there may be an early repayment charge.

The scheme provider will insist that you have buildings insurance to cover the property. It will also require you to keep the property in good repair, so you should allow for the cost of regular maintenance work. If you do not carry out repairs as required, the scheme may organise the repairs itself and send you the bill.

Moving home

Equity release schemes are designed to run until you die, but you should check what happens if you want to (or have to) move before then – for example, if you decide to move closer to relatives or have to move into a care home.

Most schemes are transferable if you move, provided that the new home is acceptable to the scheme provider. If you trade down to a cheaper home or sell up completely, the provider gets back some of its money early. In that situation, some reversion schemes pay you an extra cash sum. But, with a lifetime mortgage, there might be an early repayment charge.

Bear in mind that if the provider owns a large chunk of your home and is not prepared to transfer the scheme to a new home, you might not have enough capital left to buy somewhere new after paying off the scheme. This can be a particular problem with roll-up schemes (see page 177).

Other changes in your circumstances

If you have taken out an equity release in your single name, you are unlikely to be able to transfer it to joint names if you subsequently marry or start living with someone. This means your partner could become homeless if you die first.

You will need the scheme provider's permission before someone new can move in and share your home, for example a family member, carer or lodger.

If your financial situation worsens, you might want to borrow more against your home or sell another chunk. Schemes usually prohibit you going to another provider, but the original provider might be prepared to come to an additional arrangement.

Effect on tax

If you sell part or all of your home for more than you originally paid, you make a gain, but this is exempt from capital gains tax provided that the home is your only or main residence.

Money you receive through taking out a loan is not taxable, but, if it is used to buy an investment, income from the investment usually is taxable (but see Chapter 14 for examples of tax-free investments).

Equity release schemes commonly provide income through a purchased life annuity (see page 144). The 'income' you get is made up of two parts: the bit-by-bit return of your capital, which is tax-free, and true income produced by investing the capital – this part is taxable. The capital element of the annuity is basically the price you pay divided by the average life expectancy for someone of your age. The older you are, the higher the tax-free capital element of the annuity.

If you are aged 65 or over and your income is in or close to the region where you lose age allowance (see page 217), check your position carefully before opting for extra income from an equity release scheme. The extra income will count for the purpose of working out your age allowance. If it causes you to lose allowance, you could effectively be paying tax at a high rate on the extra income. However, this is unlikely to be a major problem if you receive income by way of a purchased life annuity. The taxable (income) part of the annuity is relatively small. Only that part comes into the age allowance calculation and so the loss of age allowance is likely to be small.

From 6 April 2005, the government is introducing a new tax called the 'pre-owned asset tax' (POT). This can land you with an income tax bill where you have given something away – like your home – but continue to use it or benefit from it. You are not affected if you have taken out a lifetime mortgage and you are not affected if you have taken out a home reversion scheme with a commercial company. But you may well be caught by the new tax if you arrange your own home reversion scheme by selling all or part of your home to a family member or friend who pays you money now but lets you carry on living in the home. See Chapter 16 for more information.

Increasingly, financial advisers are recommending equity release schemes as a way of reducing a potential inheritance tax bill after death. Taking out a mortgage or selling part of your home immediately reduces the value of your estate to the extent of the charges and profit being transferred from you to the equity release company and reduces it further as you spend or give away the money released. If

---

CASE HISTORY: ARIF

In 2004–5, Arif, who is 65, has an income of £18,900. He qualifies for age allowance of £6,830 and his tax bill for the year is £2,413, leaving him with an after-tax income of £16,487.

He takes out an equity release scheme, which provides him with extra income before tax of £4,434 a year. The taxable part of this income is only £1,309. He pays tax at 20 per cent on this. It also reduces his age allowance to £6,830 – (£1,309/2) = £6,176 (see Chapter 14 for an explanation of this calculation).

Arif's tax bill for the year increases by £406, which is 31 per cent of the £1,309 increase in his taxable income. But he also receives the tax-free capital element of his annuity and his total after-tax income increases to £20,515. Arif is prepared to accept the loss of age allowance in light of the substantial rise in his after-tax income.

---

your main motive in taking out an equity release scheme is to give away the proceeds, you will not necessarily succeed in saving tax if you die soon after making the gifts. See Chapter 16.

Effect on state benefits

If your income is low enough for you to be claiming means-tested state benefits, such as pension credit and council tax benefit (see Chapter 13), you may lose benefit for every £1 of income you receive from an equity release scheme. If you lose your whole entitlement to means-tested state benefits, you may also have to pay more for things like dental treatment and glasses.

Eligibility for some means-tested benefits also depends on the amount of capital you have, excluding the value of your home but including any lump sum you realise through an equity release scheme.

Before committing yourself to an equity release scheme, check how much you stand to lose in benefits. Does the scheme still look value for money when taking into account the extra income and/or lump sum from the scheme less the amount lost in benefits? If you need help working out the effect on your benefits, see page 183.

Home reversion schemes

Home reversion schemes are the most popular type of equity release scheme for older people. They generally provide a higher income than a lifetime mortgage.

Providers are usually insurers or specialist home reversion companies. Generally, you sell a percentage of your home – say, between 30 and 95 per cent. Some providers are willing to buy the whole property. The larger the proportion you sell, the higher the income or lump sum you get. If you sell only part of your home, you may be able to sell another chunk later on to the same provider in exchange for additional income or cash.

With most schemes, you have the right to continue living in your home until you die, either rent-free or for a nominal rent of, say, £1 a month. Your tenancy rights reduce the value of the home, so you will not receive the full market value for the part you sell. The younger you are when you start the scheme, the longer the provider has to wait to get its money back and the lower the proportion of the market value you get. For example, you might get around 35 per cent of the value if you are in your 60s, up to, say, 60 per cent if you are in your 80s.

With a few schemes, you pay a higher rent and get a higher proportion of the value of your home. This is suitable only if you are confident that you will be able to pay the rent both now and in the future.

The provider benefits from any appreciation in the value of the part of your home that you sell, from the start of the scheme to the home being sold. You benefit from any appreciation in the value of any part of the home that you keep. If future house prices rise steeply, you might – with hindsight – feel that you have paid a high price for your income or cash. This is a risk you should consider before committing yourself to a scheme.

Lifetime mortgages

Lifetime mortgages have been available since the 1970s. In their original form as home income plans, they worked in a very straight-forward manner. You took out a mortgage for life and the money borrowed was used to buy a purchased life annuity (see page 144). The annuity provided a fixed income. Interest on the mortgage was

---

CASE HISTORY: ANGELA

In autumn 2004, Angela, 70, has a home worth £120,000 on the open market. She decides to sell half (50 per cent) to a home reversion company. The company offers her a lump sum of £36,000. This represents £36,000 / (50% × £120,000) = 40 per cent of the market value. Angela has the right to remain in the home rent-free until she dies.

Angela spends £3,000 on double-glazing and invests the remaining £33,000 to provide an income. If she buys a purchased life annuity, she can get an income of around £2,550 a year (just under £50 a week) before tax.

When Angela dies eight years later, the value of her home has risen to £210,000. The home reversion company takes 50% × £210,000 = £105,000. The remaining £105,000 passes to Angela's heirs.

---

paid at a fixed rate out of the income and what was left provided the extra income you needed.

In the late 1980s, new types of home income plan came onto the market. Taking advantage of booming stock markets and soaring house prices, they aimed to provide a much higher income. They did this in either or both of two ways. First, instead of paying the mortgage interest monthly, the interest was rolled up and added to the outstanding loan. This meant that the loan was constantly growing, but, as house prices were rising, this was manageable. Second, instead of buying an annuity, the loan was used to buy a bond whose return was linked to the stock market. The firms selling these schemes generally failed to point out what might happen if market conditions changed. But the risks came home to roost when stock markets fell and house prices slumped. Suddenly, many people who had bought these schemes found their income falling and the outstanding loan rising well above the value of their home (a situation called 'negative equity'). The schemes became unsustainable and many purchasers were faced with the prospect of losing their homes. The regulators stepped in and ordered compensation where the schemes had been mis-sold, and these high-risk versions of lifetime mortgages largely disappeared from the market.

The safer versions of home income plans – where both income and interest payments were fixed – continued and proved useful until March 1999. Until then, an important feature of home income plans was that the interest paid on the mortgage qualified for tax relief. But, in his 1999 Budget, the chancellor abolished mortgage interest relief. Home income plans taken out before 9 March 1999 continue to get the relief, but not any new plans started on or after that date. The abolition of mortgage interest relief meant that the interest payments on the loan increased, leaving less to be paid out as income.

To compensate for the loss of tax relief, new versions of lifetime mortgages have been devised that aim to provide a higher income than a traditional home income plan. However, there is usually a price to pay for the higher income. That price is risk, and the form it takes varies depending on the way the plan works. Whether it is worth taking the extra risk is a personal decision you will need to make in the light of your own circumstances. See page 183 if you need help making the decision.

Table 11.1 Summary of main types of lifetime mortgages

Type of lifetime mortgage	How the mortgage part works	How you might get an income
Traditional home income plan	• Take out mortgage at fixed rate of interest. • Pay interest monthly. • Loan repaid when you die.	• Buy purchased life annuity. • Annuity provides fixed (sometimes increasing) income. • You get income left after paying mortgage interest.
No-interest plan	• Take out mortgage. • No interest charged on loan. • Loan repaid when you die.	• Buy purchased life annuity. • Annuity provides fixed (sometimes increasing) income, which is set at a lower level than you would get with a traditional plan but there is no mortgage interest to deduct.
Roll-up scheme	• Take out mortgage. Make sure this is at a fixed or capped rate of interest. • Interest is added to the outstanding loan to be repaid when you die. • Loan repaid when you die.	• Buy purchased life annuity. • Annuity provides fixed (sometimes increasing) income. There is no interest to deduct, so you get a higher income than from a traditional plan.
Shared appreciation mortgage (SAM)	• Take out mortgage either at low fixed rate or no interest at all. • If any interest is due it is paid monthly out of your income. • In return for waiving part or all of the interest, the lender takes part of any increase in the value of your home. • Loan and part of increase in value of home repaid when you die.	• Buy purchased life annuity. • Annuity provides fixed (sometimes increasing) income. There is little or no interest to deduct, so you get a higher income than from a traditional plan.
Protected appreciation mortgage (PAM)	• Take out mortgage at fixed rate of interest. • Interest over the whole life of the loan (assuming you live until the age expected on average for someone of your current age) is worked out and added as a lump sum to the outstanding loan. • Loan and interest repaid when you die.	• Buy purchased life annuity. • Annuity provides fixed (sometimes increasing) income. There is no interest to deduct, so you get a higher income than from a traditional plan.

A summary of the main types of lifetime mortgage is given in Table 11.1, and the following sections highlight the pros and cons of each.

Traditional home income plan

With the loss of tax relief on mortgage interest, traditional home income plans became uneconomic at younger ages. The income from an annuity is higher the older you are when you buy the annuity (see Chapter 5). With a traditional home income plan, only by about age 78 or so is the income sufficient to cover the higher mortgage interest payments and leave a realistic income.

Provided you are old enough for these plans to be economic, they are the simplest and safest form of lifetime mortgage. You can usually borrow up to 70 per cent or so of the value of your home.

No-interest plan

No interest is charged on the mortgage loan, but the annuity you buy pays out a lower than normal income. The net effect would be little different from a traditional home income plan, except for the effect of tax.

With a purchased life annuity, the 'income' you receive is made up of two parts: the bit-by-bit return of your capital, which is tax-free, and true income produced by investing the capital – this part is taxable. With a no-interest home income plan, the lower income is met through a reduction in the taxable part of the annuity which is reduced to a very low or negligible amount. So, provided you are

---

CASE HISTORY: MICK (1)

Mick is 80 and a basic-rate taxpayer. He owns his own home outright, and, in early 2005, it is worth £80,000. He takes out a home income plan, which comprises a fixed-rate mortgage of £45,000 used to buy an annuity that provides a fixed and level income. After the mortgage interest and tax have been deducted, Mick receives £3,275 a year.

Mick dies ten years later. His home is then worth £170,000. The home income plan provider takes £45,000 as the loan repayment and the remaining £170,000 – £45,000 = £125,000 is passed to Mick's heirs.

---

a taxpayer, a no-interest plan can offer a slightly better after-tax income than a traditional home income plan.

CASE HISTORY: MICK (2)

If Mick (see previous case history) could have chosen a no-interest plan, his income after tax would be around £3,425 a year, which is £150 a year more than from a traditional home income plan.

Roll-up scheme

You get a higher income from a roll-up scheme than a traditional home income plan because there is no mortgage interest deducted from the income. Instead, the interest is added to the outstanding loan.

The downside of roll-up schemes is that the outstanding loan can grow at an alarming rate because you are charged interest not just on the amount you originally borrowed, but also on the interest already added to the loan. The higher the rate of interest, the faster the outstanding loan grows – see Table 11.2.

To prevent a roll-up scheme becoming unmanageable, you should make sure it has the following safeguards:

- **a fixed or capped interest rate** With a fixed rate, you know in advance exactly how the outstanding loan will grow. With a capped rate, you know how the loan will grow in the worst case and, in practice, it might grow more slowly
- **a no-negative-equity guarantee** The lender guarantees never to recover more than the value of your home even if the loan, without the guarantee, would have grown to more than the home's value.

In the absence of a no-negative-equity guarantee, once the outstanding loan had reached the value of your home, interest would stop being added to the outstanding loan and usually you would have to start paying it monthly. Because the loan and rolled-up interest would then be a large sum, the monthly interest payment would be high – possibly more than you could afford to

Table 11.2 How the outstanding loan might grow with a roll-up scheme assuming you initially borrow £50,000

Years since plan taken out	Rate of interest (fixed for duration of plan)				
	3% p.a.	5% p.a.	7% p.a.	9% p.a.	11% p.a.
Initial loan	£50,000	£50,000	£50,000	£50,000	£50,000
1	£51,500	£52,500	£53,500	£54,500	£55,500
2	£53,045	£55,125	£57,245	£59,405	£61,605
3	£54,636	£57,881	£61,252	£64,751	£68,382
4	£56,275	£60,775	£65,540	£70,579	£75,904
5	£57,964	£63,814	£70,128	£76,931	£84,253
6	£59,703	£67,005	£75,037	£83,855	£93,521
7	£61,494	£70,355	£80,289	£91,402	£103,808
8	£63,339	£73,873	£85,909	£99,628	£115,227
9	£65,239	£77,566	£91,923	£108,595	£127,902
10	£67,196	£81,445	£98,358	£118,368	£141,971
11	£69,212	£85,517	£105,243	£129,021	£157,588
12	£71,288	£89,793	£112,610	£140,633	£174,923
13	£73,427	£94,282	£120,492	£153,290	£194,164
14	£75,629	£98,997	£128,927	£167,086	£215,522
15	£77,898	£103,946	£137,952	£182,124	£239,229
16	£80,235	£109,144	£147,608	£198,515	£265,545
17	£82,642	£114,601	£157,941	£216,382	£294,755
18	£85,122	£120,331	£168,997	£235,856	£327,178
19	£87,675	£126,348	£180,826	£257,083	£363,167
20	£90,306	£132,665	£193,484	£280,221	£403,116
21	£93,015	£139,298	£207,028	£305,440	£447,458
22	£95,805	£146,263	£221,520	£332,930	£496,679
23	£98,679	£153,576	£237,026	£362,894	£551,313
24	£101,640	£161,255	£253,618	£395,554	£611,958
25	£104,689	£169,318	£271,372	£431,154	£679,273

CASE HISTORY: DAPHNE

Daphne, aged 60, has a home worth £250,000. She is considering a roll-up equity release scheme. The maximum she is allowed to borrow is 20 per cent of the value of her home, in other words 20% × £250,000 = £50,000. She is charged fixed interest at 7 per cent a year. After five years, the loan has grown to £70,128. After ten years, it has nearly doubled to £98,358.

After 15 years, Daphne moves into a care home. The house, then worth £400,000, is sold. The roll-up loan, which has grown to £137,952, is paid off, leaving £400,000 – £137,952 = £262,048. The loan, which started as 20 per cent of the value of the home, had grown to 34 per cent by the time it was paid off. If house prices had risen more slowly, repayment would have taken an even higher percentage of the proceeds.

---

pay. If you could not pay the interest, you could lose your home. Even then, you could still be left owing money if the proceeds from selling the home were not enough to pay off the loan and rolled-up interest in full. A no-negative-equity guarantee protects you from the risk of losing your home and being faced with unmanageable debt.

Even with safeguards, a roll-up scheme can result in the bulk of the value of your home passing on death to the plan provider. This means your heirs will inherit little or nothing from the property on your death. But bear in mind that it is more important to ensure your own well-being while you are alive than to concern yourself with what might happen after your death.

The maximum initial sum you can borrow with a roll-up scheme is lower than the maximum with a traditional plan.

Shared appreciation mortgage (SAM)

A SAM aims to give you more income than a traditional home income plan, but with less risk than a roll-up scheme.

You either pay no interest on the loan, or you pay interest monthly but only at a very low rate. Instead of receiving interest, the provider eventually takes a share of any increase in the value of your home between the time you take out the loan and it being repaid. The share the provider takes is usually a multiple (for example, three times) of the percentage loan you take at the outset. For example, you might borrow 20 per cent of the value of your home now and, when the plan comes to an end, the provider eventually gets back both the initial loan and $3 \times 20\% = 60\%$ of any increase in the value of the home.

You – or your heirs – retain the remainder of the value of the home, so you still have some capital and there is no risk of negative equity.

However, if house prices boom – as they have done in the early 2000s – a SAM arrangement can, with hindsight, seem very expensive. The initial loan may have been small but the provider stands to receive a very large lump sum when the plan comes to an end. But bear in mind that, had house prices risen by less, the provider would have received a more modest repayment and possibly less than the original loan plus the interest you would otherwise have paid. You cannot know in advance whether the SAM will turn out to be cheaper or more expensive than a plan where you pay interest. That uncertainty is the price you pay for receiving a higher income than you would have had from a traditional home income plan. It's a gamble and you need to decide at the outset whether you are prepared to accept this uncertainty and the fact that the gamble might go against you.

Protected appreciation mortgage (PAM)

This is a variation on the roll-up scheme. During your lifetime, you pay no interest on the loan. This means you get a higher income than you would have done with a traditional home income plan.

However, interest at a fixed rate is charged. The provider works out how much interest would be due if you survive for the number of years that the average person of your age can expect to live. The total interest is converted to a lump sum and added to the initial loan to arrive at the sum that must be repaid when the loan comes to an end.

If you live longer than average, a PAM will turn out to be a good deal, because you will pay less interest than you would have done with a traditional home income plan. But if you die sooner than the average for someone of your age, you will turn out to have had a worse deal. Of course, you do not know in advance how the deal will turn out.

However, PAMs have a feature which lets you remove some of the uncertainty. In return for a lower income, you can protect yourself against paying all of the interest in the event that you die within a few years of starting the PAM. The interest is divided into instalments, which are added to the outstanding loan at yearly intervals. When the plan ends, only the interest already added to the loan has to be paid; the rest is waived. The more instalments you choose, the longer it takes to add all the interest to the loan, so the greater the protection you get. Table 11.3 shows how this works. But the greater the protection, the more income you sacrifice.

Taking in lodgers

If your home is large enough, you might be able to rent out one or more rooms to lodgers. Apart from the income this can generate, the arrangement might have other benefits, such as company if you

Table 11.3   Interest payment protection with a PAM

	No protection	Moderate protection	High protection
Interest added to loan in this many yearly instalments:	1	5	10
If you die after this many years	Percentage of the full interest you would have paid		
1	100%	20%	10%
2	100%	40%	20%
3	100%	60%	30%
4	100%	80%	40%
5	100%	100%	50%
6	100%	100%	60%
7	100%	100%	70%
8	100%	100%	80%
9	100%	100%	90%
10	100%	100%	100%

live alone, help with small domestic jobs, someone to keep an eye on your home while you are away on holiday, and so on.

Under the government's 'rent-a-room-scheme', you can receive up to £4,250 a year in rents from lodgers (and the cost of any associated services, such as providing meals or doing laundry), without having to pay tax on this income. Using the scheme also saves on paperwork, because you just need to keep a record for tax purposes of the rents you receive and not any of your expenses.

If you receive rents of more than £4,250 a year, you can still use the rent-a-room-scheme, in which case the first £4,250 is tax-free income and the rest taxable. In this case, you cannot deduct any of the expenses you incur through taking in lodgers. The alternative is to keep records of all your expenses as well as rental income and pay tax just on the profit (income less expenses). If your expenses come to less than £4,250 a year, you will be better off using the rent-a-room scheme.

For information about the legal aspects and guidance on how to find a lodger, see *The Which? Guide to Renting and Letting* from Which? Books★. For information about the rent-a-room scheme, see Inland Revenue★ leaflets IR87, *Letting and your home* and IR150, *Taxation of rents*.

Selling part of your garden

If you have a large garden, you might consider selling part of it to raise money. You will raise most money if the garden is suitable for building.

Provided the size of your garden is no more than half a hectare (about 1¼ acres), or, if larger, not considered excessive for your home, there is normally no capital gains tax on any profit you make from selling part of it (assuming the home is your only or main residence). This applies even if you have already obtained planning permission for building to go ahead on the plot. However, the tax exemption is lost if you yourself start to build on the plot. The government has indicated that sometime in the future it might introduce a tax on the gain due to obtaining planning permission, but no firm proposals had been announced at the time of writing.

For more information, see Inland Revenue★ leaflet CGT1, *Capital gains tax – an introduction* and Inland Revenue helpsheet IR283, *Private residence relief*.

Where to get more information

To find out about equity release schemes, either contact providers direct or get advice from an independent financial adviser (IFA)*. Equity release providers who belong to Safe Home Income Plans (SHIP)* abide by a code of practice. You are strongly advised to employ a solicitor* to check the terms of the contract.

The equity release scheme provider or IFA should advise about the effect an equity release scheme might have on your tax position and eligibility for state benefits. Your local social security office* or Citizens Advice Bureau (CAB)* can also advise on state benefits.

You should also employ a solicitor if you are considering any other transaction that involves selling part of your home or its garden. For information about getting planning permission, contact the planning department of your local authority*.

Consumer protection and equity release schemes

Since 31 October 2004, lifetime mortgages are regulated by the Financial Services Authority (FSA). It has set up a detailed code of business that providers and advisers must by law observe. It includes giving you standard documents that set out clearly the risks and charges involved, and ensuring that a lifetime mortgage is suitable for you given your circumstances and needs. If something goes wrong, you can take a complaint about a lifetime mortgage to an independent complaints scheme (the Financial Ombudsman Service*) and you might qualify for redress from a compensation scheme.

The FSA is due to regulate home reversion schemes from a future date (possibly in 2006) but does not do so yet. At present, the main protection when you buy these schemes is just a voluntary code of conduct imposed on its members by SHIP*.

Part 3

Support from the state

Chapter 12

State benefits if you have a disability

With advancing years, many people develop health problems that limit their ability to get around or take care of themselves – see Table 12.1. The state offers a range of different types of help, including financial payments to help you with the extra costs of coping with a disability. The main forms of cash support are disability living allowance (DLA) and attendance allowance. If you are under 65 when you first claim, DLA applies. If you are 65 or over, you claim attendance allowance instead.

Claims are assessed according to your need for help from, or supervision by, other people. However, there are no restrictions on how you use the money and no requirement that you actually spend the money on care. For example, you might prefer to try to cope alone and instead spend the money on aids or adaptations to help you do that; you could just spend the money on luxuries; or you could save it. How you use it is entirely up to you. But the amount of DLA or attendance allowance that you get may be taken into account in deciding whether, and how much, you must pay for care services provided by the state (see page 191). To prevent the state paying twice over for your care, you will lose DLA or attendance allowance if you have to spend a prolonged period in hospital or move into a care home with state funding. But you keep the benefit if you move into a care home and pay the full fees yourself.

Both DLA and attendance allowance are tax-free benefits. As there is no tax to pay on them, they cannot affect the amount of age allowance you get (see Chapter 14), and you do not have to declare them to your tax office.

Table 12.1 Incidence of health problems as you get older

Task	Percentage of people in each age group who cannot manage the tasks without help									
	65–69		70–74		75–79		80–84		85 and over	
	Men	Women	Men	Women	Men	Women	Men	Women	Men	Women
Domestic tasks	17%	26%	17%	35%	28%	45%	46%	58%	56%	80%
Self care	13%	24%	16%	33%	28%	40%	47%	54%	51%	67%
Mobility	7%	9%	5%	15%	11%	21%	22%	28%	24%	52%

Source: Office of National Statistics.

Disability living allowance (DLA)

This is the main disability benefit for people who are under 65 when they first claim. Awards can be made for a limited or indefinite period. If you are already getting DLA upon reaching your sixty-fifth birthday, you carry on receiving it – you do not switch to attendance allowance.

DLA is not means-tested, so you can get it regardless of how much income and savings you have. And, unlike some other benefits, there are no contribution conditions for DLA, so you need not have paid or been credited with National Insurance contributions in order to be eligible. To qualify, you must normally have satisfied the conditions below for at least three months prior to claiming and be expected to continue to satisfy them for at least the next six months. However, the time limits may be relaxed if you are suffering from a terminal illness.

The DLA has two components: a care component and a mobility component. If you satisfy the relevant conditions for each, you may receive both components. Alternatively, you might receive just one of the components.

You may qualify for the care component if:

- you need frequent help with personal care
- you need continual supervision to avoid endangering yourself or others, or
- you cannot prepare a main meal without help.

You may qualify for the mobility component if:

- you cannot walk
- you have great difficulty walking, or
- you can walk but need continual supervision to avoid endangering yourself or others.

The care component is paid at one of three levels. You are entitled to the highest level if you need help with care or supervision both during the day and at night. You receive the middle rate if you need care or supervision only at night or only during the day. The lower rate is paid if you need some care during the day – for example, just when getting up or going to bed – or you are unable to prepare a main meal.

The mobility component is paid at a higher rate if you cannot walk or have great difficulty walking, and at a lower rate if you can walk but need supervision.

Table 12.2   Rates of disability living allowance in 2005–6

	Weekly rate in 2005–6
Care component	
Higher rate	£60.60
Middle rate	£40.55
Lower rate	£16.05
Mobility component	
Higher rate	£42.30
Lower rate	£16.05

Attendance allowance

This is the main disability benefit for people who are aged 65 or over when they first claim.

Attendance allowance is not means-tested, so you can get it regardless of how much income and savings you have. And, unlike some other benefits, there are no contribution conditions for attendance allowance, so you need not have paid or been credited with National Insurance contributions in order to be eligible. To qualify, you must normally have satisfied the conditions below for at least six months prior to claiming and be expected to continue to satisfy them in future. However, the time limits may be relaxed if you are suffering from a terminal illness. You can qualify if:

- you need frequent help throughout the day with personal care
- you need continual supervision throughout the day to avoid endangering yourself or others, or
- you need prolonged or repeated attention at night to help with personal care, to avoid danger to yourself and others, or to watch over you.

Attendance allowance is paid at a higher or a lower rate. You get the higher rate if you need care or supervision during both the day and night. You get the lower rate if you need care or supervision either only at night or only during the day.

Table 12.3   Rates of attendance allowance in 2005–6

	Weekly rate in 2005–6
Higher rate	£60.60
Lower rate	£40.55

Claiming DLA or attendance allowance

Claim through your local Jobcentre Plus★ if you are under state pension age, The Pension Service★ otherwise, or the DWP Benefit Enquiry Line★.

What is personal care?

You might qualify for DLA or attendance allowance if you need help with dressing, washing, going to the toilet, getting up or going to bed, transferring, say, from bed to chair, walking, communication, eating or drinking, or taking medicines. Your difficulties might stem from a physical or mental disability.

State help for carers

If you spend 35 hours a week or more looking after someone who gets the middle or higher rate of DLA, attendance allowance or some other state disability benefits, you may be able to claim carer's allowance. This is a taxable benefit.

You do not have to meet any contribution conditions in order to claim carer's allowance – in other words, eligibility does not depend on having paid or been credited with National Insurance contributions.

Carer's allowance was originally available only to carers under the age of 65 when they first claimed. Since 28 October 2002, you can claim it even if you are aged 65 or over. However, you are not eligible if you have earnings over a certain limit (£82 a week in 2005–6) or you are getting other state benefits – including state retirement pension – that provide you with more than the rate of carer's allowance (£45.70 a week in 2005–6). But, for example, if your state pension is less than £45.70 a week, you may be able to claim carer's allowance to bring your total benefit up to that level.

How to claim Carer's Allowance

Claim through your local social security office* or the DWP Carer's Allowance Unit*.

Care services

Local authorities are the bodies responsible for delivering care services and help in paying for such services. This area of work is carried out by your local authority social services department*. The local authority has a duty to carry out a 'needs assessment' of anyone who it seems may need the local authority's services. (If you are disabled, the local authority *must* carry out a needs assessment.) Based on the assessment, a care plan may be drawn up which may involve providing services in your own home or your moving into a care home.

Your needs should be assessed without reference to your ability to pay. But, in deciding whether the local authority will fund the services you require, you will normally be means-tested and expected to pay a contribution towards the cost, or the full cost, if it is judged that you can afford to do so.

It is sensible to ask for a needs assessment to include an assessment of the ability of any informal carer you rely on to continue providing care. Since April 2001, carers are able to ask for such an assessment independently of a needs assessment of the person being cared for.

191

Care in your own home

There is a wide range of services that can be provided to help you to remain independent and living in your own home, for example:

- special equipment, such as easy-to-use taps, a hoist to assist with sitting up in bed, aids to help with getting in and out of the bath, and so on
- adaptations to your home, for example grab rails and ramps
- meals on wheels
- a place at a day centre where you can meet other people socially, have a meal, or receive specialist care
- a sitter to keep an eye on you while your main carer has a break
- longer respite care, either in your own home or in a care home, while your carer goes on holiday or has a break.

Local authorities normally charge for these services. The charges may be reduced or waived if your income and savings are low. (In working this out, the value of your home should be ignored if you're receiving care in your own home.) It's up to each local authority to set its own charges and decide what means tests it will use. There is considerable variation across the country. However, in April 2003, new government guidelines came into effect with the aim of reducing the variations.

As an alternative to the local authority arranging for services and payment for them, the authority can pay money direct to you. In this case, you can shop around and select the service providers. Unlike DLA or attendance allowance, you *must* use this local authority money to buy the care you need.

Moving to a care home

The outcome of the needs assessment might be a recommendation that you move into a care home. Since October 2001, the state pays for nursing care (up to limits) even if you are well-off. But state help paying for personal care, board and lodging is means-tested, except in Scotland where the state covers personal care up to a limit whatever your financial circumstances.

You get no state help with fees if you have to move into a care home unless your income is low and your savings and other capital come to no more than an upper threshold – see Table 12.4. If your income is between the limits shown in the table, you are deemed to receive £1 a week of income from every £250 (or part £250) of capital above the lower limit. This deemed income is added to your income and if that exceeds the means-test limit, you'll have to pay part of the care home fees.

If your income and capital are too high for you to get state help, you'll have to meet care costs either out of your income or by using up your savings. State help will kick in only when your capital has fallen below the upper limit.

In assessing your capital, the value of your home is ignored if you're receiving care in your own home. It's also ignored if you go into a care home but your home will still be occupied by your husband, wife, partner, a dependent child or a relative who is over 60 or incapacitated. In other circumstances, your home will usually count as part of your capital and may have to be sold to pay for care costs.

Since April 2001, your home is left out of the equation for the first 12 weeks after moving into a residential or care home. This gives a breathing space to work out whether you are likely to return home at some stage.

Instead of selling your home, you may be able to borrow from the state to pay for care. The state then recoups the loan out of the eventual sale of your home. Another option might be for you to privately rent out your home and use the rental income to pay the care home fees.

If you can see that you might soon have to move into a care home, you might be tempted to give away some of your capital to bring it under the means-test limit. Similarly, personal possessions

Table 12.4 Capital limits in 2004 used to determine eligibility for state help with care home funding

	Lower limit	**Upper limit**
England	£12,250	£20,000
Scotland	£11,750	£19,000
Wales	£13,500	£20,500
Northern Ireland	£12,250	£20,000

do not usually count towards the means test, so you might be tempted to spend a large chunk of your savings. However, if the local authority suspects that your main motive in making gifts or spending your savings was to manipulate the means test, it can treat you as still owning the capital.

Protecting your capital

You may be able to reduce the need to use up your capital in payment for care by taking out a long-term care plan. These are designed to pay out an income if you become reliant on help because of ill-health or disability. There are two types of plan: 'pre-funded' and 'immediate care'.

Pre-funded plans

Pre-funded long-term care plans are either pure insurance policies or combine insurance with an investment element. In either case, the income starts to be paid if you can no longer carry out two or three 'activities of daily living' (ADLs) without help. The definitions of ADLs vary slightly from one company to another, but are typically:

- washing/bathing
- dressing
- feeding
- continence/toileting
- mobility (moving from one room to the next)
- transfer (for example, from a bed to a chair).

In general, claims are valid whatever the cause of the illness or disability, but some policies exclude, for example, depression, schizophrenia, AIDS and HIV-related conditions, alcohol and drug abuse and self-inflicted injuries.

A snag with pre-funded plans is that they are very expensive, easily costing tens of thousands of £s if you pay a single premium and hundreds of £s a month if you pay a regular premium. As a result, they have failed to take off in the UK and very few providers now offer this type of long-term care plan. An independent financial adviser (IFA)★ can check the market and tell you what, if any, plans are available.

Paying a hefty premium for a plan obviously eats into your savings – so how would this type of plan help to protect your capital?

Firstly, although the cost is great, it is a known amount. By contrast, you don't know how long you'll have to pay direct for care, so you can only guess at the overall cost. In addition, many plans pay out a lump sum when you die, which might replace part or all of the premium you paid.

Immediate care plans

Immediate care plans are aimed at people who already need care. You hand over a lump sum (which could be raised by taking out a mortgage on your home) and in return get an income for the rest of your life. The income can be paid to you, or, more often, direct to the care provider.

Alternatives to an immediate care plan are ordinary purchased life annuities (see Chapter 9), or equity release schemes (see Chapter 11). However, an immediate care plan may offer a higher income. This is because the income from all these products depends on how long you are expected to live. The greater your life expectancy, the lower the income because it will probably have to be paid out for longer. An ordinary annuity or equity release scheme usually assumes you have average life expectancy for someone of your age and sex. But, if you're already ill, your life expectancy is likely to be lower than average. An immediate care plan recognises this by offering a higher-than-average income. In addition, where the payments under the immediate care plan are paid direct to the care provider, the return is tax-free.

How to get help with care

To find out what state help is available and request a needs assessment, contact your local authority social services department★. There are various organisations that can give you free information and help in making a claim for state help. These include Citizens Advice Bureaux★ and your local branch of Age Concern★.

To find out about and buy long-term care insurance or a long-term care plan, contact an independent financial adviser★.

Other state help with health costs

If you are aged 60 or over, you qualify for free prescriptions. There are no special steps for claiming; just tick the appropriate box on the form on the back of the prescription.

People aged 60 and over also qualify for free sight tests. Again, there is no special procedure for claiming; just tick the appropriate box on the form that the optician asks you to sign.

If you are on a low income (for example, claiming income support – see Chapter 13), you may also qualify for a voucher towards the cost of glasses. This will be provided by the optician carrying out your sight test, but it can be used at other outlets. You need to complete a form available from the optician or your local social security office★.

If you are on a low income, you may be eligible to have the costs of travel to and from a hospital for treatment as an in-patient or out-patient refunded. You claim the refund from the hospital reception. You need to show proof that you are claiming a means-tested benefit (such as income support – see Chapter 13) or produce a certificate which you can obtain through your social security office★.

For details of these benefits, see Department of Health leaflet HC11, *Are you entitled to help with health costs?* available from social security offices★, doctors surgeries, hospitals, post offices, some public libraries, and so on.

Where to get more information

For information about benefits if you have a disability, contact your local social security office★ or the DWP Benefit Enquiry Line★. The DWP also operates a variety of helplines dedicated to particular types of benefit – see the Address section. If you need help working out what you might be entitled to or making a claim, contact your local Citizens Advice Bureau (CAB)★.

If you are a carer, you can get information and advice from Carers UK★.

The government publishes a wide range of free leaflets about state benefits. A selection are shown in Table 12.5 and can be obtained from the DWP leaflet unit★ as well as local social security offices★, post offices, many public libraries, and other outlets. Age Concern★, an independent charity championing older people, publishes a range of very good, free factsheets about state benefits and other topics.

Table 12.5 Selection of DWP leaflets about state benefits

Reference number	Title
DS702	Attendance allowance
DS704	Disability living allowance – you could benefit
GL12	Going into hospital?
HB5	Non-contributory benefits for disabled people
HB6	A practical guide for disabled people
HC11	Are you entitled to help with health costs?
HC12	NHS charges and optical voucher values
HC13	Help with health costs
SD3	Long-term ill or disabled?
SD4	Caring for someone?

Chapter 13

State benefits if your income is low

If your income is less than the state deems you need to live on, you may be entitled to means-tested benefits to top up your income. The main means-tested benefit for retired people is pension credit. This is made up of two parts: a guarantee credit and a savings credit.

If you qualify for pension guarantee credit, you automatically also qualify for housing benefit to help with your rent and council tax benefit (see below). However, you might still qualify for these benefits even if you cannot get the pension guarantee credit.

Means-testing means that you can get a benefit only if your income, and in some cases your savings, are less than certain amounts.

The pension credit

The pension credit started in October 2003. It is designed to top up the resources of current pensioners whose income is low and has two parts: a guarantee credit and a savings credit. Depending on your circumstances, you might qualify for either or both of these elements.

The guarantee credit

Any person aged 60 or over whose income is less than a certain amount – the minimum guarantee (£109.45 a week for a single person and £167.05 for a couple in 2005–6) – is entitled to claim a top-up to bring their income up to that level. The minimum guarantee is higher for people who are severely disabled and for carers, and can include extra to cover mortgage interest and certain other housing costs (but not rent for which you might be able to claim housing benefit instead – see page 202). The minimum guarantee is increased each year in line with national average earnings.

Pension credit and couples

At the time of writing, 'couple' means either a married couple or partners living together as man and wife. From a future date (expected to be late 2005 or early 2006), it will also include same-sex couples who have registered their relationship as a civil partnership and unregistered same-sex partners living together as if they were civil partners. Until the new law comes into effect, same-sex partners are treated as single people.

The savings credit

A problem inherent in the pension guarantee credit is that it discourages people who do not expect to have much income in retirement from saving anything at all. What is the point of saving enough to provide, say, £20 a week in retirement if it will simply replace money you could otherwise have claimed through the guarantee credit? To tackle this problem, pension credit also has a savings credit which is designed to reward you for making your own savings for retirement.

If you are aged 65 or over, you can claim a credit of 60p for each £1 of income that you have between two thresholds. The lower threshold at which savings credit starts is the same as the maximum state basic retirement pension (£82.05 a week for a single person and £131.20 for a couple in 2005–6). The upper threshold is the minimum guarantee described above (£109.45 a week for a single person and £167.05 for a couple in 2005–6). This gives a maximum savings credit of £16.44 a week in 2005–6 if you are single and £21.51 if you are a couple. But the savings credit is reduced by 40p for each £1 of income above the minimum guarantee. In this way, the savings credit is tapered away to nothing for single people with an income of £150 or more and couples with an income of £220 or more. Tables 13.1 and 13.2 gives some examples of how much you can get depending on your retirement income.

Table 13.1   Examples of pension credit if you are single in 2005–6

Your income from all sources	Income above threshold at which savings credit starts	Pension credit		Your income including pension credit
		Guarantee credit	Savings credit	
£40	£0	£69.45	£0.00	£109.45
£50	£0	£59.45	£0.00	£109.45
£60	£0	£49.45	£0.00	£109.45
£70	£0	£39.45	£0.00	£109.45
£82.05[1]	£0	£27.40	£0.00	£109.45
£90	£7.95	£19.45	£4.77	£114.22
£100	£17.95	£9.45	£10.77	£120.22
£109.45[2]	£27.40	£0.00	£16.44	£125.89
£120	£37.95	£0.00	£12.22	£132.22
£130	£47.95	£0.00	£8.22	£138.22
£140	£57.95	£0.00	£4.22	£144.22
£150.55[3]	£68.50	£0.00	£0.00	£150.55

[1] Threshold at which savings credit starts (equal to full state basic pension).
[2] Minimum guarantee (and threshold at which savings credit starts to be lost).
[3] Income level at which all savings credit lost.

The means test for pension credit

The rules are complicated and this description gives just a broad outline. Income from most sources is taken into account, including state pensions, occupational pensions, personal and stakeholder pensions, earnings if you carry on working, profits if you are self-employed, rent from lodgers, and so on. However, income from many state benefits does not count and neither does your actual income from any savings and investments, such as building society

Table 13.2 Examples of pension credit if you are a couple in 2005–6

Your income from all sources	Income above threshold at which savings credit starts	Guarantee credit	Savings credit	Your income including pension credit
£80	£0	£87.05	£0.00	£167.05
£90	£0	£77.05	£0.00	£167.05
£100	£0	£67.05	£0.00	£167.05
£110	£0	£57.05	£0.00	£167.05
£120	£0	£47.05	£0.00	£167.05
£131.20[1]	£0	£35.85	£0.00	£167.05
£140	£8.80	£27.05	£5.28	£172.33
£150	£18.80	£17.05	£11.28	£178.33
£160	£28.80	£7.05	£17.28	£184.33
£167.05[2]	£35.85	£0.00	£21.51	£188.56
£170	£38.80	£0.00	£20.33	£190.33
£180	£48.80	£0.00	£16.33	£196.33
£190	£58.80	£0.00	£12.33	£202.33
£200	£68.80	£0.00	£8.33	£208.33
£220.83[3]	£89.63	£0.00	£0.00	£220.83

[1] Threshold at which savings credit starts (equal to full state basic pension).
[2] Minimum guarantee (and threshold at which savings credit starts to be lost).
[3] Income level at which all savings credit lost.

accounts and unit trusts. Instead you are treated as receiving a deemed amount from savings and investments of £1 a week from every £500 of savings over £6,000 (or £10,000 if you live in a care home). The first £6,000 (or £10,000) of savings and investments is ignored.

CASE HISTORY: ELSIE

In 2005–6, Elsie, who is 66, has a state pension of £80 a week and £6,700 in a building society savings account. She makes a claim for pension credit. The interest from her savings account is ignored but she is treated as getting £1 a week for each £500 (and part-£500) of savings above £6,000, so she has a deemed income from savings of £2 a week. This brings her income up to £82 a week. This is less than the minimum guarantee of £109.45 a week, so she gets a guarantee credit of £109.45 – £82 = £27.45 a week.

Although Elsie has some savings income, it is not quite enough to bring her income above the threshold (£82.05 a week in 2005–6) at which she would qualify for savings credit. In a way, her savings are wasted since they earn her no savings credit and, without the £2 a week deemed income, she would simply qualify for £2 more guarantee credit. On the other hand, the actual interest she gets on her savings (including the £6,000 that was ignored for pension credit purposes) is equivalent to about £6 a week, so her total income is £109.45 + £6 = £115.45.

CASE HISTORY: JACK AND RHIANNON

In 2005–6, Jack and Rhiannon together get state pensions of £140 a week plus £35 a week from Joe's personal pension, taking their total weekly income to £175 a week. This is more than the minimum guarantee for a couple (£167.05), so they do not qualify for any guarantee credit. However, their income of £175 is more than the threshold at which savings credit starts (£131.20 in 2005–6), so they may qualify for some savings credit.

Initially the savings credit is worked out as the maximum amount of (£167.05 – £131.20) × 60p = £21.51. But, because their £175 income is £7.95 higher than the minimum guarantee (£167.05), they lose 7.95 × 40p = £3.18, reducing their savings credit to £21.51 – £3.18 = £18.33. This increases their weekly income to £175 + £18.33 = £193.33.

CASE HISTORY: KEVIN

In 2005–6, Kevin has a state pension of £82.05 a week and a small occupational pension of £20 a week, making a total weekly income of £102.05. This is £7.40 less than the minimum guarantee for a single person of £109.45, so he qualifies for a guarantee credit of £7.40. His income is £20 more than the £82.05 threshold at which the savings credit starts, so he is also entitled to a savings credit of 20 × 60p = £12. The pension credit has boosted his weekly income to £102.05 + £7.40 + £12 = £121.45.

Help with home-related costs

Mortgage interest

If you qualify for the pension guarantee credit, the amount you get can be adjusted to include interest (but not capital repayments) on a mortgage you have taken out to buy your home or to make certain improvements to it. The interest payments are covered from the start of your claim (in contrast to claims for means-tested benefits for under-60s where there is usually a delay of nine months before interest payments are met by the state).

The amount you get will not cover the whole of your interest payments if either your mortgage is larger than £100,000 or your housing costs are considered excessive for your needs. Normally the pension credit for interest payments is paid direct to your lender.

Rent

Pension credit does not cover rent. Instead, you may be eligible to claim housing benefit.

If you are a tenant and qualify for the pension guarantee credit (or if you are under 60 either income support or income-based jobseekers allowance), you automatically also qualify for full housing benefit, though you still have to put in a separate claim. If you do not qualify for any of these benefits, you may still be eligible for housing benefit – whether you are and the amount you get will be worked out according to a means test that looks at your income and savings (see overleaf).

Housing benefit can cover up to the full amount of your rent. But it may cover only part if you live with anyone else who can be expected to contribute or your rent is considered excessive or covers items (such as fuel) which are not considered to be housing costs.

Council tax benefit

If you qualify for the pension guarantee credit (or if under 60 either income support or income-based jobseekers allowance), you automatically also qualify for full council tax benefit, though you still have to put in a separate claim. But, again, if you do not get any of these benefits, you might still qualify for council tax benefit if you pass a means test which is worked out in the same way as for housing benefit (see below). Council tax can cover up to the whole of your eligible council tax bill.

The means test for housing benefit and council tax benefit

You cannot get housing benefit or council tax benefit at all if your capital comes to more than £16,000. Below that limit, your capital is assumed to produce £1 of income for each £500 (or part £500) in excess of £6,000 (£10,000 if you live in a care home) if you are aged 60 or over (or £1 for each £250 if you are younger). This is called 'tariff income' and is added to your other income for the purpose of the means test. If you are married or living with someone of the opposite sex as man and wife, the limits apply to your joint capital, but note that the limits are the same as those for single people – they are not increased for couples.

If you have passed the capital test, the next stage of the means test is to assess your income. You include all types of income unless they are specifically disregarded. For example, include: your state pension; any other pensions; income from annuities (though if this is an annuity from a lifetime mortgage, you deduct any part that pays monthly interest on the mortgage); earnings from a job; state benefits, such as invalid care allowance and bereavement allowance, but not any benefits that are specifically disregarded, such as disability living allowance, attendance allowance and winter fuel payment. Note in particular that your income includes any pension credit you get, but that an adjustment is made (see below) to prevent you losing benefit as a result. You do not include actual income from investments, but instead add on any tariff income (see above).

Your income is then compared to an amount of income you are deemed to need to cover your basic living expenses, which is called the 'applicable amount'. The amount varies depending on your circumstances. For example, the standard applicable amount for a single pensioner aged 65 or over in 2005–6 is £125.90 a week and £188.60 for a couple, and this includes allowance for the maximum amount of any pension saving credit you could get. Your applicable amount could be increased if, say, you have a disability. If your income is less than your applicable amount, you qualify for housing benefit and council tax benefit in full. If your income is greater than your applicable amount, your benefits are reduced by a percentage of the income over the applicable amount (65 per cent in the case of housing benefit and 20 per cent for council tax benefit).

Tax credits

If you are working but on a low income, or you are caring for children, you may qualify for working tax credit and/or child tax credit. Despite the name 'tax credit' these are means-tested state benefits and nothing to do with your tax bill.

These are tax-free, non-contributory benefits. Whether you qualify and for how much depends on a means test based on your household income calculated in more or less the same way as for income tax purposes (see Chapter 14).

A household without children may qualify for working tax credit if:

- you or your partner work at least 30 hours a week
- you or your partner work at least 16 hours a week and either of you has a disability that disadvantages you in getting a job, or
- you work at least 16 hours a week, are aged 50 or over and have recently started work after a period on specified state benefits.

You can work out the standard amount you might get by adding up the elements for which you qualify in Table 13.3. Next take your income and subtract from this the income threshold (£5,220 in 2005–6). The standard amount is reduced by 37p for each £1 of income above the threshold.

Table 13.3 Working tax credit for a household without children in 2005–6

Element	Yearly amount
Basic (applies to all claimants)	£1,620
Lone parent or couple	£1,595
Working 30 hours per week	£660
Disabled worker	£2,165
Severe disability	£920
50-plus working 16–29 hours per week	£1,110
50-plus working 30+ hours per week	£1,660
Income threshold	£5,220
Withdrawal rate	37p in the £1

CASE HISTORY: TERRY

Terry is 62 and still works full-time, earning £10,000 a year. He lives with his wife Claire, who does not work and receives a small state pension of £1,250 a year. They have no other income. Terry qualifies for a standard amount of working tax credit as follows: basic element £1,620 + couple element £1,595 + 30-hour element £660 = £3,875. The household income is £10,000 + £1,250 − £5,220 = £6,030 above the income threshold. This reduces the standard credit by 6,030 × 37p = £2,231. Therefore Terry is able to claim working tax credit of £3,875 − £2,231 = £1,644 a year.

Where to get more information

For information about pension credit, contact The Pension Service★ or the Pension Credit Application Line★. For information about housing benefit or council tax benefit, contact your local authority★. (If you are claiming housing benefit or council tax benefit at the same time as pension credit, you can use the forms supplied in the pension credit application pack.) For working tax credit, contact the Inland Revenue★.

State benefits are complicated, and if you need help working out what you might be entitled to, contact your local Citizens' Advice Bureau (CAB)★ or charities specialising in helping older people, such as Age Concern★ and Help the Aged★.

The government publishes a wide range of free leaflets about state benefits. A selection is shown in Table 13.4 below and can be obtained from the DWP leaflet unit★ as well as social security offices★, post offices, many public libraries and the DWP★ website. Age Concern★ publishes a range of very good, free factsheets about state benefits.

Table 13.4 Selection of DWP leaflets about state benefits

Reference number	Title
PC1L	Pension credit – pick it up it's yours
PC10S	A guide to pension credit
GL16	Help with your rent
GL17	Help with your council tax
GL23	Social security benefit rates
RR2	Housing benefit and council tax benefit

Part 4

Navigating the tax system

Chapter 14

Income tax

Sadly, stopping work does not mean an escape from income tax. However, you might see a big drop in your tax bill if a fall in income takes you into a lower tax bracket and on reaching age 65 when you qualify for a higher tax allowance.

Tax basics

Income tax is charged on your taxable income, less certain allowable deductions, if the total comes to more than your personal allowance and any other tax allowance for which you are eligible.

You are taxed on your income for a 'tax year'. This runs from 6 April in one year to 5 April in the next. For example, the 2005–6 tax year runs from 6 April 2005 to 5 April 2006.

What income is taxed?

Income from most sources is taxable. This includes state pensions, occupational pensions, personal pensions, interest from savings accounts, dividends from shares, distributions from unit trusts, rents from property (net of expenses) and earnings or profits from any work you continue to do.

However, some income is tax-free. The main sources of tax-free retirement income are shown in Table 14.1. And some types of income are taxed in a special way, for example life-insurance policies (see page 214).

Payments you get on leaving a job

You may have received various lump sums on leaving a job, especially if you were made redundant or encouraged to retire early.

Table 14.1 Main sources of tax-free retirement income

Savings and investments (see Chapter 9)	• Individual savings accounts (ISAs)★ • National Savings & Investments certificates • Part of the income from a purchased life annuity • Pay-out from some friendly society plans★ • Personal equity plans (PEPs)★ • Premium bonds
State pensions and benefits (see Chapters 12 and 13)	• Attendance allowance • Bereavement payment • Christmas bonus paid to state pensioners • Home renovation and repair grants • Housing benefit and council tax benefit • Over-70s payment to help with countil tax bill • Pension credit • Payments from the social fund • Severe disablement allowance • Winter fuel payment
Other	• Letting a room in your home under the rent-a-room scheme (see Chapter 11) • Lottery winnings • Maintenance from a former husband or wife • Interest on a tax rebate

★ Depending on the investments within the account or plan. Dividends and similar income from investments in a stocks-and-shares ISA are paid with tax equivalent to 10 per cent already deducted and this cannot be reclaimed.

Some such payments, in particular the lump sum from an occupational pension scheme, are tax-free, but others count as part of your earnings from the job and are taxable.

The general rule is that any payment that is a reward for services, due under the terms of your contract, or habitually paid by your employer to people who leave, is part of normal pay and taxable. This covers, for example, pay in lieu of notice as specified in your contract, holiday pay, a bonus in respect of work you have done, and sums that your employer normally pays to every employee on, say, completion of so many years' service.

With some other payments, there is no tax to pay on the first £30,000 received, but you are taxed on any excess over £30,000. For example, this applies to non-contractual pay in lieu of notice, genuine compensation for redundancy, compensation for unfair dismissal, and so on. If you receive an item rather than cash – say, a car – its value is taken into account instead.

This is a complicated area of tax, but your employer should ensure that the correct amount of tax is deducted before you receive the payment.

Interest from bank and building society accounts

Interest from bank and building society accounts and some other investments, such as purchased life annuities, is normally paid with some tax already deducted. If you are a non-taxpayer, you can claim a tax refund. This involves filling in a form R40 which is a bit like a mini tax return. Far simpler, you can instead register to receive the interest 'gross' (without any tax deducted). You do this by completing a very simple form, R85, available from the bank or building society concerned or your tax office.

Taxpayers whose highest rate of tax is the starting rate (see page 222) can claim back part of the tax already deducted from bank and building society accounts.

See Chapter 9 for more information about these investments, including how they are taxed.

Dividends from shares and distributions from unit trusts and open-ended investment companies investing in shares

These types of income are also paid with some tax already treated as paid (and the dividend or distribution comes with a tax credit for that amount). You cannot reclaim the tax deducted even if you are a non-taxpayer. The tax credit is taken to satisfy your liability to pay tax at the starting rate or the basic rate, so if you are a basic-rate taxpayer there is no more tax to pay. If you are a higher-rate taxpayer, extra tax is due at a special rate of 32.5 per cent less the 10 per cent tax credit.

Life-insurance policies

Life-insurance policies that build up a cash value are used as investments. There are three main types of policy.

Tax-efficient policies

These include some friendly society plans and insurance individual savings accounts (ISAs). The return used to be completely tax-free, but since 6 April 2004 any dividends from shares or similar income from share-based investments within the policy are paid with the equivalent of tax at 10 per cent already deducted, and you cannot reclaim this even if you are a non-taxpayer.

Qualifying policies

These include most regular premium whole-life policies and most regular premium endowment policies with a life of at least ten years.

The insurance company invests your premiums and the return you get is directly or indirectly linked to the return on the investments. The insurance company pays tax on both income and gains made by the investments, so it is not correct to call the return you get tax-free. However, there is no tax for you personally to pay on the proceeds from the policy.

If you are a non-taxpayer you cannot reclaim any of the tax already paid by the insurance company.

A qualifying policy that is surrendered within the first ten years or, if fewer, within the three-quarters of its term, becomes a non-qualifying policy.

Non-qualifying policies

If a policy is neither tax-free nor qualifying, it will generally be a non-qualifying policy. This includes, for example, single premium endowment policies, single premium whole-life policies and regular premium endowment policies with a life of fewer than ten years.

The insurance company invests your premiums and the return you get is directly or indirectly linked to the return on the investments. The insurance company pays tax on both income and gains made by the investments. You cannot reclaim any of this tax even if you personally would pay less tax on income or gains or no tax at all.

The tax paid by the company is treated as satisfying any tax due at the savings rate. So if you are a basic-rate taxpayer, there is no tax for you personally to pay on the proceeds from a non-qualifying policy.

If you receive a pay-out from the policy that counts as a 'chargeable gain' and you are a higher-rate taxpayer, you do have to pay income tax on the gain but only at the excess over the savings rate (40% – 20% = 20% in 2004–5).

If adding the chargeable gain to your other income for the tax year takes you from the basic-rate band into the higher-rate band, you can claim top-slicing relief. Broadly, this lets you divide the gain by the number of years the policy has run to find the average yearly gain. You add the average gain to your income and work out the tax due on that. The tax due on the average gain is then multiplied by the number of years the policy ran to find the tax due on the whole gain. For example, if adding the average gain to your other income left you in the basic-rate band, there would be no tax to pay on the whole gain.

A 'chargeable gain' is, in general terms, a pay-out either on maturity or earlier that exceeds the amount you have paid in premiums. The rules can be complicated, but, since 6 April 2002, insurance companies must tell you if a payout is a chargeable gain.

However, not all pay-outs are chargeable. You can each year withdraw up to one-twentieth of the premiums paid (up to an overall maximum of 20 twentieths). If you do not make the maximum withdrawal in one year, you can carry the unused limit forward and take a higher amount in subsequent years. Whatever your tax position, there is no tax to pay at the time you make the withdrawals. Any tax bill is deferred until the policy is finally cashed in. If, at that time, you are not a higher-rate taxpayer, you will not have to pay any tax. This withdrawal facility is widely used to enable insurance bonds to provide a regular income with no immediate tax bill.

Whatever your tax position, a chargeable gain from a non-qualifying insurance policy does count as part of your income for the purpose of working out age allowance (see page 217). This means that even if you have no tax to pay directly on the gain, it could nevertheless cause your tax bill to rise.

CASE HISTORY: JUNE (1)

June, who is 58 and a higher-rate taxpayer, buys a single premium with-profits insurance bond. It is designed to pay her a regular income and, provided it grows as expected, to return her capital on maturity. She pays £10,000 for the bond. She can withdraw an income of up to $1/20 \times £10,000 = £500$ a year. Even though she is a higher-rate taxpayer, there is no tax for her to pay on this income because it falls within the special rules for withdrawals for non-qualifying life-insurance policies. The bond matures ten years later. June is by then a basic-rate taxpayer, so again there is no tax for her to pay on the bond. However, the maturing bond does cause her tax bill to rise because she loses age allowance (see case history on page 218).

Allowable deductions

Having added up all your taxable income for the year, you can deduct certain payments that qualify for tax relief (sometimes called 'outgoings'). There used to be a lot more of these, but only a few remain. The most relevant are likely to be:

- contributions to retirement annuity contracts (see Chapter 4). Also contributions to occupational pension schemes (see Chapter 3), though your employer will usually already have made this deduction
- interest on a loan taken out to invest in your business
- losses made as a result of being self-employed or in a part-nership that you have opted to set off against other income
- the value of gifts to charity of shares, land and property.

Deducting an expense from your income before tax is worked out gives you tax relief on the expense up to your top rate of tax.

Other payments that qualify for tax relief

Some other payments you make also qualify for tax relief, but relief is given in other ways.

Payments to personal pensions (including stakeholder schemes) are treated as being made after deducting tax relief at the basic rate.

The tax relief is then claimed by the pension provider and added to your plan (see Chapter 4). If you are a higher-rate taxpayer, you are eligible for extra relief and this is given by extending your 'basic-rate band' (see page 222) by the amount of the contribution plus basic-rate relief. This ensures that less of your income is taxed at the higher rate.

Tax relief on contributions to charity or community amateur sports clubs through the gift aid scheme is given in the same way. Your donation is treated as being made after the deduction of tax relief at the basic rate. The charity or sports club claims the relief from the Inland Revenue, boosting the total sum it receives. If you are a higher-rate taxpayer, you qualify for extra relief, which is given by extending your basic-rate band.

Investments you make in venture capital trusts (VCTs) and enterprise investment schemes (EISs) qualify for income tax relief and this is given by deducting the relief from your tax bill. This means that the maximum relief you can get may be capped at the amount of tax you would otherwise have paid.

Gift aid donations

If you pay tax at less than the basic rate, the Inland Revenue can reclaim some or all of the basic-rate tax relief treated as deducted from your donation. Therefore, do not use gift aid if you are a starting-rate taxpayer or non-taxpayer.

Personal allowance and age allowance

Everyone gets a personal allowance, which means that the first slice of otherwise taxable income is tax-free. Table 14.2 sets out the personal allowances for 2004–5 and 2005–6.

Older people qualify for extra personal allowance and this higher total is usually referred to as 'age allowance'. However, the extra amount is reduced if 'total income' exceeds a set limit (£18,900 in 2004–5 and £19,500 in 2005–6). The allowance is lost at a rate of £1 for every £2 of income over the limit. But the remaining allowance is never reduced below the amount someone under 65 can get. Table 14.3 shows the range of incomes at which you are losing age allowance.

Table 14.2   Personal allowances

Your age	Allowance in 2004–5	Allowance in 2005–6
Under 65	£4,745	£4,895
65 to 74	£6,830	£7,090
75 and over	£6,950	£7,220

Table 14.3   Income range at which age allowance is being lost (single person or married woman)

If you are aged:	You are losing age allowance if your income is in this range:	
	2004–5	2005–6
65 to 74	£18,901 to £23,070	£19,501–£23,890
75 and over	£18,901 to £23,310	£19,501–£24,150

CASE HISTORY: RICHARD

In 2005–6, Richard has a taxable income of £17,000. He is 76 and qualifies for a personal allowance of £7,220. This means he is taxed on only £17,000 – £7,220 = £9,780 of his income.

CASE HISTORY: JUNE (2)

June is 68 and initially qualifies for a personal allowance of £7,090 in 2005–6, but her income (including the gain from a maturing life insurance bond – see case history on page 216) at £20,100 is over the limit at which age allowance is reduced. Her age allowance is reduced by (£20,100 – £19,500) / 2 = £300 to £6,790. This means she pays tax on £20,100 – £6,790 = £13,310 of her income.

CASE HISTORY: HUBERT

In 2005–6, Hubert has an income of £40,000. He is aged 70 and this would normally qualify him for an age allowance of £7,090, but his income is well over the £19,500 limit at which age allowance is reduced. Therefore he gets only the same allowance, £4,895, that a younger person would get. He is taxed on £40,000 – £4,895 = £35,105 of his income.

'Total income' for the purpose of working out age allowance is your taxable income less allowable deductions and less the 'grossed up' amount of any contributions to personal pensions or stakeholder schemes or gift aid donations. ('Grossed up' means you add the basic-rate tax relief you have had to the amount you actually paid.)

You qualify for age allowance for the whole tax year in which you reach the relevant age. For example, if you were born on 5 April 1941, your allowance is £7,090 for the whole year from 6 April 2005 to 5 April 2006.

Married couple's allowance

If you or your husband or wife were born before 6 April 1935, you can claim married couple's allowance. The allowance has been abolished for younger couples and does not apply at all to unmarried couples. If you and your spouse were born on or after 6 April 1935, you do not need to read this section.

Married couple's allowance is not deducted from your taxable income. Instead it is given at a rate of 10 per cent as a reduction in your tax bill.

There are two different amounts of allowance depending on the age of you and your spouse (see Table 14.4). However, the extra allowance is reduced if your 'total income' exceeds a set limit (£18,900 in 2004–5 and £19,500 in 2005–6). The allowance is lost at a rate of £1 for every £2 of income over the limit. But the remaining allowance is never reduced below a set amount, which is £2,210 in 2004–5 and £2,280 in 2005–6. See above for the definition of 'total income'.

The allowance is made up of two parts: the basic allowance of £2,210 (£2,280), and an age-related addition (the excess). The age-related addition is always given to the husband and any reduction is

Table 14.4 Married couple's allowance

Age of you or your spouse during tax year	Allowance in 2004–5	Allowance in 2005–6
70 to 74	£5,725	
71 to 74		£5,905
75 or older	£5,795	£5,975

based on the husband's income. His personal age allowance is reduced before any reduction is made to the married couple's allowance.

Either the husband or wife can receive the whole basic married couple's allowance, or they can elect to share it equally between them.

CASE HISTORY: JACK AND SYBIL

Jack is 64 but his wife, Sybil, is a bit older at 71. Jack is too young to qualify for an age-related personal allowance, but because of Sybil's age he is eligible for married couple's allowance of £5,905 in 2005–6. This is made up of a basic allowance of £2,280 and an age-related addition of £3,625. Sybil is still working, so the couple opt to transfer the basic allowance of £2,280 to Sybil.

CASE HISTORY: TED AND HANNAH

Ted and Hannah are married. Ted is aged 77 and Hannah is 75. Ted qualifies for an age-related personal allowance of £7,220 and the married couple's allowance of £5,975 in 2005–6. But Ted's income exceeds the £19,500 threshold at which age allowance starts to be lost. His income is £27,000, which means he loses (£27,000 – £19,500) / 2 = £3,750 of age-related allowances. First he loses personal allowance and this is reduced by £2,325 to £4,895. Next, he loses the married couple's age addition so the married couple's allowance falls by £3,750 – £2,325 = £1,425 from £5,975 to £4,550.

Same-sex couples

In 2004, new legislation was passed which will give the same rights as married couples to same-sex partners who register their relationship as a civil partnership. The legislation did not cover tax issues but the government has indicated that changes to tax law will be made in future, possibly from April 2006. It is expected that civil partners will then be entitled to married couple's allowance where one or both partners were born before 6 April 1935.

How tax is worked out

The following steps show broadly how your tax bill is worked out. However, if your circumstances are unusual – for example, you have income from a trust – your affairs will be more complicated.

Step 1 Your taxable income

Add up your taxable income from all sources. Do not include any tax-free income. Keep a separate note of:

- income that does not fall into any of the groups below (this would include pensions, earnings, profits and rents)
- interest from bank and building society accounts, interest from gilts and bonds, the taxable element of purchased life annuities (see page 144) and distributions from unit trusts and open-ended investment companies that invest largely in gilts or bonds
- dividends from shares and distributions from unit trusts and open-ended investment companies that invest in shares
- chargeable gains from life-insurance policies (see page 214).

Often you will have received income from which tax has already been deducted. You need to 'gross up' this income by adding back the tax already paid and include this gross (tax-inclusive) amount in your calculation.

Step 2 Make allowable deductions

If you have any expenses that can be set off against your taxable income (see page 216), deduct these now. Deduct them from income in this order:

- other income not in any of the groups below
- interest from bank accounts, and so on, as above
- dividends from shares, and so on
- chargeable gains from life-insurance policies.

Step 3 Deduct your personal allowance or age allowance

Again, deduct them from income in this order:

- other income not in any of the groups below
- interest from bank accounts, and so on, as above
- dividends from shares, and so on
- chargeable gains from life-insurance policies.

Step 4 Allocate your income to tax bands

Table 14.6 shows the tax bands and rates for 2004–5. If you have made contributions to personal pensions or stakeholder schemes or gift aid donations during the tax year, you need to 'gross up' these payments by adding back the tax relief and then add the gross (tax-relief-inclusive) amount to the basic-rate band. This process will ensure that you get higher-rate tax relief for the payments.

You now need to allocate your income to each band. Again, you do this in the following order of income:

- other income as above
- interest from bank accounts, and so on, as above
- dividends from shares, and so on
- chargeable gains from life-insurance policies.

Multiply the income in each band by the tax rate that applies to each type of income.

Table 14.6 Tax bands and rates for 2004–5

Tax band	Size of band in 2004–5	Type of income	Tax rate in 2004–5
Starting-rate band	£2,020	Life-insurance gains	0%
		All other income	10%
Basic-rate band	£29,380	Life-insurance gains	0%
		Dividends and similar income	10%
		Interest, for example, from savings accounts	20%
		Other income	22%
Higher-rate band	The rest	Life-insurance gains	20%
		Dividends and similar income	32.5%
		Other income	40%

Step 5 Deduct tax already paid or credited

For each type of income, add together the tax on each band to find the total. Deduct any tax that you have already paid or been credited with.

If the answer is less than zero, you may be due a tax refund, but note that you cannot reclaim the 10 per cent tax already deducted from dividends and similar income.

If the answer is more than zero, deduct any allowances or tax credits that give you relief as a reduction in your tax bill, such as VCT investments or married couple's allowance (but the maximum you can deduct is the amount that reduces your tax bill to zero). What remains is the tax you have to pay.

Tips on saving income tax in retirement

- If you are a non-taxpayer, register to receive interest from savings accounts without any tax deducted. This will save you the administrative bother of claiming tax back.

- If your highest rate of tax is the starting rate, make sure you claim back part of the tax already deducted from interest from savings accounts.

- If you are a taxpayer, consider tax-free sources of income, such as cash ISAs and some National Savings & Investments products (see Chapter 9) and the rent-a-room scheme (see Chapter 11).

- Especially consider tax-free investments if your income is in the region where you are losing age allowance (see pages 212 and 218).

- Another way to cut any loss of age allowance is to contribute to a personal pension or stakeholder scheme for yourself or make gift aid donations. These reduce your 'total income' and so can increase the age allowance you get.

- Life insurance bonds can be a useful way of providing an income on which there is no immediate tax to pay (see page 214). Provided the income is no more than one-twentieth a year of the premium(s) you paid, any tax bill is deferred until the bond matures or you cash it in. Any gain is then taxed only if you are a higher-rate taxpayer. But be aware that a gain on maturity or cashing in is added to your 'total income' for that year and could cause you to lose tax allowance.

CASE HISTORY: DOREEN

Doreen works through the steps to calculate her tax bill for 2004–5.

Step 1

In 2004–5, Doreen has the following income:

- state pension of £3,926 before tax
- building society interest of £5,000. Adding back the tax already deducted, the gross amount is £6,250
- share dividends of £6,000. Adding back the tax credit, the gross amount is £6,666
- life-policy gain of £1,500.

Step 2

Doreen recently gave £500 of shares to a charity. She deducts the value of these shares from the pension income, leaving £3,926 − £500 = £3,426.

Step 3

Doreen is 63 and has a personal allowance of £4,895. She sets this first against her pension income, which is reduced to zero, and the remaining £4,895 − £3,426 = £1,469 against her building society interest.

Step 4

Doreen allocates the remaining taxable income to the tax bands for 2004–5. None of her pension income is taxable because it is more than covered by deductions and allowances, so the starting-rate band is set against her building society interest. The rest of her income falls within the basic-rate band. The basic-rate band has been extended by £256 because Doreen made a £200 gift aid donation to a local charity (which claimed £56 tax relief from the Inland Revenue), but this does not give Doreen any extra tax relief because she has too little income in any case to use her full basic-rate band.

Step 5

Doreen adds up the tax due on each type of income. She then subtracts the tax she has already paid. This comes to more than the tax due, so Doreen is due a rebate. Bearing in mind that no tax on dividends can be reclaimed, the rebate is £1,250 − £754.20 = £495.80.

- Even if you are already retired, provided that you are under age 75, consider saving through a stakeholder pension scheme. You get tax relief on what you pay in and can quickly take the proceeds, including part as a tax-free lump sum. Stakeholder schemes must have low charges, so the deductions from your investment will be relatively small. See Chapter 4 for details.

- Only part of the return from a purchased life annuity (see page 144 and case history below) counts as taxable income and this part is taxed at the savings rate. The rest is treated as return of your capital. This means it can make sense to swap taxable pension for a tax-free lump sum (see pages 50 and 65), which is then used to buy a purchased life annuity. You can end up with a higher after-tax income as a result.

- Often one partner in a couple has a lower income than the other. If the lower-income partner is not using his or her full personal allowance, consider transferring income-producing assets to the lower-income partner. Similarly, you may collectively be able to save tax by transferring assets if one of the couple pays tax at a higher rate than the other. Note, though, that gifts between unmarried partners could trigger a capital gains tax bill (see Chapter 15), and have implications for inheritance tax (see Chapter 16).

CASE HISTORY: MARK

In November 2004, Mark, aged 65, has a pension fund of £40,000. He needs as much income as possible and considers converting the whole fund into pension. After tax at the basic rate (22 per cent), he would get £2,293 a year.

Alternatively, he could take a quarter of the fund (£10,000) as a tax-free lump sum. The remaining £30,000 would provide an after-tax pension of £1,718 a year. With the £10,000, he buys a purchased life annuity. Part of the income from this counts as a return of capital and is not taxed; the rest is taxed at the savings rate of 20 per cent. After tax, the annuity provides £640 a year income. Adding this to his pension, he has a total of £640 + £1,718 = £2,358. Because of the difference in the ways pensions and purchased life annuities are taxed, this strategy increases Mark's overall income by nearly £65 a year.

Where to get more information

The Inland Revenue★ produces a wide range of free leaflets explaining how income tax works. Table 14.7 lists those that you might find particularly useful during retirement.

If you need help working out your tax, completing your tax return or dealing with the Inland Revenue, consider using an accountant★ or other tax adviser★. If you can't afford to use a tax professional, you might be eligible for help from Tax Aid★ or Tax Help for Older People★.

Table 14.7   Selection of Inland Revenue leaflets

Reference number	Title
IR65	Giving to charity: how individuals can get tax relief
IR78	Personal pensions. A guide for tax
IR110	Bank and building society interest – are you paying tax when you don't need to?
IR121	Income tax and pensioners
IR143	Income tax and redundancy
IR2008	ISAs and PEPs

Chapter 15

Capital gains tax

When you sell or give away something (or dispose of it in some other way), there could be a tax bill on any increase in its value during the time you owned it. The increase is called a capital gain and the tax you might incur is capital gains tax (CGT). But there are various exemptions, reliefs and allowances that either eliminate or reduce the tax bill.

An introduction to CGT

This section gives a brief introduction to capital gains tax (CGT). It does not cover the many complications of CGT. In particular, this chapter assumes you are disposing of an asset on or after 6 April 1998 and that the asset was acquired no earlier than 31 March 1982. If you acquired an asset before then, you can opt to treat it as if it had been acquired on that date for the purpose of working out the CGT due, but an alternative method may be available if this would produce a lower tax bill. For details of the alternative method and further information about CGT, see the Inland Revenue publications mentioned on page 235.

Tax basics

CGT is charged on your chargeable gains, less allowable losses and certain other allowances and reliefs, if they come to more than your annual allowance.

You are taxed on the gains you make during a 'tax year'. This runs from 6 April one year to 5 April in the next. For example, 2004–5 runs from 6 April 2004 to 5 April 2005.

Which gains are taxed?

CGT could apply to virtually anything you own – land, buildings, paintings, furniture, shares, unit trusts, gilts, and so on – but some assets are specifically exempt. They include:

- money in sterling
- foreign currency for your own personal use
- chattels (also called 'tangible moveable objects') that have a useful life of 50 years or less and have not been used by you in a business. These chattels include personal possessions such as clothes, books and household goods
- chattels with a useful life of more than 50 years – for example, antique furniture, paintings, and so on – are exempt if the item disposed of is worth no more than £6,000. If it's worth more, special rules apply – see box on page 226
- your main or only home, including the garden up to half a hectare (more if the style and size of the home warrants a larger plot). If you have more than one home, you must nominate one as your main residence. A husband and wife may have only one main residence between them. A gain on your home could be partly taxable if you have used part of it exclusively for business or you have lived away from home for long periods
- motor vehicles for private use (cars, motorbikes, and so on)
- some investments, such as National Savings & Investments products, premium bonds, gilts, many corporate bonds, investments held in individual savings accounts (ISAs) or personal equity plans (PEPs), venture capital trusts (VCTs) and enterprise investment schemes (EISs), provided that certain conditions are met
- life-insurance policies you take out (though any gain might be subject to income tax – see page 214). But a gain on a policy you bought from someone else could be taxable
- a right you have to receive income from, say, an annuity or the right to benefit under a trust. But if you bought the right from someone else, there could be tax on any gain you make.

Regardless of the asset involved, some transactions are also free of capital gains tax. They include:

- transfers between husband and wife, provided that the couple live together. (The periods of time that the donor and recipient each own the asset are added together and treated as a continuous period for working out the tax)
- gifts to charities, community amateur sports clubs, and various other institutions such as museums, art galleries and universities
- gifts on death, whether under the terms of a will or the intestacy rules
- gifts of things you acquired in the UK that you make while resident abroad, provided that you are outside the UK for at least five years.

When you dispose of an exempt asset or make an exempt transaction, there is no chargeable gain for tax purposes. In most cases, there is no allowable loss either.

When you make a gift, there could also be an immediate or potential inheritance tax bill (see Chapter 16).

Same-sex couples

In 2004 new legislation was passed which will give the same rights as married couples to same-sex partners who register their relationship as a civil partnership. The legislation did not cover tax issues but the government has indicated that changes to tax law will be made in future, possibly from April 2006. It is then expected that transfers between civil partners will be free of capital gains tax.

Working out the basic gain or loss

If you dispose of an asset which is not covered by any of the exemptions above, the first step in working out whether you have any CGT to pay is to:

- take the final value of the item. This is, usually, the proceeds you received or the item's market value on the day you disposed of it

- deduct the initial value. This is usually what you paid or the market value, of the item on the day you first acquired it
- deduct any allowable expenses. These include costs incurred in acquiring or disposing of the asset, such as commission to a broker, valuation fees and solicitor's fees. You can also deduct costs associated with enhancing the value of the asset, such as adding an extension to a building or laying a water supply to a field, but not spending on maintenance and repairs.

If this calculation produces a positive figure, you have made a gain. If it produces a negative figure you have made a loss.

CASE HISTORY: PHYLLIS (1)

In September 2004, Phyllis sells a holiday cottage she has owned since December 1987. She sells it for £151,200 – this is the final value. The initial value at which she bought the cottage is £62,000. When she bought the cottage she incurred valuation fees and solicitor's costs of £1,200 and stamp duty of £6,200. The fees on selling were £2,800. She also spent £4,000 in May 1995 adding a conservatory to the cottage. Her basic gain is £151,200 – £62,000 – £1,200 – £6,200– £2,800 – £4,000 = £75,000.

Indexation allowance

If you owned the asset before 6 April 1998, you can claim an indexation allowance in respect of the period up to that date. The aim of indexation allowance was to ensure that you were not taxed on increases in value that were purely due to inflation. From 6 April 1998 onwards, indexation allowance was replaced by taper relief (see page 228).

You can claim indexation allowance in respect of the asset's initial value and each allowable expense. In each case, you find the allowance by multiplying each initial value or expense by the appropriate factor. Table 15.1 shows the factor you should use if you dispose of the asset on or after 6 April 1998.

Subtract the indexation allowance from the basic gain you have made. The answer is your 'indexed gain'. The maximum indexation

Table 15.1 Indexation allowance for disposals on or after 6 April 1998

Year you acquired the asset or incurred the expense	Month you acquired the asset or incurred the expense											
	Jan	Feb	Mar	Apr	May	Jun	Jul	Aug	Sep	Oct	Nov	Dec
1982	–	–	1.047	1.006	0.992	0.987	0.986	0.985	0.987	0.977	0.967	0.971
1983	0.968	0.960	0.956	0.929	0.921	0.917	0.906	0.898	0.889	0.883	0.876	0.871
1984	0.872	0.865	0.859	0.834	0.828	0.823	0.825	0.808	0.804	0.793	0.788	0.789
1985	0.783	0.769	0.752	0.716	0.708	0.704	0.707	0.703	0.704	0.701	0.695	0.693
1986	0.689	0.683	0.681	0.665	0.662	0.663	0.667	0.662	0.654	0.652	0.638	0.632
1987	0.626	0.620	0.616	0.597	0.596	0.596	0.597	0.593	0.588	0.580	0.573	0.574
1988	0.574	0.568	0.562	0.537	0.531	0.525	0.524	0.507	0.500	0.485	0.478	0.474
1989	0.465	0.454	0.448	0.423	0.414	0.409	0.408	0.404	0.395	0.384	0.372	0.369
1990	0.361	0.353	0.339	0.300	0.288	0.283	0.282	0.269	0.258	0.248	0.251	0.252
1991	0.249	0.242	0.237	0.222	0.218	0.213	0.215	0.213	0.208	0.204	0.199	0.198
1992	0.199	0.193	0.189	0.171	0.167	0.167	0.171	0.171	0.166	0.162	0.164	0.168
1993	0.179	0.171	0.167	0.156	0.152	0.153	0.156	0.151	0.146	0.147	0.148	0.146
1994	0.151	0.144	0.141	0.128	0.124	0.124	0.129	0.124	0.121	0.120	0.119	0.114
1995	0.114	0.107	0.102	0.091	0.087	0.085	0.091	0.085	0.080	0.085	0.085	0.079
1996	0.083	0.078	0.073	0.066	0.063	0.063	0.067	0.062	0.057	0.057	0.057	0.053
1997	0.053	0.049	0.046	0.040	0.036	0.032	0.032	0.026	0.021	0.019	0.019	0.016
1998	0.019	0.014	0.011	0	0	0	0	0	0	0	0	0
1999 or later	0	0	0	0	0	0	0	0	0	0	0	0

CASE HISTORY: PHYLLIS (2)

Phyllis (see Case History on page 224) can claim indexation allowance when she sells her holiday cottage for the initial value and each of the allowable expenses (apart from the selling costs since they were incurred at the same time as the sale). Table 15.2 shows the allowances she claims.

Table 15.2   Phyllis's indexation allowances

A Expense	B Initial value or allowable expense	C Date incurred	D Indexation factor from Table 15.1	E Allowance (B × D)
Initial value	£62,000	Dec 1987	0.574	£35,588
Buying costs	£7,400	Dec 1987	0.574	£4,248
Conservatory	£4,000	May 1995	0.087	£348

Adding the indexation allowances together comes to £40,184. Phyllis deducts this from her basic gain of £75,000 to leave an indexed gain of £75,000 − £40,184 = £34,816.

Special rules for chattels

If you dispose of a personal possession with a useful life of 50 years or more, there is no CGT if the final value is £6,000 or less. If the final value exceeds £6,000, special rules apply that limit the chargeable gain after indexation allowance but before taper relief (see page 228) to five-thirds of the excess of the final value over £6,000. These rules apply to items such as antiques, paintings, jewellery, and so on.

allowance you can claim is the amount needed to reduce the gain to zero. You cannot use indexation allowance to create or increase a loss.

CASE HISTORY: MARIA

Maria sells a painting in May 2004 for £9,000. She inherited it in November 1992 when it was valued at £2,400. The basic gain is £9,000 − £2,400 = £6,600 and she can claim indexation allowance of 0.164 × £2,400 = £394. Therefore the indexed gain is £6,600 − £394 = £6,206. However, under the special rules, the chargeable gain is capped at 5/3 × (£9,000 − £6,000) = 5/3 × £3,000 = £5,000.

Loss relief

If you have sold or disposed of other assets in the same year and made an allowable loss on them, you must deduct the losses from your chargeable gains. Any losses that cannot be used up against this year's gains are carried forward to be used in subsequent years.

If, after deducting your losses for the year, you still have chargeable gains, you next deduct any allowable losses brought forward from earlier years. However, you only set off so much of these as is needed to reduce your chargeable gains to the level of the annual allowance (see below), which was £8,200 in 2004–5.

Where you have several gains, losses are set off first against those assets which qualify for the lowest taper relief (see page 228).

CASE HISTORY: PAUL

In February 2005, Paul sells an antique table, making a gain of £12,000. He also sells some shares, making a loss of £2,000. His net gains for 2004–5 are £12,000 − £2,000 = £10,000. He has losses brought forward from previous years of £5,000. He sets £1,800 of these against his gains reducing them to £8,200, which equals the annual allowance for 2004–5. Therefore he has no CGT to pay on the gain he made on the table. He carries the remaining £3,200 of losses forward to subsequent years.

Taper relief

In respect of periods you have owned an asset from 6 April 1998 onwards, you may be eligible for taper relief. In general, the longer you have owned an asset, the greater the amount of taper relief you get. However, some things count as 'business assets' and qualify for much more generous taper relief than 'non-business assets'. Tables 15.3 and 15.4 set out the taper relief rates for each type of asset. (The CGT taper relief described here has nothing to do with the inheritance tax taper relief discussed in Chapter 16.)

If you owned a non-business asset on 17 March 1998, on disposal you treat the asset as if you had held it for one extra year for the purpose of calculating the taper relief.

Since taper relief on business assets builds up much more quickly and is given at higher rates, it is important to know which of your possessions qualify as business assets. Broadly they are:

- items you use in your business if you are a sole trader or partner
- items used by a 'qualifying company'
- from 6 April 2005, items you own used by a sole trader or partner in their business (for example, premises you rent out)

Table 15.3 Taper relief on non-business assets

If you have held the asset for this many complete years since 6 April 1998:	Your net chargeable gain is reduced by this much:	Only this much of the gain is chargeable:	For example, each £100 of chargeable gain is reduced to:
0	No reduction	100%	£100
1	No reduction	100%	£100
2	No reduction	100%	£100
3	5%	95%	£95
4	10%	90%	£90
5	15%	85%	£85
6	20%	80%	£80
7	25%	75%	£75
8	30%	70%	£70
9	35%	65%	£65
10 or more	40%	60%	£60

Table 15.4   Taper relief on business assets disposed of on or after 6 April 2002[1]

If you have held the asset for this many complete years since 6 April 1998:	Your net chargeable gain is reduced by this much:	Only this much of the gain is chargeable:	For example, each £100 of chargeable gain is reduced to:
0	No reduction	100%	£100
1	50%	50%	£50
2 or more	75%	25%	£25

[1]Business asset taper relief built up more slowly where you disposed of an asset before 6 April 2002. If this applies to you, ask your tax office for details.

- something you are required to have as a result of your employment
- shares in a 'qualifying company'.

From 6 April 2000 onwards, the definition of 'qualifying company' changed, as shown in Table 15.5.

Importantly, the post-April 2000 definition includes any shareholdings in unlisted trading companies whether or not you work for the company and regardless of the size of your holding. 'Unlisted'

Table 15.5   Definition of qualifying company for taper relief

Before 6 April 2000	From 6 April 2000 onwards
• a trading company where you controlled 25% of the voting rights, or • provided you were a full-time officer or employee, a trading company where you controlled at least 5% of the voting rights.	• any unlisted trading company • a quoted company where you control at least 5% of the voting rights • provided you are an officer or employee (full- or part-time), any quoted trading company • provided you are an officer or employee (full- or part-time), any quoted non-trading company where you control no more than 10% of the voting rights, income or assets

includes companies quoted on the Alternative Investment Market (AIM). Also, the relaxation in the conditions where you work for a company means that nearly all shares acquired through employee share schemes and employee share option schemes qualify as business assets from 6 April 2000 onwards.

Change in definition mean that some assets that have been non-business assets in the past became business assets from 6 April 2000 or 6 April 2004. This means that you might dispose of an asset that had been a business asset for only part of the time since 6 April 1998 (or the date you acquired the asset if later). Similarly, you might have an asset that you used in your business for a while, but which either before or after was a personal belonging. In these cases, you split the asset into business and non-business parts, according to the length of time the asset counted as a business asset, and apply separate rates of taper relief to each part; see the case history on page 231 for an example of how this works.

CASE HISTORY: PHYLLIS (3)

In September 2004, Phyllis (see case histories on pages 224 and 226) made an indexed capital gain of £34,816 on the sale of her holiday cottage. It counts as a non-business asset for taper relief. She had owned the cottage for six years since 6 April 1998 and, since she owned it on 17 March 1998, she can claim seven years' worth of taper relief. This means her gain is reduced by 25%. Therefore, the chargeable gain becomes 75% × £34,816 = £26,112.

CASE HISTORY: SYED

Syed, who is self-employed, sells one of his shops in September 2004, making a gain of £36,625. He has owned the shop – which counts as a business asset – for three years, which is long enough to qualify for 75 per cent taper relief. Therefore the chargeable gain is reduced to 25% × £36,625 = £9,156.

CASE HISTORY: ALBERT

Albert has held shares in Megagrowth Ltd, a trading company listed on the AIM since March 1996. He is just a small investor – he does not work for Megagrowth or hold a sizeable proportion of its total shares. The shares were originally a non-business asset, but became a business asset from 6 April 2000 onwards when the definition was changed to include shares in AIM-listed and other unquoted trading companies.

Albert sells the shares in February 2005, making £30,000 after allowable expenses and indexation allowance. He has owned the shares for six complete years since 6 April 1998. For two of these six years – in other words, a third of the total time – the shares counted as non-business assets. So Albert divides the shareholding into two parts of £10,000 and £20,000.

The first £10,000 counts as a gain on a non-business asset. Albert qualifies for seven years' non-business taper relief on this part (including the extra year for having held the shares on 17 March 1998). So his chargeable gain is reduced to 75% × £10,000 = £7,500.

The second £20,000 counts as a gain on a business asset. Albert qualifies for the maximum 75 per cent relief, so the chargeable gain is reduced to 25% × £20,000 = £5,000.

Albert's total chargeable gain on the shares is £7,500 + £5,000 = £12,500.

Annual allowance

Having arrived at your net chargeable gains for the tax year, you still might escape a tax bill if the gains come to no more than the annual CGT allowance for the year, which is £8,200 in 2004–5. If your gains come to more than the allowance, you are taxed only on the excess.

> **CASE HISTORY: PHYLLIS (4)**
>
> In 2004–5, Phyllis (see case histories on pages 224, 226 and 230) made a chargeable gain of £26,112 after deducting all allowances and reliefs. She has an annual allowance of £8,200, so she will be taxed on £26,112 – £8,200 = £17,912.

Working out the tax bill

Your taxable gains after deducting all the allowances and reliefs are added to your taxable income for the same tax year. The gains are then taxed as if they are the top slice of your income. Tax is charged at the following rates:

- **starting rate** If your combined taxable income and gains come to no more than the starting-rate band (£2,020 in 2004–5), 10 per cent

> **CASE HISTORY: PHYLLIS (5)**
>
> Phyllis (see case histories on pages 224, 226, 230 and above) has taxable income of £22,000 in 2004–5. She has made a taxable gain of £17,912 on the sale of a holiday cottage. The gain is added to her income, making a combined total of £39,912. The gain has taken her over the higher-rate threshold, so part of the gain is taxed at 20 per cent and part at 40 per cent. Tax is worked out as follows:
>
> - unused basic-rate band: £31,400 – £22,000 = £9,400. Therefore £9,400 of the gain is taxed at 20 per cent, i.e. 20% × £9,400 = £1,880
> - remaining gain: £17,912 – £9,400 = £8,512. This is taxed at 40 per cent. 40% × £8,512 = £3,404.80.
>
> Total tax on the gain is £1,880 + £3,404.80 = £5,284.80. After paying selling costs and tax, Phyllis's net sale proceeds from selling the cottage are £151,200 – £2,800 – £5,284.80 = £143,115.00.

- **savings rate** If your combined taxable income and gains come to no more than the top of the basic-rate band (£31,400 in 2004–5), 20 per cent
- **higher rate** if your combined taxable income and gains come to more than the top of the basic-rate band (£31,400 in 2004–5), 40 per cent.

If adding the gains to your income takes you over a tax threshold, part of the gain is taxed at one tax rate, while the part in excess of the threshold is taxed at another.

Special rules for shares, unit trusts and similar investments

If you have a holding of shares, unit trusts and similar investments (for convenience referred to as 'shares' in this section) that you bought all at the same time, when you dispose of the shares the gain is worked out in the way described in this chapter. If you sell only part of the shareholding, you simply scale down the sums by the same fraction that the part you are selling bears to the whole transaction. For example, if you sell only half the shares, take into account only half the initial cost of the total holding.

The fun starts when you have a holding of identical shares that you acquired on more than one date. When you dispose of some of the shares, special rules require you to identify the shares being disposed of with the shares you acquired in a set sequence, as follows:

- shares you acquire within the next 30 days. This measure is designed to stop the practice of 'bed and breakfasting', where you sell shares one day and buy them back the next day in order to save tax by realising a capital gain (for example, to use up your annual allowance) or loss (to set against other gains)
- shares acquired since 6 April 1998, matching the shares you sell to your most recent acquisitions first
- shares acquired after 6 April 1982 up to 5 April 1998. The shares are pooled and an average initial value and indexation allowance calculated
- shares acquired on or after 6 April 1965 (the date on which CGT was first introduced) up to 5 April 1982. The shares are

pooled and an average initial value and indexation allowance calculated

- shares you acquired before 6 April 1965, starting with the shares bought most recently. (You can opt instead to include these in the pool of shares acquired from 6 April 1965 to 5 April 1982.)

The matching rules were slightly different where you disposed of shares before 6 April 1998.

Tips for saving capital gains tax

- If you can, use your annual allowance every year.
- If you currently do not use your capital gains tax allowance, consider choosing investments that produce gains which could be tax-free instead of investments that produce taxable income.
- If, say, a husband will be liable for CGT but the wife is not using her annual allowance, the couple may be able to save tax if the husband transfers some assets to the wife before disposal. Transfers between husband and wife are tax-free.
- If you have made a large taxable gain on one asset, consider selling assets that are showing a loss to set off against the gain.
- If you want to make gifts to charity, bear in mind that gifts of assets are tax-free. If you give something on which you have made a gain, you will not be taxed on it and you might get income tax relief on the gift (see page 216). But do not give assets on which you have made a loss – instead, sell the asset to realise the loss and give the charity the resulting cash.
- Check whether assets count as business assets for taper relief. If they do, you can claim higher relief.
- Keep a careful record over the years of all the costs that can be claimed as allowable expenses and all the losses you make.
- The share identification rules have stopped traditional 'bed and breakfasting' (selling shares one day and buying them back the next to crystallise a gain or loss), but there are other ways to achieve the same effect. For example, sell shares you own direct and buy them back within an ISA; sell shares you own and get your spouse to buy them back; or sell shares in one company and buy shares in another similar company in the same sector.

Where to get more information

The Inland Revenue★ publishes free leaflets about CGT. It also provides helpsheets that are designed to aid people filling in a tax return. But, even if you do not need to declare your gains for tax (see Chapter 15), you may find it helpful to look at the helpsheets. Table 15.6 lists the main leaflets and helpsheets.

You may find the following Which? Book★ helpful: *The Which? Guide to Giving and Inheriting*.

Table 15.6   Selection of Inland Revenue leaflets and helpsheets

Reference number	Title
Leaflets	
CGT1	Capital gains tax – an introduction
CGT/FS1	Capital gains tax – a quick guide
Helpsheets	
IR279	Taper relief
IR280	Re-basing – assets held at 31 March 1982
IR284	Shares and capital gains tax
IR287	Employee share schemes and capital gains tax
IR293	Chattels and capital gains tax

Chapter 16

Saving inheritance tax

One of the most punishing of UK taxes can be inheritance tax on
what you leave to your heirs when you die. Up to 40 per cent of
your estate may have to be handed over to the Inland Revenue in
tax. (Your 'estate' is the value of all the things you own less anything
you owe someone else.) However, with careful planning, an inheritance tax bill can be reduced or eliminated.

How does inheritance tax work?

Inheritance tax is a tax on the value of your estate when you die and
on certain gifts you make during your lifetime. Tax is charged on the
running total of chargeable gifts you make over seven years. What
you leave when you die is treated as your final gift and added to
other gifts made in the seven years before death.

However, there is no tax on the first slice of the running total of
gifts – called the 'nil-rate band'. In 2004–5, the nil-rate band is
£263,000. So, if you died in 2004–5 and the value of your estate and
taxable gifts in the seven years before death came to no more than
£263,000, there would be no inheritance tax on your estate.

In addition, many gifts are tax-free either on death, during your
lifetime or both (see below). Tax-free gifts are not included in your
seven-year running total. Some gifts – called 'potentially exempt
transfers' (PETs) – are part of the running total only if you die
within seven years of making the gift (see page 247).

Most people want to ensure that they pass on as much as
possible to their heirs and that any inheritance tax bill is as low as
possible. There are two main ways of achieving this, but each has
its drawbacks:

- **make tax-free gifts on your death** All right up to a point, but often you'll want to leave your estate to, say, children and grand-children and these sorts of gift are not automatically tax-free
- **reduce the value of your estate before death** The problem is that giving away your assets before death might leave you short of income or capital that you need for your own use. Special 'gift with reservation' tax rules and a new 'pre-owned asset tax' prevent you making an effective gift for inheritance tax purposes if you continue to benefit from the thing you have given away – see page 253.

As a result, there are many tax planning devices that aim to reduce or avoid an inheritance tax bill while avoiding the drawbacks above.

CASE HISTORY: MARTIN

Martin dies in February 2005, leaving an estate valued at £103,000. He made two chargeable gifts in the seven years before his death of £10,000 and £60,000 respectively. His running total at death is £10,000 + £60,000 + £103,000 = £173,000. This is less than the nil-rate band for 2004–5 of £263,000. Therefore no inheritance tax is payable.

Tax-free gifts

Table 16.1 lists the gifts that are free of inheritance tax when you make them during your lifetime. However, there could be capital gains tax to pay on something you give away if it has risen in value during the time you have owned it (see Chapter 15). There is no capital gains tax on gifts of money.

Table 16.2 lists the gifts that are free of inheritance tax when made on death (under either the terms of your will or the intestacy rules). There is no capital gains tax on the things you leave on death.

CASE HISTORY: CHARLES

Charles makes the following gifts in 2004–5. They are all free of inheritance tax:

- £10,000 to his wife Jacqueline (spouse exemption)
- unit trusts worth £4,000 to his daughter on the occasion of her marriage (gift in consideration of marriage)
- birthday and Christmas presents to family members. No person receives more than £250 in total (small gift exemption)
- £8,000 to his ex-wife to support his two children by her (maintenance of family).

CASE HISTORY: POLLY

When Polly dies, she leaves an estate of £500,000. She has made no gifts in the seven years before death. She leaves £100,000 to charity and the rest to her husband. These are both exempt gifts, so there is no inheritance tax on her estate.

Same-sex couples

In 2004 new legislation was passed which will give the same rights as married couples to same-sex partners who register their relationship as a civil partnership. The legislation did not cover tax issues but the government has indicated that changes to tax law will be made in future, possibly from April 2006. It is expected that civil partners will then be able to use the spouse exemption (see Table 16.1) to make gifts which are free of inheritance tax.

Table 16.1   Main lifetime gifts that are free of inheritance tax

Tax-free gift	Description and main conditions
Annual exemption	Up to £3,000 of any gifts each year. If you do not use the full exemption, the unused part can be carried forward to the next year (but no subsequent year). The current year's exemption is used before any carried-forward amount.
Normal expenditure out of income	Gifts that form a regular pattern of giving, are made out of income and do not reduce your standard of living. An example would be regular premiums for a life-insurance policy that would pay out to someone else. Note that the capital element of an annuity or capital withdrawals from an investment-type life-insurance policy do not count as income.
Small gifts up to £250 per person	Outright gifts to any number of people. But this exemption cannot be combined with other exemptions. For example, you cannot claim that a gift of £3,250 is covered partly by the annual exemption and partly by the small gift exemption.
Gifts in consideration of marriage	Up to £5,000 if the gift is from a parent. Up to £2,500 if the gift is from a grandparent or remoter ancestor. Up to £2,500 if the gift is from one of the people getting married to the other. Up to £1,000 if the gift is from anybody else.
Spouse exemption	Any number of gifts, in general of any amount, from a husband to a wife or vice versa. However, if the recipient is not domiciled in the UK, the exemption is limited to a cumulative total over seven years of £55,000 worth of gifts. The spouse exemption does not apply to unmarried couples or divorced couples. (But separated spouses can use this exemption until the grant of a decree absolute.)
Gifts for the maintenance of your family	Applies to gifts of any amount to maintain your spouse or a dependent relative, or to maintain, educate and train your children. 'Child' includes adopted and stepchildren who live with you, and illegitimate children whether they live with you or not.
Gifts to charity	All gifts of any value to any number of charities and similar bodies regardless of the amount involved.
Gifts to housing associations	All gifts of UK land or property of any value to any number of housing associations regardless of the amount involved.
Gifts to political parties	All gifts of any value to qualifying political parties (broadly a party that had at least two MPs elected at the last general election, or at least one MP elected and the party polled at least 150,000 votes).
Gifts for the national benefit	Any number of gifts of any value to certain national bodies, including museums, art galleries, libraries, and so on, run to preserve items for the public benefit or to advance teaching or research in universities.

Table 16.2 Main gifts on death that are free of inheritance tax

Spouse exemption	Gifts of any amount from a husband to a wife or vice versa. However, if the recipient is not domiciled in the UK, the exemption is limited to a cumulative total of £55,000, including the seven years preceding death. The spouse exemption does not apply to unmarried couples or divorced couples. (But separated spouses can use this exemption until the grant of a decree absolute.)
Gifts to charity	Gifts of any value to any number of charities and similar bodies regardless of the amount involved.
Gifts to housing associations	Gifts of UK land or property of any value to any number of housing associations regardless of the amount involved.
Gifts to political parties	Gifts of any value to qualifying political parties (broadly a party that had at least two MPs elected at the last general election, or at least one MP elected and the party polled at least 150,000 votes).
Gifts for the national benefit	Any number of gifts of any value to certain national bodies, including museums, art galleries, libraries, and so on, run to preserve items for the public benefit or to advance teaching or research in universities.
Death on active service	Death from injury or disease contracted while on active service against an enemy. A certificate from the Inland Revenue Capital Taxes Office is required to claim the exemption.
Non-resident bank accounts	Foreign currency bank accounts and National Savings accounts if the deceased was not resident, ordinarily resident or domiciled in the UK.

Domicile and residence

Whether or not inheritance tax is due can depend on a person's domicile, residence and ordinary residence. These terms are not well defined in tax law, but broadly have the following meaning:

- **domicile** The country you regard as your permanent home, regardless of where you actually live
- **residence** Where you live for the majority of the tax year
- **ordinary residence** Where you are normally resident year after year.

Potentially exempt transfers (PETs)

Most lifetime gifts that are not tax-free are potentially exempt transfers (PETs). This means there is no inheritance tax on them at the time they are made and a PET becomes completely tax-free provided you survive for seven years after making the gift.

If you die within seven years of making the gift, there could be an inheritance tax bill, but only if your running total of chargeable gifts over the seven years up to the date you made the PET exceeds the nil-rate band. See 'Working out the tax bill' on page 249 for details of how this works.

The following gifts count as PETs:

- gifts to people
- gifts to trusts that include an interest in possession (see page 258)
- gifts to accumulation and maintenance trusts (see page 259)
- gifts to trusts for disabled people.

CASE HISTORY: PETER

Peter had already used up his nil-rate band when he gave £100,000 to his daughter, Rose, on 5 October 2004. However, there is no inheritance tax to pay at the time, because the gift counts as a PET. There will be no tax at all, provided Peter survives until 5 October 2011.

Business property relief and agricultural relief

There is often no inheritance tax on a gift of business assets or shares in a business either during your lifetime or on death, because gifts of business property can qualify for relief against inheritance tax. Relief is 100 per cent for unincorporated businesses (such as sole traders and partnerships) and shares in unlisted companies (including those quoted on the Alternative Investment Market) and 50 per cent for a controlling interest in a listed company and in some other cases. Various conditions must be met.

A similar relief applies to gifts of agricultural property either in lifetime or on death. Relief is usually 100 per cent, but only 50 per cent where you let out the farm on leases lasting a year or less. To qualify, various conditions must be met.

The aim of these reliefs is to ensure that businesses and farms can be handed on intact from one generation to another, without part being sold to raise money to pay inheritance tax.

Chargeable lifetime gifts

With a few types of gift made during your lifetime, there is an immediate inheritance tax bill and, if you die within seven years of making the gift, there may be extra tax to pay (see page 250).

Probably the most common chargeable gifts are gifts to discretionary trusts (see page 259).

What is taxed?

Inheritance tax is charged on the loss to the giver, in other words the reduction in the donor's estate as a result of making the gift. Often, this will simply be the market value of the thing you give away, but not always. For example, suppose you own a set of six antique chairs valued at, say, £20,000, and you give one away. The market value of a single chair is, say, £2,000, and the market value of the remaining five is only £12,000. The loss to you as a result of breaking up the set and giving one chair away is £20,000 − £12,000 = £8,000. So inheritance tax is chargeable on £8,000, not the £2,000 market value of the chair that you gave away.

If the person making a gift pays any inheritance tax due on it, the tax paid counts as part of the gift.

Working out the tax bill

Table 16.3 shows the rates of inheritance tax for gifts made, and deaths occurring, in 2004–5.

Table 16.3 Rates of inheritance tax in 2004–5

	Lifetime rates	Death rates
First £263,000 of your running total	0%	0%
Excess over £263,000	20%	40%

PETs

No inheritance tax is due on a PET at the time the gift is made. However, if you die within seven years of making a PET, the gift is reassessed as a chargeable gift and any tax is charged at the death rates. Tax will be due if the running total of all your chargeable gifts up to and including the PET come to more than the nil-rate band at the time of death.

If you survived more than three years after making the PET, inheritance tax 'taper relief' (nothing to do with the capital gains tax taper relief discussed in Chapter 15) reduces any inheritance tax due on the reassessed PET. See Table 16.4.

The recipient of the gift is responsible for paying the tax. But if he or she cannot or will not pay up, the Inland Revenue will instead collect the tax from your estate.

Table 16.4 Inheritance tax taper relief

Period between making the PET and death	Percentage of tax rate payable
Up to 3 years	100%
More than 3 and up to 4 years	80%
More than 4 and up to 5 years	60%
More than 5 and up to 6 years	40%
More than 6 and up to 7 years	20%
More than 7 years	No tax

CASE HISTORY: MALCOLM

Malcolm dies in December 2004. He had given £106,000 to his son, Philip, in August 2000. At the time, the gift counted as a PET and no tax was payable. But on Malcolm's death the gift is reassessed as a chargeable gift. Malcolm had already made £220,000 of other gifts in the seven years before the making of the PET. His annual exemptions for 2000–1 and 1999–2000 reduce the value of the chargeable gift to £106,000 – £6,000 = £100,000. The nil-rate band at the time of death is £263,000. £220,000 of this is used up by the earlier gifts, leaving £43,000 to set against the PET. The PET exceeds this by £100,000 – £43,000 = £57,000. Tax at the death rate is 40 per cent, but because Malcolm died between four and five years after making the PET, taper relief reduces the tax rate to 60% × 40% = 24%. Therefore tax on the gift is 24% × £57,000 = £13,680. Philip is liable for this tax bill.

Lifetime chargeable gifts

If you make a gift during your lifetime and it is neither tax-free nor a PET, inheritance tax is due at the time of the gift if the total of all your chargeable gifts over the seven years up to and including the current gift exceeds the nil-rate band. Tax is charged at 20 per cent on the amount of the current gift in excess of the nil-rate band.

If you die within seven years of making a chargeable gift, tax on the gift is recalculated using the death rates. Provided that you survived more than three years after making the gift, inheritance tax 'taper relief' reduces the reassessed tax. If this comes to more than the tax paid when the gift was made, there is an inheritance tax bill for the excess. If it comes to less, there is no extra tax to pay but no refund either.

The recipient of the gift is responsible for paying any extra tax on the gift on your death. But if he or she cannot or will not pay up, the Inland Revenue will instead collect the tax from your estate.

CASE HISTORY: MUNIR

In January 2002, Munir puts £500,000 into a discretionary trust. He has used up his nil-rate band and annual exemption, so the whole gift is chargeable at the lifetime rate. Tax comes to 20% × £500,000 = £100,000.

In February 2005, Munir dies. Tax on the chargeable gift is recalculated at the death rates. This would be 40 per cent, but because Munir died between three and four years after making the gift, taper relief reduces the tax rate to 80% × 40% = 32%. The tax bill is 32% × £500,000 = £160,000. However, tax of £100,000 was paid in Munir's lifetime, so only the excess of £160,000 – £100,000 = £60,000 is now due. The trustees of the discretionary trust are liable to pay this tax out of the trust property.

Your estate on death

Inheritance tax is charged on the excess over the nil-rate band of your estate plus chargeable gifts made in the seven years before death. This includes PETs in the seven years before death because they have been reclassified as chargeable due to your death.

The nil-rate band is used up by earlier chargeable gifts before later ones and by the lifetime gifts before the estate. A PET being reclassified as a chargeable gift can result in some of the nil-rate band being used up by the PET, which means more of the estate may become taxable.

Note that tax on the estate is entirely separate from the extra tax on PETs and chargeable gifts that may become due as a result of the death of the giver. In particular, taper relief is not available to reduce tax due on the estate even if the existence of PETs within the last seven years causes extra tax on the estate.

CASE HISTORY: PATRICK

Patrick dies in November 2004, leaving an estate worth £180,000 to his son, Sean. The only gift he made in the seven years before death was £100,000 to Sean. At the time, the gift counted as a PET, but on Patrick's death it is reassessed as a chargeable gift and becomes part of his running total of £100,000 + £180,000 = £280,000. The nil-rate band for the year of death is £263,000. The reassessed PET uses up £100,000 of this. £163,000 of nil-rate band is left to set against the estate. The remainder of the estate £180,000 – £163,000 = £17,000 is taxable. Tax comes to 40% × £17,000 = £6,800 and is paid by Patrick's executors out of the estate.

Tax avoidance

Inheritance tax used to be viewed as a tax paid only by the rich. But rising house prices have brought into the tax net many families who do not consider themselves to be wealthy. There are many inheritance tax exemptions and loopholes that have in the past provided opportunities for people legitimately to plan away an inheritance tax bill. But it has always been hard to take advantage of these if you do not have spare assets to give away and in particular if your only substantial asset is the home you live in. If you try to give something away but carry on using it, you fall foul of the gift-with-reservation (GWR) rules – see opposite.

Tax and legal advisers have for years devised clever schemes to get around the GWR rules. Many sailed close to the legal wind and the Inland Revenue mounted many challenges – some successful, some not. By and large, the schemes were aimed at a relatively small pool of wealthy clients. But, as the less wealthy began to be drawn into inheritance tax, avoidance schemes started to be mass-marketed, particularly schemes designed to enable people to give away their homes tax-effectively yet still live in them without triggering the GWR rules. The government decided enough was enough.

From 6 April 2005, the government is introducing a new income tax – pre-owned assets tax – to plug the inheritance tax avoidance loopholes. The effect of the new tax will be 'retroactive' (see opposite for what the government means by this) and the government has said it is prepared in future to introduce other retroactive steps to close successful avoidance loopholes. The new tax makes many avoidance schemes ineffective. The threat of further retroactive measures means there can be no certainty that complex tax planning schemes will save you tax.

The government has also introduced new rules that require advisers and others who devise tax avoidance schemes to give early details to the Inland Revenue so giving the government a chance to block such schemes with new legislation. At present, these new reporting rules do not apply to inheritence tax, but could be extended to inheritance tax in future.

Gifts with reservation

These rules have been a feature of the tax system since 18 March 1986. Normally the size of your estate shrinks by the value of the gift, when you give something away. But if you give something away and the recipient either does not take possession of the gift or cannot enjoy it without your continuing to benefit from the item, the gift is called a gift with reservation (GWR). The value of a GWR remains as part of your estate for inheritance tax purposes for as long as you continue to benefit from it. This is despite the fact that legal ownership of the asset has passed from you to the recipient. Examples of GWRs include:

- giving your home to your children but continuing to live there yourself unless you pay your children the market rent or share the home with them and bear your full share of the costs
- giving away a lump sum in a bank account but continuing to receive interest on it
- giving away a painting that continues to hang in your home.

The GWR rules do not apply to most of the tax-free gifts listed on page 246. However a gift covered by the annual exemption or normal expenditure out of income exemption can be caught by the GWR rules.

Pre-owned assets tax

Using the tax-free gifts to which the GWR rules do not apply together with trusts and loans, many clever schemes were devised which have enabled people to give away their homes and other possessions and continue to enjoy them without falling foul of the GWR rules. The government decided not only to stop future use of these sorts of scheme but also to stem the tax savings from past use of many such schemes by introducing the pre-owned assets tax (POT).

POT is an income tax. It applies where you occupy or enjoy land or personal possessions (chattels) without the GWR rules applying and either:

- you disposed of all or part of your interest in the land or possessions at any time on or after 18 March 1986 (the date the GWR rules were introduced), or
- you funded the purchase by someone else of the land or possessions.

Some arrangements are excluded from the new tax, for example, where you sold the asset in a genuine arm's-length deal (which can include a sale at full value to a friend or family member), the asset was given to your husband or wife, or the gift of cash was made at least seven years before you started to enjoy the asset purchased with it. The Inland Revenue has also specifically stated that equity release schemes where you have sold all or part of your home to a commercial equity release firm are not caught by the new tax, but equity release schemes you arranged yourself by selling to, say, a family member are potentially caught.

POT is charged on the value you are deemed to receive from your use or enjoyment of the asset. For example, if you live in a home you gave away, the taxable value would be the market rent you would otherwise pay to live in such a property. In the case of possession, the taxable value is the capital value of the asset multiplied by a percentage interest rate set by the government (5 per cent at the time of writing). But no POT is charged if the total value of your benefit from all such land and possessions is £5,000 or less.

If the gross value of your benefit exceeds £5,000, POT is due but you can deduct any amount you actually pay for using or enjoying the asset. The net values count as part of your income for the tax year and are taxed along with any other income under the rules described in Chapter 14.

POT is a difficult tax. It imposes an income tax bill on deemed income that you do not actually have, so you might not be able to afford the bill. And it is 'retroactive' in that it imposes a charge from 6 April 2005 on arrangements that you may have set up many years in the past (right back to 18 March 1986). There are two ways to escape a POT charge and both involve accepting the risk of inheritance tax instead:

- you can unravel the arrangement so that the land or possessions are after all caught by the GWR rules. However, because the assets are now legally owned by someone else, reversing the deal might not be possible
- you can keep the arrangements as they are but elect for the assets to be treated as if the GWR rules do apply. The election must normally be made by 31 January following the end of the tax year in which you first become liable for the POT. Exceptionally, for assets you already own when POT is introduced on 6 April 2005, you have until 31 January 2007 to make the election.

This is a complicated area, so get professional advice from an accountant*, for example a member of the Society of Trust and Estate Practitioners (STEP)*.

Ways to plan for or reduce an inheritance tax bill

It will be clear from the discussion above that new government measures have restricted the scope for planning during your lifetime to minimise an inheritance tax bill. Nevertheless, there are still some steps you can take. The descriptions below are brief outlines, and should not be used as a DIY kit. Get professional help from a solicitor*, accountant* or independent financial adviser (IFA)*, especially where a scheme involves the use of trusts. It is very important that the wording of trust deeds is accurate, otherwise the trust might not achieve the aim you intended.

Think about your pension arrangements

With most pension arrangements, you do not directly own the assets building up in your pension fund so, on death, it is up to the trustees or similar organisers to decide who should receive any lump sum or survivor's pension from your scheme or plan. Nearly always, you will be asked to complete a form nominating the people you would like to benefit and in most cases the trustees/organisers will follow your wishes. (However, they may consider claims from other people – for example, a former spouse who has not remarried – if they have a valid claim that they were financially dependent on you.) Payments made in accordance with such nominations bypass your estate and so are not subject to inheritance tax or probate delays.

Life insurance

The extra tax on a reassessed PET or chargeable gift due to the giver dying within seven years can come as a nasty shock to the recipient. However, you could plan for the possible tax bill by taking out a reducing term insurance policy at the time of the gift. The insurance lasts exactly seven years and pays out a lump sum on death within that term. The policy is designed so that the lump sum equals the estimated tax bill on the gift as a result of death.

The policy can be taken out by the recipient based on the giver's life. Alternatively, it can be taken out by the giver on his or her own life, but with the benefit being paid in trust to the recipient of the gift. In the latter case, each premium paid is itself a gift from the giver to the recipient. The premiums can count as a tax-free gift if they fall within, say, the annual exemption or normal expenditure out of income. Otherwise, the premiums would count as PETs.

Similarly, you could take out a whole life policy to pay out a lump sum whenever you die of enough to meet an estimated inheritance tax bill on your estate. By writing the policy in trust, the pay-out can go direct to your heirs without being included as part of your estate. This has two advantages: first, there will be no inheritance tax on the pay-out; secondly, your heirs can pay the inheritance tax straight away and without having to take out a loan to cover the bill.

Spouse exemption and the nil-rate band

By leaving everything to your husband or wife, you ensure there is no inheritance tax bill on your estate if you die first. This strategy has the advantage of maximum security for the surviving spouse, who has full access to the family's income and capital.

CASE HISTORY: FRED

When Fred dies, he leaves his whole £400,000 estate to his wife Betty. There is no inheritance tax on Fred's estate because bequests to a husband or wife are tax-free. When Betty dies in September 2004, her estate, valued at £600,000, is left to the couple's grown-up children. Tax is due on the excess over the nil-rate band: £600,000 – £263,000 = £337,000. The tax bill is 40% × £337,000 = £134,800. The children inherit £600,000 – £134,800 = £465,200.

The family would have saved tax if Fred had left £263,000 direct to the children and the remaining £137,000 to Betty. There would still have been no tax on Fred's estate because the gift to the children is within the nil-rate band and the gift to Betty is covered by the spouse exemption. When Betty dies, her estate would total £337,000. The excess over the nil-rate band is £337,000 – £263,000 = £74,000 and tax is 40% × £74,000 = £29,600. Tax of £105,200 has been saved and the children inherit £263,000 + £337,000 – £29,600 = £570,400.

However, leaving everything to your husband or wife means wasting the nil-rate band of the first to die and can create an unnecessarily large tax bill when the second spouse dies. Provided the surviving spouse does not need all the family's assets, consider leaving part of your estate to, say, your children or grandchildren and the remainder to your spouse. In 2004–5, this can save the family up to £105,200 in tax.

Consider a discretionary will trust

If you are not sure at this stage what your husband or wife might need if you were to die first, you could rewrite your will so that on death an amount up to the amount of your tax-free slice is bequeathed to a 'discretionary will trust'. This is a discretionary trust – see box overleaf – set up in the terms of your will. Your spouse and other heirs should be named as the beneficiaries, and the trustees (who you can appoint in your will – for example, the same people who are your executors and who can also be beneficiaries) can decide how the trust money and assets or income produced by them are given out (or even lent interest-free).

Make lifetime gifts

You can reduce the tax bill on death by giving away your assets during your lifetime and so reducing the value of your estate. By using tax-free gifts (see page 245), you can ensure there is no inheritance tax to pay when you make the gift or if you die within seven years. If you can reasonably expect to live for at least another seven years, you can give away even large sums by making PETs. To save the most tax, give away things that you expect to increase in value.

However, do not make gifts you cannot afford; for example, do not give away money or assets that you rely on for your standard of living or may need in the future.

Use trusts for lifetime gifts

You might be reluctant to make an outright gift to someone if, for example, you think the recipient is too young to make good use of the gift or you fear you might want the gift back at some future time. An alternative to making an outright gift is to make a gift to a trust.

What is a trust?

A trust is a legal arrangement where one or more people (the trustees) hold money or other assets to be used for the benefit of one or more other people (the beneficiaries) in accordance with the terms of the trust. The person who gives the assets to the trust is called the settlor and it is the settlor who usually decides who the beneficiaries will be and under what circumstances they are to receive or use the trust property. However, the settlor can give the trustees a power of appointment, which means the trustees decide who the beneficiaries will be, usually from a group of people defined by the settlor.

There are two main sorts of trust:

- **interest in possession trust** At least one beneficiary has the right to the income from the trust or to use the trust property. The person (or people) who have the interest in possession are treated for inheritance tax purposes as if they own the trust

---

assets outright. The trust will say what happens to the trust
assets when the interest in possession ends. Whoever then
gets the assets is said to have the 'reversionary interest'

- **discretionary trust** No-one has an interest in possession and,
  within the trust's rules, the trustees decide how the income and
  capital are distributed.

Discretionary trusts (see box above) are the most flexible form of
trust, but, in general, they are treated less favourably for inheritance
tax purposes than interest in possession trusts. However, accumulation and maintenance trusts (designed to benefit children and
young people) and disabled trusts (designed to benefit people who
may need financial help due to a disability) are both types of discretionary trust, but do benefit from favourable inheritance tax
treatment.

The gift with reservation rules (see page 253) mean that a gift to a
trust will not usually be effective for saving inheritance tax if the
settlor can be a beneficiary of the trust. However, the settlor can
have the reversionary interest in an interest in possession trust
without triggering the reservation rules. A gift you make to a trust of
which your husband or wife is a beneficiary is not a gift with reservation provided that you do not benefit in any way from your
spouse's share of the trust assets.

Loans

Another way to make a gift but retain the option to get it back is to
make an interest-free loan – usually of money – instead of an
outright gift. The loan remains part of your estate so there is no gift,
but the recipient can invest the money and keep the income or gains
it generates. To prevent the Inland Revenue arguing that you are
making a gift of the right to receive the income, it is essential that the
loan is repayable on demand and on your death. Loan schemes like
this are sometimes called 'estate freezing', because any growth in
value of the loaned assets goes to someone else and so does not
increase the value of your own estate.

Equity release schemes

When you take out an equity release scheme – see Chapter 11 – the value of your estate is reduced (by either the amount of the mortgage or the value of the part of your home you have sold, less any of the proceeds that you keep). Therefore, some financial advisers have been promoting these schemes as a method of inheritance tax planning.

Certainly, equity release schemes can reduce a potential inheritance tax bill, but bear in mind that you give up a much larger share of your home than you get back as a lump sum or income. If you do not mind moving, a more efficient plan would be to sell your home and move to somewhere smaller. That way you would realise a sum much closer to the full value of equity previously locked in your home. In order to reduce the value of your estate, you must spend or give away the money released. See earlier in this chapter for the factors to think about when making lifetime gifts.

Deed of variation

Provided that all the beneficiaries of a will agree and they are all adults of sound mind, the terms of your will can be altered after you have died. This could be worth doing if, for example, the gifts you made in your will are not tax-efficient. To make the change, the beneficiaries must draw up a deed of variation identifying your will, specifying how the bequests are to be changed and making clear if inheritance tax (and, if relevant, capital gains tax) are to be affected. This must be done within two years of your death.

It is better to get your will right than to rely on your heirs using a deed of variation, because:

- previous governments have considered abolishing deeds with variation. Although they did not go ahead, there's no guarantee that they will still be allowed when your heirs need one
- some of the beneficiaries of your will might not be adults or of sound mind. This would make it much more difficult to effect a variation, as a court would have to be involved
- although you can save inheritance tax, there can be income tax problems. If a parent wants to renounce a bequest in favour of his or her child, any income (unless it was less than £100 a year)

that the child earned from the inherited assets would be treated as income of the parent.

Where to get more information

For a more detailed guide to planning how your heirs can inherit tax-efficiently, see *The Which? Guide to Giving and Inheriting* available from Which? Books★.

Unless your affairs are very straightforward, you are advised to get professional help with inheritance tax planning. For example, contact an accountant or solicitor who is a member of the Society of Trust and Estate Practitioners (STEP)★.

Addresses

Accountants

Look in *Yellow Pages* under 'Accountants', or for a list of members in your area contact:

- Association of Chartered Certified Accountants, 29 Lincoln's Inn Fields, London WC2A 3EE.
  Tel: 020–7396 5700
  Website – www.acca.co.uk

- Institute of Chartered Accountants in England and Wales, Chartered Accountants' Hall, PO Box 433, London EC2P 2BJ.
  Tel: 020–7920 8100
  Website – www.icaew.co.uk

- Institute of Chartered Accountants in Ireland, Chartered Accountants' House, 83 Pembroke Road, Dublin 4, Republic of Ireland.
  Tel: (00 353) 1 637 7200
  Website – www.icai.ie

- Institute of Chartered Accountants of Scotland, CA House, 21 Haymarket Yards, Edinburgh EH12 5BH
  Tel: 0131 347 0100
  Website – www.icas.org.uk

Age Concern Information Line

Freepost (SWB 30375)
Ashburton
Devon TQ13 7ZZ
Tel: 0800 00 99 66 (freephone)
Website – www.ace.org.uk

Age Positive Campaign

Website –
www.agepositive.gov.uk

Carers UK

20/25 Glasshouse Yard
London
EC1A 4JS
CarersLine: 0808 808 7777
(Wed –Thu 10am-12pm and 2–4pm)
Website –
www.carersonline.org.uk

Citizens' Advice Bureaux
Look in *The Phone Book* under
'Citizens' Advice Bureau'.
Websites –
www.citizensadvice.org.uk
www.adviceguide.org.uk

*Debt Management Office
(DMO)*
Eastcheap Court
11 Philpot Lane
London EC3M 8UD
Tel: 0800 376 9232
(publications)
Website – www.dmo.gov.uk

*Debt Management Office's
Purchase and Sale Service*
Computershare Investor
Services plc
PO Box 2411
The Pavillions
Bridgwater Road
Bristol BS3 9WX
Tel: 0870 703 0143
Website – www-
uk.computershare.com

*Department of Trade and
Industry*
• TIGER (Tailored Interactive
  Guidance on Employment
  Rights) www.tiger.gov.uk

• DTI Response Centre,
  1 Victoria Street,
  London SW1H 0ET
  Tel: 020–7215 5000
  Minicom 020–7215 6740
  Website – www.dti.gov.uk

Discount brokers (examples)
• Hargreaves Lansdown,
  Kendal House,
  Brighton Mews,
  Clifton,
  Bristol BS8 2NX
  Tel: 0117 900 9000
  Website –
  www.hargreaveslansdown.
  co.uk

• The ISA Shop,
  Star House,
  6 Garland Road,
  Stanmore,
  Middlesex HA7 1NR
  Tel: 0870 870 8558
  Website – www.hcf.co.uk

*Department for Work and
Pensions*
Website – http:
//www.dwp.gov.uk
• DWP Benefit Enquiry Line
  0800 88 22 00
  Textphone 0800 24 33 55
• DWP Carer's Allowance
  Unit,
  Palatine House,
  Lancaster Road,
  Preston PR1 1HB Tel: 01253
  856 123
• DWP Direct Payment
  Helpline: 0800 107 2000
  Textphone: 0800 107 4000
• DWP Disability Living
  Allowance and Attendance
  Allowance Helpline: 08457
  12 34 56

- DWP Leaflet Unit: DWP Pensions,
Freepost BS5555/1,
Bristol BS99 1BL
Pensions Info-Line 08457 313 233
- DWP winter fuel hotline 08459 15 15 15
Textphone 08456 01 56 13

Financial Ombudsman Service
South Quay Plaza
183 Marsh Wall
London E14 9SR
Tel: 0845 080 1800
Website – http://www.financial-ombudsman.org.uk

Financial Services Authority (FSA)
25 The North Colonnade
London E14 5HS
Tel: 020–7066 1000
FSA Consumer Helpline: 0845 6061234 (calls charged at local rates)

To check whether a firm is authorised: Consumer Helpline as above or use the Firm Check Service on the consumer website below
Website – http://www.fsa.gov.uk
Consumer website – http://www.fsa.gov.uk/consumer
Comparative tables – http://www.fsa.gov.uk/tables

Financial Services Compensation Scheme
7th Floor
Lloyds Chambers
1 Portsoken Street
London E1 8BN
Tel: 020–7892 7300
Website – www.fscs.org.uk

Fund supermarkets (examples)
www.chasedevere.co.uk
www.egg.com
www.fidelity.co.uk (Funds Network)
www.hargreaveslansdown.co.uk
www.tqonline.co.uk

Help the Aged
207–221 Pentonville Road
London N1 9UZ
Tel: 020–7278 1114
SeniorLine: 0808 800 6565
(Mon–Fri 9am –4pm)

(for factsheets and booklets, written requests preferred)
Website – www.helptheaged.org.uk

Independent financial adviser (to find one)
- IFA Promotion Tel: 0800 085 3250 Website – www.unbiased.co.uk

- The Institute of Financial Planning
Whitefriars Centre,
Lewins Mead,
Bristol BS1 2NT

Tel: 0117 945 2470
Website –
www.financialplanning.
org.uk

- Matrix Data UK IFA
  Directory Website – http:
  //www.ukifadirectory.co.uk

- Personal Finance Society
  (PFS)
  20 Aldermanbury,
  London EC2V 7HY
  Tel: 020–8530 0852
  Website – www.thepfs.org

Independent financial advisers specialising in annuities (examples)
- The Annuity Bureau,
  The Tower,
  11 York Road,
  London SE1 7NX
  Tel: 0845 602 6263
  Website – www.annuity-
  bureau.co.uk

- Annuity Direct,
  32 Scrutton Street,
  London EC2A 4RQ
  Tel: 0500 50 65 75
  Website –
  www.annuitydirect.co.uk

- William Burroughs Annuities
  Tel: 020–7421 4545
  Website –
  www.williamburrows.com

Inland Revenue
- For local tax enquiry centres
  look in *The Phone Book* under
  'Inland Revenue'.
- For your own tax office,
  check your tax return, other
  tax correspondence or check
  with your employer or
  scheme paying you a pension.
- Website –
  www.inlandrevenue.gov.uk
- To get Inland Revenue
  leaflets, phone the Orderline:
  0845 900 0404 (minicom
  available on this number)
- ISA Helpline: 0845 604 1701
- Inheritance Tax and Probate
  Helpline: 0845 302 0900
- National Minimum Wage
  Helpline: 0845 600 0678
- Self Assessment Helpline:
  0845 900 0444
- Self-employed Contact
  Centre: 0845 915 4655
- Tax Credits Helpline: 0845
  300 3900 (Northern Ireland:
  0845 603 2000)
- Ten Percent Helpline (for
  taxpayers paying tax onlt at
  the starting rate): 0845 307
  5555

Inland Revenue (Capital Taxes)
- Forms and leaflets: 0845 234
  1000
  - (England and Wales)
    Ferrers House,
    PO Box 38,
    Nottingham NG2 1BB
    Tel: 0115 974 2400.

- (Northern Ireland)
  Level 3, Dorchester House,
  52–58 Great Victoria Street,
  Belfast BT2 7QL
  Tel: 0289 050 5353.

- (Scotland)
  Meldrum House,
  15 Drumsheugh Gardens,
  Edinburgh EH3 7UG
  Tel: 0131 777 4050/4060.
  Website –
  www.inlandrevenue.gov.uk/
  cto

Jobcentre Plus

For local office, look in *The Phone Book* under 'Jobcentre Plus' or 'Social security'.
Website –
www.jobcentreplus.gov.uk

Local authority planning department

Look in *The Phone Book* under 'Councils' or the name of your District, Metropolitan, London Borough or Unitary Council.

Local authority social services department

Look in *The Phone Book* under 'Councils' or the name of your County, Metropolitan, London Borough or Unitary Council.

Local law centre

For local centre, see *The Phone Book* under 'Local law centre' or contact:

- The Law Centre Federation,
  Duchess House,
  18-19 Warren Street,
  London W1P 5DB
  Tel: 0171 387 8570
  Website –
  www.lawcentres.org.uk

- Community Legal Service
  Direct Tel: 0845 345 4 345
  Website –
  www.clsdirect.org.uk

Moneyfacts

Moneyfacts House
66–70 Thorpe Road
Norwich NR1 1BJ
Subscriptions: 0870 2250 100
Website
–www.moneyfacts.co.uk

Moneyfacts faxback services

(calls charged at maximum of 75p per minute):

- Compulsory purchase annuities (pension annuities) 090 607 607 31
- National Savings & Investments: 090 607 607 12
- Purchased life annuities 090 607 607 32
- Savings: 090 607 607 11

National Savings & Investments

- For Easy Access Savings Account, Investment Account, Ordinary Account, Children's Bonus Bonds, Capital Bonds, contact: National Savings and Investments, Glasgow G58 1SB
- For Premium Bonds, Guaranteed Equity Bonds, Pensioners Bonds, Income Bonds, contact: National Savings and Investments Blackpool FY3 9YP
- For Cash mini ISA, TESSA ISA, Fixed Interest Savings Certificates, Index-linked Savings Certificates, Fixed Rate Savings Bonds, Deposit Bonds, contact: National Savings and Investments, Durham DH99 1NS
- Tel: 0845 964 5000
- Website – www.nsandi.com

Pension Credit Application Line
Tel: 0800 99 1234
Textphone: 0800 169 0133

Pension scheme administrator (occupational pension scheme)
See pension statement, scheme handbook, recent benefit statement, annual report or noticeboard at work for contact details of pension scheme administrator or trustees. Alternatively, contact your personnel department.

Pension Schemes Registry
PO Box 1NN
Newcastle upon Tyne NE99 1NN
Tel: 0191 225 6316
Website – www.opra.gov.uk

The Pension Service
For local office, look in *The Phone Book* under 'The Pension Service' or 'Social security'.
Tel: 0845 60 60 265
Textphone: 0845 60 60 285
Website – www.thepensionservice.gov.uk

Personal Finance Society (PFS)
20 Aldermanbury,
London EC2V 7HY
Tel: 020–8530 0852
Website – www.thepfs.org

Safe Home Income Plans (SHIP)
PO Box 516
Preston Central PR2 2XQ
Tel: 0870 241 6060
Website – www.ship-ltd.org

Social security office
Look in *The Phone Book* under
'Social security', 'Jobcentre
Plus' or 'The Pension Service'.

*Society of Trust and Estate
Practitioners (STEP)*
26 Grosvenor Gardens,
London SW1W 0GT
Tel: 020–7838 4890
Website – www.step.org

Solicitor (to find one)
- (England and Wales) Law
  Society,
  113 Chancery Lane,
  London WC2A 1PL
  Tel: 020–7242 1222
  Website – www.lawsoc.org.uk

- (Scotland) Law Society of
  Scotland
  26 Drumsheugh Gardens,
  Edinburgh EH3 7YR
  Tel: 0131 226 7411
  Website –
  www.lawscot.org.uk

- (Northern Ireland) Law
  Society of Northern Ireland,
  Law Society House,
  98 Victoria Street,
  Belfast BT1 3JZ
  Tel: +44 (0) 28 90 231 614
  Website – www.lawsoc-ni.org

State Pension Claims Line
Tel: 0845 300 1084
Textphone: 0845 300 2086

State Pension Forecast
State Pension Forecasting
Team,
Tyneview,
Whitely Road,
Newcastle upon Tyne
NE98 1BA
Tel: 0845 3000 168
Textphone: 0845 3000 169
Website:
www.thepensionservice.gov.uk

Stockbroker (to find one)
Association of Private Client
Investment Managers and
Stockbrokers (APCIMS)
114 Middlesex Street
London E1 7JH
Tel: 020–7247 7080
Website – www.apcims.co.uk

Tax advisers
- See *Yellow Pages* under 'Tax
  advisers'.

- The Chartered Institute of
  Taxation
  12 Upper Belgrave Street
  London W1X 8BB
  Tel: 020–7235 9381
  Website – www.tax.org.uk

TaxAid
Room 304
Linton House
164–180 Union Street
London SE1 0LH
(personal callers only by
appointment)
Tel: 020–7803 4959 (Mon-Thu
10am-12pm)
Website – www.taxaid.org.uk

Tax Help for Older People
Tel: 0845 601 3321
Website – www.litrg.org.uk

Tax office
See *Inland Revenue* above

Television text services
• BBC1 for share prices
• BBC2 for city news, share
  prices and stock exchanges
• C4 for bonds, borrowing, city
  news, mortgages, savings and
  share prices
• Website – www.teletext.com

Volunteering (examples)
• Contact local branches of
  charities direct
• Do-It Website –
  www.thesite.org/do-it

• National Centre for
  Volunteering,
  Regents Wharf,
  8 All Saints Street,
  London N1 9RL
  Tel: 0845 305 6979
  Website –
  www.volunteering.org.uk

• Retired and Senior Volunteer
  Programme (RSVP),
  237 Pentonville Road,
  London N1 9NJ
  Tel: 020–7643 1385
  Website – www.csv-
  rsvp.org.uk

• Scottish Council for
  Voluntary Organisations
  Tel: (Glasgow) 0141 221 0030
  (Edinburgh) 0131 556 3882
  (Inverness) 01463 235 633
  Website – www.scvo.org.uk

Which? Books
Freepost
PO Box 44
Hertford X
SG14 1SH
Tel: 0800 252100 (freephone)
Website – www.which.co.uk

Index

Budget 2005

The following Budget 2005 measures may affect readers of this book. The measures may be changed by Parliament before becoming law. After a general election, an incoming government might announce further tax changes.

- **Individual savings accounts (ISAs)** Availability extended to 5 April 2010. The investment limits of £7,000 a year overall and £3,000 for cash will apply for the whole period.
- **Shari'a-compliant financial products** Mark-ups and profit-sharing are to be taxed in a comparable way to interest.
- **Unclaimed assets** Financial institutions must come up with ways actively to reunite unclaimed assets (such as old bank accounts) with their owners. Money then still unclaimed is likely to be used for the benefit of society.
- **National minimum wage** Increases to £5.05 per hour from 1 October 2005 and £5.35 from 1 October 2006.
- **State benefits if you go into hospital** From 6 April 2006 onwards, state pension will not be cut if you are in hospital for a prolonged period. But attendance allowance and carer's allowance will continue to be reduced.
- **Help with council tax** Households that pay at least some council tax and have a person aged 65 plus will receive a tax-free £200 with their 2005 winter fuel payment. Households that pay no council tax with a person aged 70 plus will get £50.
- **Free bus pass** Over 60s in England will qualify for free local, off-peak bus travel from 6 April 2006.
- **Income tax bands and rates** Rates unchanged. New bands are: starting-rate £2,090; basic-rate £30,310; higher-rate anything over £32,400.
- **Same sex couples** From 5 December 2005 couples who register as civil partners will be treated for tax the same as married couples.
- **Married couple's allowance** If you get married or form a civil partnership on or after 5 December 2005, any married couple's allowance will be based on the income of the person with the highest income (not the husband's). Existing marriages are not affected.
- **Capital gains tax** Annual allowance for 2005-6 is £8,500 (previously £8,200).
- **Inheritance and tax** Nil-rate band for 2005-6 is £275,000 (previously £263,000). For the following two tax years it is £285,000 and £300,000.

160 Letters that Get Results

Ever been frustrated by a garage over-charging? A shop selling faulty goods? Inexplicable debits from your bank account? Writing a letter of complaint will stop you feeling helpless when you know you are in the right.

The new and expanded edition of this guide, provides carefully worded **model letters** for dealing with a wide range of service providers from financial institutions and mail order companies, to doctors and solicitors.

It explains your rights for each kind of problem and the obligations of the individual or organisation serving you, together with a summary of the relevant legislation and details of proposed changes in the law. Solving common consumer problems through tried-and-tested methods, the letters are written in the language your solicitor would use if acting for you.

The book covers:

- how long to allow respondents to reply to your letter
- which Act of Parliament to cite in which situation
- how to take your claim through the small claims track
- which ombudsman, trade association or arbitration scheme to approach for help.

With this book you can fight back effectively and no longer have to take no for an answer.

Paperback   216 x 135mm   320 pages   £11.99

Available from bookshops, or post free from
Which? Phone FREE on (0800) 252100
quoting Dept BKLIST and your credit card details
or buy on line from **www.which.co.uk** (Bookshop).

Wills and Probate

If you die without making a will your wealth could go
to the very person you least want to have it and your
loved ones could lose out, perhaps to the Inland
Revenue.

The practical, easy-to-follow advice contained in *Wills
and Probate* has already helped thousands of people to
make their wills. Whether you are single, married,
divorced or co-habiting, it will show you how to write
your will in such a way that your wishes can be carried
out without any complications.

The second part of the book covers probate: the
administration of the estate of someone who has died.
The book will enable you to decide whether you can
make your own will or administer an estate confidently
by yourself or whether you should call on professional
help.

Covering the law and procedure in England and Wales,
and outlining the main differences which apply in
Scotland and Northern Ireland, this revised edition
contains sample forms and also describes what happens if
there is no will.

Paperback   216 x 135mm   256 pages   £11.99

Available from bookshops, or post free from
Which? Phone FREE on (0800) 252100
quoting Dept BKLIST and your credit card details
or buy on line from **www.which.co.uk** (Bookshop).

What to Do When Someone Dies

For many people, the first experience of making the sorts of arrangements that are necessary following a death comes only when they have been bereaved and least feel like finding out what needs to be done. *What to Do When Someone Dies* guides readers through the process practically, sympathetically and informatively. The book covers:

- how to register a death
- the role of the coroner
- choosing between burial and cremation
- how to claim any state benefits that may be due
- arranging a funeral without a funeral director
- humanist and other non-Christian funerals
- organ donation
- arranging your own funeral if you want to plan ahead.

The book covers the law and practice in England and Wales and highlights in separate sections the important differences which apply in Scotland. A list of useful addresses is also included.

Paperback   216 x 135mm   192 pages   £10.99

Available from bookshops, or post free from
Which? Phone FREE on (0800) 252100
quoting Dept BKLIST and your credit card details or buy on line from **www.which.co.uk** (Bookshop).

450 Legal
Problems Solved

This question-and-answer handbook shows you where you stand on a multitude of common problems of consumer law, and how to deal with them, without resorting to costly legal services.

If your tour operator goes bust while you're on holiday, your application for credit has been turned down, if you regret signing that timeshare contract or you've been bitten by your neighbour's dog, you want to know what to do right away, and preferably without the expense of hiring a lawyer.

This book tells you what to do. It covers:

- eating out
- holidays, travel and transport
- finance and credit
- neighbours
- public utilities
- buying on the Internet
- personal data, injuries and complaints about medical treatment

and much more. It explains how and to whom to make an effective claim and how to use mediation and arbitration schemes. The book provides you with the ammunition to fight your own consumer battles and to use the law to your advantage.

Paperback   216 x 135mm   320 pages   £11.99

Available from bookshops, or post free from
Which?, Phone FREE on (0800) 252100
quoting Dept BKLIST and your credit-card details
or buy on line from **www.which.co.uk** (Bookshop).

Be Your Own Financial Adviser

From education to dental care, retirement to home ownership, increasingly you are expected to take a more active role
to ensure the financial wellbeing of you and your family.

Whether you want to manage your money yourself or simply be in the driving seat when you get advice, this guide
will equip you with the knowledge and techniques you
need.

In simple language, with numerous case studies, tips and flow
charts, Be Your Own Financial Adviser shows you how to
identify your financial goals and create a plan to meet them
without falling into the traps of unsuitable products, high
charges and hidden risks. It will help you:

- Save for emergencies.
- Protect your family.
- Protect your income.
- Insure against illness and dental bills.
- Buy a home.
- Help your children.
- Save and invest for growth or income.
- Build up retirement income.
- Pass on your money tax efficiently.

Paperback   216 x 135mm   368 pages   £11.99

Available from bookshops, and post free from
Which? Phone FREE on (0800) 252100
quoting Dept BKLIST and your credit card details
or buy on line from www.which.co.uk (Bookshop).